THE ABINGDON
PREACHING
ANNUAL
1997

THE ABINGDON PREACHING ANNUAL 1997

COMPILED AND EDITED BY

Michael Duduit

ABINGDON PRESS
Nashville

THE ABINGDON PREACHING ANNUAL 1997

Copyright © 1996 by Abingdon Press

This book is printed on recycled, acid-free paper.

ISBN 0-687-01988-5
ISSN 1075-2250

96 97 98 99 00 01 02 03 04 05 — 10 9 8 7 6 5 4 3 2 1

MANUFACTURED IN THE UNITED STATES OF AMERICA

To James Robert

CONTENTS

AUGUST

SEPTEMBER

CONTENTS

CONTENTS

CONTENTS

INTRODUCTION

એ

Edgar DeWitt Jones once commented that the preacher for this day "must have the heart of a lion, the skin of a hippopotamus, the agility of a greyhound, the patience of a donkey, the wisdom of an elephant, the industry of an ant, and as many lives as a cat." A clerical menagerie!

The person who is called by God to stand in the pulpit and proclaim the Word of God requires an enormous combination of gifts and talents. None of us has all that is required; some of us, late on Saturday nights, wonder if we have any!

There is, however, one element without which we had best stay out of the pulpit: that is the anointing power of the Holy Spirit. Unless God has called us, and unless we constantly seek God's empowering presence, our homiletical gems are more likely to be revealed as fool's gold than as authentic treasures.

The *Abingdon Preaching Annual* cannot replace the hours of study, prayer, and preparation that are required for powerful preaching. My prayer is that it will provide you with a helpful, practical, and worthy resource which will help you to focus more quickly and directly on some of the unique preaching riches in Scripture.

This volume does not contain full sermon manuscripts, but instead features "sermon briefs"—suggested homiletical approaches to the text. The combination of sermon briefs and suggested worship resources for each Sunday offers a useful starting point for your own preparation. Through the *Abingdon Preaching Annual,* you'll have the opportunity to "look over the shoulder" of some gifted preachers who have struggled with these texts. Their insights may serve as seeds, which can bloom into homiletical fullness in your own anointed imagination.

May God's richest blessings be on your preaching in the year ahead!

Michael Duduit
Editor

15

SERMONS FOR SPECIAL DAYS

MOTHER'S DAY
The Ultimate Home Security System

❧

DEUTERONOMY 6:4-9

A few months ago I baptized two of the heirs to one of America's great fortunes in the chapel on their family estate. The estate was protected by an elaborate security system. My wife, Barbara, and I were impressed by the steep wall surrounding the property, the tall iron gates that swung open after a private security guard cleared us for admission, and the cameras that followed our every move as we drove up the driveway toward the house.

When I say we were "impressed," I mean we were firmly convinced we would not want to live like that. It was a startling contrast from our rural Mississippi student pastorate, where people in the community felt secure enough to leave their doors unlocked and their car keys in the ignition.

Unfortunately, few communities like this remain in our country. Even people not listed in Forbes 400 sleep behind dead bolts and install home security systems. No ordinary security system, however, can protect us from the intrusion of our most treacherous enemy. There is a thief whose primary target is not your money, or securities, or jewelry. He wants to steal your mind. He wants your children. Jesus says, "The thief comes only to steal and kill and destroy; I have come that they may have life, and have it to the full" (John 10:10 NIV).

A newspaper ran a story about a burglar who broke into a house and lived there for four years before the residents discovered him. When the family was home, the intruder lived quietly in the attic. When they went out, he had the run of the house. He cooked his meals in their kitchen, ate their food, read their books, and watched their television. The residents had no idea someone was living with them.

Perhaps your worst enemy is already living in your house and you don't realize it. His presence is proved by the television programs you watch, or the books and magazines you read. He subtly seduces your soul, and you have not even noticed that he lives with you.

If that is the case, I must tell you that God has already provided you with "divine power to demolish [your enemy's] strongholds . . . [by taking] captive every thought to make it obedient to Christ" (2 Cor. 10:4-5 NIV). In other words, if within the walls of your home there are programs, books, magazines, conversations, or toys that detract from your honor of the One who died on the cross to take away your sins, do your soul a favor: destroy them now.

This is the essence of what Moses writes to the Israelites. Recognizing that this thing called "faith in God" is, at every moment in history, only one generation away from extinction and does not automatically transfer from parents to children, he says the most important security system guards your home against moral corruption.

When Moses writes, "Talk about them when you sit at home" (Deut. 6:7 NIV), he speaks of the commandments and promises God intends to secure our families against our greatest enemy. It is another way of saying that if you want your children to grow up loving God, don't expect the schools to teach them Christianity. And don't presume the church will do that either in one or two hours a week. Rather, demonstrate the excitement of the Christian life in your everyday living by conquering despair with hope, hatred with love, lethargy with enthusiasm, anger with peace, rage with reason, and fear with confidence, and all things with love, so that God may be Master where you live. In short, by word and by deed, let your children know that Jesus, who died on the cross and rose again, makes a positive difference in life.

I am where I am today largely because of my maternal grandmother's influence. Abruptly widowed with six children on the eve of the Great Depression, she demonstrated to me through testimony and example the positive difference God's Son, Jesus Christ, makes to living. In short, Christ was not just part of her life; Christ *was* her life.

As I remember my grandmother, my mind's eye sees an embroidered message prominently displayed on her wall: "Christ is the head of this house; the unseen guest at every meal; the silent listener to every conversation." He was! Wouldn't it be wonderful if that was the case in every home!

Some newspaper columnists decry the decay of our society. However, societies don't disintegrate unless families do. Our society is in a mess because our families are in a mess. Our country is in jeopardy.

A little girl cried out, "Mummy, Mummy, you know that vase in the china cabinet you said was handed down from generation to generation?"

"Yes," her mother replied.

"This generation just dropped it!"

That may be true of America's Christian heritage. This generation is dropping it, and we are already paying the price for our carelessness.

Our children's souls are being stolen on a scale sensible people will not ignore. In thirty years we have experienced a fourfold increase in divorce, a 560 percent increase in illegitimate births (despite the legalization of abortion), and a 200 percent increase in teenage suicide rates. In this age our schools, which were once safe havens for children, are often war zones. "Impress [the commandments] on your children" (v. 7). Clothe them in "the full armor of God, so that when the day of evil comes [to them, as it surely will], [they] may be able to stand [their] ground" (cf. Eph. 6:13).

Your home can be protected by the world's ultimate home security system. How? Take God's commands and, "Write them on the doorframes of your houses" (Deut. 6:9 NIV). Counteract the terrorism of the times by releasing God's power upon your house. That will come only as you pray for it, study God's Word at home, and release yourself to God.

Moses itemizes God's commandments that give people life, hope, and prosperity. He prescribes God's program for spiritual sanitization. For some of us it means cleaning up our act before our partners, children, friends, and our God!

The ultimate home security system company is the church of Jesus Christ. If you want to own it, be active in a church where God's Word is central. Then take God's Word seriously in your home. Almost a quarter century of pastoral ministry has demonstrated that parents who openly invite Christ to be the center of their family life have invested in a security system money can never buy. They endow their children with a trust no bank can value. If you have not done it before, you can do it now, in his name, as we pray together. *(Robert Leslie Holmes)*

THANKSGIVING

Learn the Secret of Thanksgiving

૨૦

PHILIPPIANS 4:13

Recently on a college campus I asked a group of college students this question: "What do you plan to be doing ten years from now?" Some of them needed time to think before they could answer. They had not thought that far ahead. Others had no difficulty at all answering my question. They had already been thinking about it.

The student who impressed me most was a young man in his midtwenties who said, "What am I going to be doing ten years from now? Simple! I'm going to be sitting back, taking it easy, raking in the dough. I'm going to be so rich I will never have to work again!"

One reason this young man impressed me was because he reminded me of myself when I was younger. When I left Ireland to come to America, I was motivated in part by the stories of the Mellons and other Irish immigrants who were greatly blessed in their new home. Today I thank the Lord that I have been allowed to discover his idea of riches. It is far better than mine. The riches I had in mind, like the riches the college student spoke about, are very temporal. But God's riches last forever and ever.

Let me hasten to add that there is certainly nothing wrong with financial wealth. Some people I know have a gift for using their wealth wisely and generously. They achieve their wealth honestly and manage it very well. They are wise enough to understand that wealth can be a good thing but that it is certainly not the answer to all of life's situations. They would probably agree with me that for many of us, one of the worst things that could happen would be to wake up one morning and find ourselves extremely wealthy. Like the college student, we might be tempted to dream that monetary wealth would solve all our problems. Not all of us want to be wealthy. Not all of us need to have great financial holdings to feel we are successful.

A newspaper cartoon pictures two mountaineers climbing a high mountain. One of them has "Cost of Living" written across his back. With his hands shading his eyes, he is looking up and saying to his partner, "What peak? There is no peak!" The message of the cartoon is this: the cost of living (or perhaps I should say, the cost of the privilege of living in the greatest nation in the history of the world) never stops rising.

"There is no peak!" Maybe those of us who are expecting miracles from our government leaders need to be reminded of that. When America's cost of living stops rising America will be dead. I believe that one day we may need to earn millions of dollars every year just to make ends meet!

In this season we call Thanksgiving, we are called upon to be thankful! All across the world, in a variety of different forms, people pause at this time of the year to give thanks. One of my fondest memories of home is the annual Harvest Thanksgiving Service. Once a year we gathered with friends to lay crops at the front of our church sanctuary. We sang praise songs glorifying God for his many blessings. Later, we distributed the crops we gathered to needy people.

David sings, "It is good to give thanks to the LORD" (Ps. 92:1). Thanksgiving is one of those good emotions we all need to experience more often. The depth at which we feel thankful is a good indicator of how much we really appreciate ourselves, our loved ones, our blessings in life, and our prospects for eternity.

The apostle Paul has a tremendous lesson for us about thanksgiving. Paul's letters testify to a life that is a collage of good and bad. He grew up as a hate-filled zealot. One of his great joys was ferreting out Christians for arrest, and ultimately, stoning. One day Paul himself was suddenly arrested by the power of the risen Christ. The beater became the beaten. The scorner became the scorned. Perhaps the passage Paul himself would use to illustrate the complexity of his life is Romans 7. There he describes himself like a walking civil war—he wants to do right but often ends up doing wrong.

This same Paul, who planted more churches and brought the gospel to more people than anyone else in the history of the church except Christ himself, tells his favorite congregation from a Roman prison cell: "[F]or I have learned, in whatever state I am, to be content. I know how to be abased, and I know how to abound. Everywhere and in all things I have learned both to be full and to be hungry, both to abound and to suffer need. I can do all things through Christ who strengthens me" (Phil. 4:11-13 NKJV).

Writing from prison as he approaches his life's end, Paul's secret of thanksgiving is, "I have learned, in whatever state I am, to be content." Is not contentment what is missing from the lives of many of us? Many people who are single want to be married. Some married people say they would rather be single again. Folk who have children sometimes wish they were childless. Some folk with no children wish they could be parents. Poor folk wish they could be millionaires. One young millionaire I know was so unhappy about his life that he decided to give all his money away. Our universal lack seems to be a lack of contentment. This thing called contentment is scarce in our society, a fact that is well attested by the high level of alcoholism, drug abuse, immorality, and crime.

A friend told of meeting with a psychoanalyst as a prerequisite for admission to a doctoral program. The psychoanalyst asked, "What is your goal in life?" My friend had already learned to always answer that kind of question with a question, so he replied, "What do you mean by that?" The counselor responded, "Well (and he had to think for a minute to see what he did mean), what do you want out of life?" My friend answered, "More of the same."

My friend said the psychoanalyst looked at him quizzically and said, "What do you mean by that?" My friend responded, "Well, I am satisfied with life the way it is. I have a great wife, two marvelous children, and good friends. I really do not need anything else. If I must have more, I'd like to have more of what I have right now—more time with my wife, and children, and friends. There is nothing I don't have that I want."

The psychoanalyst scratched his head and said, "Frankly, I don't know what to do with someone who is satisfied with life as it is!"

What a sad commentary on our society! My friend—who, by the way, uses a wheelchair—knows Paul's secret for thanksgiving. He knows what it means to be content in "any and all circumstances."

Paul's secret to thanksgiving is threefold. First, he believed in God. He believed that his circumstances in this world, whether as a member of the Sanhedrin or as a prisoner of the Romans, were not unknown to God. He knew that God was interested in his life.

Second, Paul knew that his God was sovereign. God can do anything God wants, even going as far as rescuing Paul from prison. In Acts 16, we read that Paul had experienced God doing that very thing once before. Paul knew that God is in control of everything, even prisons.

In the movie *Star Wars* a number of references are made to a force that stays with those who believe in it. The greatest blessing that one could bestow upon his friends was, "May the force be with you." Paul's force was not an *it*. Paul's force was a personal, living, loving force who promises to be with us forever.

Third, Paul knew that God is limitless. Not only can God open prison doors, he can open the doors of life and death. Because Paul had encountered God personally in the risen Christ, he knew not only that God is able to do anything; he knew, moreover, that whatever God would do would ultimately be in Paul's best interests. Paul wrote, "For I am convinced that neither death, nor life, nor angels, nor rulers, nor things present, nor things to come . . . nor anything else in all creation, will be able to separate us from the love of God in Christ Jesus our Lord (Rom. 8:38-39).

Before Paul met Christ on the Damascus road he thought of God only as a lawmaker. After he met Christ, Paul found that not only is God a lawmaker, he is also our law keeper. Moreover, he is the God of love. God's love is so great that he gave his son for Paul and for "everyone who believes in him" (John 3:16).

When Paul believed Christ had died for him on Calvary and accepted Christ's death as the total sacrifice needed for salvation, he had taken the first step toward the wonderful discovery of the secret of thanksgiving. As he grew in the grace and love of Christ, Paul discovered Christ's sufficiency to control every circumstance of life. The ability to accept life as it really is, to have dreams but not to be so overcome by them that they have you, comes when we realize that God knows exactly where we are and has a plan in it all. That is the second step.

Have you taken these two steps to the secret of thanksgiving? Are you at peace with God through his son, Jesus Christ? To be a Christian is to be thankful because you realize that God has cared for you by sending Christ. You can know that now if you will turn away from sin, receive Christ as Savior, and go into the world to live as a follower of Christ. *(Robert Leslie Holmes)*

MENDING THE NET,
SHARPENING THE HOE
Monthly Meditations

ॐ

There is no shortcut to homiletical excellence. Quality preaching does not happen by accident. It comes with hard work, careful reading, research, and, of course, a clear dependence on the Holy Spirit. Charles Spurgeon and I agree that we must consider the great evil that will come upon our people if we neglect this work: they will perish! "Their blood shall be required at the watchman's hands." Therefore, it is imperative that we prepare ourselves as well as the material. As Spurgeon put it, "No man preaches his sermons well to others who does not first preach it to his own heart."

Our whole life in ministry will be affected by the level of our spiritual preparation. Jesus said to his disciples, "Let us go into the desert and rest awhile." Rest time, meditation time, and prayer time are work times. A farmer does not waste time when he sharpens his hoe, and the fisherman is working just as hard when he mends his net.

I have proposed twelve exercises to help the preacher prepare spiritually. These come from my own spiritual walk and have been of great help to me. Each one of us must make them fit his or her own style. These exercises will focus on both the preacher and the congregation. I trust they will be helpful.

I have selected a symbol for each month that moves with the Christian year. Some of these are symbols from medieval Christian art. I have also selected Scripture, and have a visualization and prayer time, as well. I hope this will prove meaningful. As Spurgeon observed, "A holy minister is an awful weapon in the hands of God."

J. H. Jowett in his Yale lectures presented in 1911 quoted the English judge, Lord Bowden, who said, "Cases are won in the chambers. Preaching that costs nothing, accomplishes nothing. Cases are won in the chambers with us too. If the study is a lounge, the pulpit will be an impertinence." Preaching is hard work in the closet, but it has its rewards in the open.

Someone asked Joe DiMaggio in the twilight years of his playing career, "Why do you play so hard?" His answer was simple: "I imagine there is a young man in the stadium today who came to see me play for the first time. I want him to see me playing hard and at my best." I think the application for the preacher is evident.

Suggestions for Using the Material

I find it helpful to do my reflection, praying, and devotional reading in the same place(s). There is a chair in my study, surrounded by materials with which I do my spiritual exercises. Other times I may walk in the woods for my quiet time and thinking time. I would suggest that quiet time be done without much variation of place and manner.

A notebook is most helpful. Keeping a journal is a helpful way to see how the movement of God is taking place in your life. Record your thoughts about texts, focus, and people. The old preacher who answered a question about his spiritual preparation was right when he said, "I read myself full, I think myself straight, I pray myself hot."

Scripture focus is not intended to be an exhaustive study of the Scriptures, but instead a devotional springboard into the theme for the month. However, as you read and think about these Scriptures, I would suggest using one a week/month. You will begin to note that God does leave fingerprints in your life, especially when you review your journal.

I would suggest that the prayer focus be a period of quiet meditation and visualization before a period of actual prayer. During this time I have found it helpful to determine prayer needs—of people for whom I am concerned, church concerns, and personal concerns—clarify them, meditate upon them, and visualize them. A time of prayer is simply implementing the focus. It is a time in which we talk to God about our focus: "Knock, and the door will be opened for you" (Matt. 7:7). It is a time to knock upon the door of God; it is bloody-knuckles time. *(Bill Self)*

JANUARY

&

Mending the Net, Sharpening the Hoe

Symbol: Door

View the new preaching year as an open-door opportunity and challenge.

Text:

"Behold, I stand at the door and knock. If anyone hears My voice and opens the door, I will come in to him and dine with him, and he with Me" (Rev. 3:20 NKJV).

Invocation:

Almighty God, look upon my life and cause all darkness and doubt to banish beneath your gaze. Look upon my ministry and banish all barriers to effectiveness and faithfulness. Fill my life and ministry with your Holy Spirit to the end that I may be led into paths of fruitful service through Jesus Christ. Amen.

Scripture Focus:

Meditate upon persons in the Bible who responded appropriately to challenges and opportunites—open doors:
- Joseph in the pit (Gen. 37:12-24)
- Moses before the burning bush (Exod. 3:1-12)
- Paul on a missionary journey (Acts 13:1ff.)
- Peter at the home of Simon the tanner (Acts 9:43; 10:6, 17, 32)
- Opportunities and open doors always expand our horizons.

Prayer Focus:
- Pray that God will reveal to you the opportunities for the new year.
- Pray that you will have a vision to see the opportunities and communicate that vision to your people.
- Make a list of the opportunities that God reveals to you as you meditate.
- Look at your choice of texts for the month. Ask God for insight to make them live.

- Ask God for courage to speak.
- Ask God to be present in worship.
- Look at your people. Call as many by name as you can. You may wish to do this in a series of meditative thoughts. Make a list of their names.
- Ask God to heal their spirits, their bodies. Visualize the people who should know God; list them and pray for them.

Prayer:

O God, as I look at another year, help me to see it as a year of opportunity, an open door for service, a chance to serve you and this church that you have entrusted to me. Help me to have the courage to seize the opportunities for service, as well as to lead our people to see and respond to them.

- Bless _____ that he/she might have his/her horizons broadened.
- Bless _____ that he/she may have his/her spirits sweetened.
- Bless _____ that he/she may have the courage to follow.
- Bless _____ that he/she may begin his/her journey.

In his strong name, Amen. *(Bill Self)*

JANUARY 5, 1997

❧

Second Sunday After Christmas

Worship Theme: Redemption and forgiveness are available to us through Christ.

Readings: Jeremiah 31:7-14; Ephesians 1:3-14; John 1:(1-9) 10-18

Call to Worship (Psalm 147:12-20):

Leader: Praise the LORD, O Jerusalem! Praise your God, O Zion!

People: For he strengthens the bars of your gates; he blesses your children within you.

Leader: He grants peace within your borders; he fills you with the finest of wheat.

People: He sends out his command to the earth; his word runs swiftly.

Leader: He gives snow like wool; he scatters frost like ashes.

People: He hurls down hail like crumbs—who can stand before his cold?

Leader: He sends out his word, and melts them; he makes his wind blow, and the waters flow.

People: He declares his word to Jacob, his statutes and ordinances to Israel.

Leader: He has not dealt thus with any other nation; they do not know his ordinances.

All: Praise the LORD!

Pastoral Prayer:

Almighty God, another year has begun for us, your children. And even as we change our calendars, we note the changing of our lives.

31

The new year brings with it new challenges. We face the challenge of building marriages and raising our children in committed Christian homes in a society that has thrown away the very idea of commitment. Some of us face the challenge and hurt of growing older without children. Some face the challenges of youth, others the challenges brought by aging. Some face the challenges of careers that may be going nowhere, while others face the challenge of careers that threaten to replace everything else in our lives. In the midst of a new year filled with challenges old and new, help us, Lord, to recognize your powerful presence. Remind us, Father, that no challenge is too great when you stand with us. Make this new year a good year, filled with your love and grace made manifest in our lives, for we ask it in the name of the One who goes with us whatever the challenge. Amen.

SERMON BRIEFS

A JOYFUL NEW BEGINNING

JEREMIAH 31:7-14

The beginning of a new year is always a period of refreshment and renewal. No matter how many bad things may have come your way in 1996—no matter how many problems, how much illness, how many family difficulties, how many notices from the IRS—that year is now history; and 1997 is here—fresh, clean, and full of promise. (Although you still have to answer those letters from the IRS!)

Even as Israel is in captivity in a foreign land, the prophet Jeremiah writes of a new beginning—a day when God will restore and renew his people, giving them a fresh start. Despite what has gone before—the nation's sin and rebellion, their lack of faith and vision—God will bring them home and establish a new covenant with them. It will be a joyful new beginning.

Could you use a joyful new beginning in your life right now? Just as God gave Israel a new beginning, God is willing to give you one as well. You can enjoy a new covenant, a new beginning with God through Jesus Christ.

What was that new covenant, that new beginning like for Israel?

I. A New Beginning Produces Praise (vv. 7-9)

God would bring a remnant back to the land of promise. None would be excluded who were willing to come—even the weakest and most vulnerable among them: the blind, the lame, those who had just had children or who were about to have children.

And what was the result of Israel's salvation? Resounding praise! They would "sing aloud with gladness" and "raise shouts." They would "give praise" and celebrate the greatness of their nation—not because of any inherent value in Israel, but because God's covenant relationship gave them significance.

Verse 9 is important because it reminds us that an important part of authentic praise is sincere repentance. Israel was to know a new kind of greatness, based not on political power or military might but based on a covenant relationship with God.

If you wish to have a new beginning with God, it must include repentance—a godly sorrow for sin and a willingness to allow God to turn your life in a new direction.

II. A New Beginning Is Based on Grace (vv. 10-11)

It was important for Israel to understand that their new beginning was not produced by their own efforts; it was a gift of God's grace—unmerited, undeserved, flowing out of divine love. And Israel was to demonstrate God's grace to all the nations.

Two important words are used here: *ransom* and *redeem*. To ransom means literally "to loose"—it involves paying a price to receive ownership of something, often something once owned or possessed. God was willing to pay the price to ransom Israel and give her a new beginning. To redeem is an act of deliverance, usually relating to a family member; for example, one might redeem a relative who had been sold into slavery by purchasing his or her freedom, or one might redeem a piece of land that had been sold away from the family.

Just as God was willing to ransom and redeem Israel, so he offers the same deliverance to us. God wants us to be a part of his covenant family, and he has already paid the price—through Christ's death on the cross.

III. A New Beginning Results in Joy (vv. 12-14)

Now freed and restored to their homeland, Israel would rejoice in celebrating God's abundant gifts. Israel was to be a new community focused on worshiping God.

A new beginning with God always results in joy. That's why Jesus said, "I came that they may have life, and have it abundantly" (John 10:10). Through a relationship with Jesus Christ, you can experience that joy which God alone can produce in the human heart.

Are you ready for a new beginning? There's no better day than today for a fresh start with the Lord. *(Michael Duduit)*

HEIRS OF THE PROMISE

EPHESIANS 1:3-14

Timothy William Hennessy, a child of the promise, was baptized on the Sunday that this scripture came up in the lectionary three years ago. And in his baptism on that particular day, we found a perfect explication of this reading from Ephesians.

Many months before that, his mother, Susan, herself a child of this church, stood up during the sharing time to announce another birth in their family. Wistfully she added, "All we need now is an heir." In due time, in God's good pleasure, an heir was born to Sue and Tim, Sr., and they requested this date for his baptism. None of us knew then what the lectionary scripture for the date was. It was thrilling to find the answer to Sue's prayer from so long before, already given beforehand by the Spirit, so clearly in the scripture for the day of their "heir's" baptism.

We could even call this passage "Susan's Song," as it rejoices in the riches of our inheritance of redemption, forgiveness, and boundless grace as heirs through Christ, which, as Paul says, is "marked with the seal of the promised Holy Spirit; [which] is the pledge of our inheritance" (v. 13).

I. Our Inheritance Is Cause for Thanksgiving

All eleven verses in this scripture seem to have leaped from Paul's heart, in one single exuberant sentence in the Greek! It is as if the effervescence of joy and thanksgiving that Paul is feeling can hardly be spoken in words. So it flows out of him in a song that his soul "speaks." The contents of God's mysterious "will" (vv. 9, 11) have been revealed to Paul, and he is overwhelmed by the generosity of his benefactor—the boundless riches of his inheritance! Here is the passionate gratitude of one who knows what it means to be truly guilty of great sin and then experience the life-restoring redemption of being made "holy and blameless before him [Christ] in love" (v. 4).

II. Our Inheritance Is Couched in Mystery

Paul also realizes the incredible synchronicity of this as a blessing for which he had long before been "chosen." This is not the kind of predestination that the Presbyterian woman was talking about when, after she fell down the stairs, she said, "Thank goodness that's over!" Rather this is the destiny that is part of a vision of spiritual blessing planned from the beginning and offered, mysteriously, as the inheritance to many. Yes, it is mysterious; but perhaps sometimes we make it more oblique than necessary.

Do you know what you get when you cross a Mafia leader and a theologian? An offer you can't understand! But that's not the kind of offer Paul wants to advise us of here. The full extent of the blessings in our inheritance is beyond our comprehension, to be sure. But these blessings are being revealed to us daily, and Paul extends God's invitation to exalt in being open to receive all that is offered to us in these blessed promises that are our rightful inheritance.

III. Our Inheritance Is the Basis for Abundant Living

It is a great sadness, and one of the most insidious forms of evil, that the systems of this world lead so many "children of the promise" into blind alleys, where the great promise and the hope that was in them are lost. Most unfortunately of all, even the church itself has often been in confusion about what it means to be called and blessed by God. Too often "Give your selfish will to God" has meant, "Give your will and resources to this person who rules in the church in the very same way others rule in the world, by imposing their will, not by helping you to find God's."

Like a child whose baptism functions also as an elucidation of this scripture, we were all created out of God's love and similarly destined for the fullness of love's expression, each in our own unique way. It is our birthright, in Christ. Praise God who has made us blessed heirs to such a glorious inheritance! *(Kathleen Peterson)*

THE GLAD SONG OF SALVATION

JOHN 1:1-18

There are days when it happens unexpectedly. When the Spirit blows like a cool breeze on a sweltering afternoon. When you hear the voice of angels in the prayers of your colleagues or friends. When you know—really know for sure—that what you hope and believe and trust in is true.

I had shuffled into my liturgy practicum a few minutes late. What we were doing—what we had been doing all semester—was rehearsing the rituals. Over the twelve weeks each student was to baptize a Cotton Patch Premie, offer a Great Thanksgiving over a fictional Eucharist, and "marry" a couple of fellow students. The professor would make suggestions and critique each student along the way, and then the class members would have their shot after the ritual was performed. It was pretty dull stuff, to tell you the truth—except on one day.

I arrived late, not altogether excited about another round of eucharistic prayers to be offered, as they were, over water and a wadded up paper towel. I slipped into my seat, only to be called on to assist a student, a candidate for episcopal orders. With a certain chagrin, I took my place at her right shoulder, ready to endure as best I could, when suddenly, almost ethereally, I heard music. Heavenly music! The celebrant was singing the prayer. Chanting it! I stood transfixed.

The usually chatty professor was speechless. The mouths of most class members hung open; they were barely able to utter the congregational responses. The celebrant's plainsong had floored us. When the ritual ended, everyone was silent. After a few moments the professor said, "And that, class, is why, in the early church, nothing was said that could be sung."

Prose comes after the poetry, explanations after the arias. Mere speech is no match for a love song, and especially when the beloved is God.

Christianity is a faith that sings. Look no further than our lesson scripture, where John the evangelist sings the beginnings of the gospel of Jesus Christ. Although this text is most often referred to as the "Prologue," I have come to regard it more as the "Overture," for in it all the themes of the balance of the gospel are sounded.

Consider it a hymn with three stanzas, with two descants regarding the Baptist thrown in for good measure. The first stanza, verses 1-5, sings of the creating God's relation to all creation through the Word. The second stanza, verses 9-13, sings of the intervening God's relation to all humanity through the Word. The third stanza, verses 14-18, sings of the redeeming God's offer of salvation to all who receive the Word.

Of course, the gracious theme of these stanzas is counterpointed with rejection, hatred, and darkness. But the overture's climax is one of mutual Christian confession; for while many, even of God's own people, did not receive the Word, "we did."

"The Word became flesh and dwelt among us, and we have seen his glory . . . we have received grace upon grace . . ." It's a song more than a syllogism, poetry more than prose. And though we have lost the original tune, we can, in faith, still find the glad rhythm of this song of salvation.

We all learn our faith by singing it. By singing our faith, we learn more of it. And the Scriptures, by example and exhortation, remind us that the Word became flesh is a truth that has to be sung to be believed. *(Thomas R. Steagald)*

JANUARY 12, 1997

❧

Baptism of the Lord

Worship Theme: The Holy Spirit empowers us for Christian living.

Readings: Genesis 1:1-5; Acts 19:1-7; Mark 1:4-11

Call to Worship (Psalm 29:1-4, 10-11):

Leader: Ascribe to the LORD, O heavenly beings, ascribe to the LORD glory and strength.

People: **Ascribe to the LORD the glory of his name; worship the LORD in holy splendor.**

Leader: The voice of the LORD is over the waters; the God of glory thunders, the LORD, over mighty waters.

People: **The voice of the LORD is powerful; the voice of the LORD is full of majesty.**

Leader: The LORD sits enthroned over the flood; the LORD sits enthroned as king forever.

All: **May the LORD give strength to his people! May the LORD bless his people with peace!**

Pastoral Prayer:

We stand in awe of your glory, O Lord of heaven and earth. We are your people, the creation of your word, and we gather together to worship your majesty and love. We are amazed at the gift of your presence, Lord. Even as you were active at the creation of our world, so we sense your hand in our own lives day by day. Even as you were with Jesus in the baptismal waters at the River Jordan, so you have been with us in the water of baptism. Even as you baptized those early believers with your Spirit, so we know that your Holy Spirit has come to reside in our lives, guiding and leading us daily. We cannot understand such love, that leads the Lord of all creation to care so about such rebellious creatures, but we praise you for your love and thank you for your presence. May we so yield our lives to you that we will be living, walking witnesses to the power of your presence. Amen.

SERMON BRIEFS

IN THE BEGINNING

GENESIS 1:1-5

What is your first memory? Some people claim to remember images from infancy; others don't recall any clear memories before age six or seven.

If the universe could speak—and perhaps in some ways it does, through natural revelation—the first memory it would have is of God, the Creator. Creation is God's handiwork. The opening verses of Genesis reveal some marvelous truths about God and his creation.

I. God Is Before Creation

Before there was anything else, God was. "In the beginning, God." Before the human mind could comprehend, before anything we know existed, God was there. Before the Big Bang or the Little Pop or anything science imagines, God was there.

God is foundational—before all, above all, beyond all, over all. That is why idolatry is a heinous sin in the Bible—because it puts the created thing above the Creator.

II. God Is the Active Agent in Creation

When the time of creation arrived, God was the agent of creation. He is the prime mover, the supreme creator. Anything that exists does so because God brought it into being.

How God creates is of little importance. When we get hung up on such questions—was it a twenty-four-hour day or an aeon?—we are majoring on minor things. What matters is that *God* is at the center, the foundation of all creation. As Madeleine L'Engle said, "To argue about *how* God made us is to argue about non-essentials.

. . . The important thing is that creation is God's and that we are part of it."

In his grace, God allows us to be part of his continuing creative work. Anyone who has held a tiny baby in his or her arms must rejoice and marvel that God allows us to be a part of his creative process.

III. God Accomplishes His Purpose in Creation

Though some people argue that the universe is a giant accident—a cosmic coincidence—the words of Genesis ring true to ears of faith. Creation has a divine purpose. God has a reason in all he creates.

God accomplishes his own purpose in creation:

- from nothing—something!
- from formless—structure!
- from darkness—light!

That is how God creates—taking what seems like nothing, and in his divine hands transforming it into an incredible something. What was once "without form and void" is now the miraculous universe in which we live.

That is also what God has done in us through Jesus Christ. He has transformed us into his children—sinners into saints, lost into found, nothing into something! *(Michael Duduit)*

HAVE YOU HEARD ABOUT THE SPIRIT?

ACTS 19:1-7

There's a wonderful true story about the brilliant pianist, Artur Schnabel. In the middle of a public performance of a Mozart piano concerto, Schnabel had a memory lapse and forgot the notes! The conductor, Toscanini, kept the orchestra playing, although there was an unexpected pause of about three minutes in the piano music. When they found out later that an unauthorized, pirated recording of the concert was going to be reproduced for distribution, Schnabel was told he would have to play the piece over. He refused, on the grounds that if he did it again he "might play it better, but it wouldn't be as good." He used the word "good" to mean moving "under the influence" of the Spirit.

I. The Spirit Brings Cleansing and Power

In Acts 19, we catch up to Paul in Ephesus, "where he found some disciples" (v. 1). He asked them if they had received the Holy Spirit and they answered: "We have not even heard that there is a Holy Spirit" (v. 2). They had experienced the water baptism of John. But Paul told them that was just a prelude, as John himself had said, to the main music of Jesus' baptism.

Outlined here are two distinct levels of religious experience. The first, water baptism, is the baptism of repentance; the humble admission of sin, which draws one to seek forgiveness and cleansing. One is then technically "better" because one is allowed to "forget" and make mistakes, as one is released from the fetters of the unforgiving law. But what then? Is that it? No, that is just the first step. Then comes the fiery baptism by the Holy Spirit, which illumines one to live in the fullness of grace, inspired to be really "good."

II. The Spirit Brings Awareness and Communication

When Paul baptized the new disciples "in the name of the Lord Jesus (v. 5), the Holy Spirit came upon them, and they spoke in tongues and prophesied" (v. 6). As at Pentecost, when the first disciples received the Holy Spirit and spoke in tongues, so too did the disciples in Ephesus. When they received the Holy Spirit they could speak to foreigners and be understood. They weren't just babbling in foreign tongues—they were communicating. The Spirit had lifted them to a new level of awareness.

This is the same Spirit that Genesis 1 tells us brooded, like a hovering bird, over the formless void and darkness of the deep. As the voice of God spoke the Spirit brought light out of the darkness. And then there was morning.

This is the same Spirit that Old Testament prophets likened to water in the desert. It brings forth new life and hope out of parched places. It makes all things new.

The Spirit releases us to go forward and then inspires us to become what we were created to be.

41

III. The Spirit Brings Unity and Growth

Christians need not act as if they have never heard of the Holy Spirit! We can move with the Spirit, beyond old assumptions, beyond ego and pride, beyond the need to look "good." The Spirit calls us as Christians to be able even to look foolish in the world's eyes. We can be open to new understandings, new connectedness, and easy access to our unity with each other. We can be ready to be amazed at how the Spirit can lift us out of deep waters, washed, renewed, and ready to be recreated in love. We can wait with assurance for this daily baptism.

My daughter told me a story that reminded me of the Spirit's presence in daily life.

One day while she was folding clothes and singing as she worked, a friend dropped by. He came into the house, sat down, and just looked at her. "What?" she asked him, thinking he must have something to tell her. He responded, "Don't stop. It makes me feel so secure when I hear you singing." No concert hall, but real "good" Spirit. (*Kathleen Peterson*)

TAKING HIS PLACE

MARK 1:4-11

A rather active layperson came to me seeking baptism. Her request caught me off-guard. Being somewhat new to the congregation, and having seen her at almost every function, I had assumed she was already a member of the congregation, perhaps of long-standing. Membership aside, it had never occurred to me to wonder whether she had ever made a public profession of her faith—in fact, she had done so regularly since my arrival!

So when she made her request I expressed my honest befuddlement. She smiled and said, "It's only been lately that I've decided I'm ready to take my place."

She went on to say that membership in the church was a sacred responsibility to her—too many people had given too much of themselves for too long for her to take it lightly. She had wanted to make sure she was ready to take her place, shoulder to shoulder with others for whom our congregation was life and home. She had wanted to be ready to give completely of herself before she took the vows of membership.

And even more to the point, she said she wanted to be sure she was ready to take her place through baptism. While she had always believed, she had not always been sure she was ready to commit in the fashion so many faithful others had. "After all," she said, "so many have died for the faith—I just wanted to be sure I could live for it. And now I am ready to take my place with them—to be one of y'all."

I. Jesus Modeled the Way for Us

Look at the text from Mark and you see a story of Jesus taking his place such as the laywoman did. He goes to the Jordan to get in line and be baptized by John. Did he need to do it? Why did he submit to such a thing? The Lord of the universe, the Word by which all that is made was made, being baptized like a common sinner? What's going on here?

These questions and others like them have haunted theologians and exegetes through the centuries. And while I have no decisive conclusions to offer , I am reminded of Frederick Buechner's observation that Jesus honored human life by living one. He hallowed human death by dying one. He created new life by being raised to one. He took his place among us that we might take our place with him.

Similarly, it would seem that Jesus commends baptism by submitting to one. Jesus takes his place with sinful Israel as a means of accepting Israel's plight onto himself. He is more ready to give himself to the task before him, there to take his distinctive place among other prophets of God who ultimately gave their lives for the restoration of God's people. That which drips off Jesus' face as he rises from the water is no less than his obedience and his commission, his commencing to do the will he came to do.

Theologians and exegetes should expect no less, then. In fact, the more speculative question might be, "Why not earlier?" All we can say is that, somehow, the time was right.

II. Our Call Is to Follow Him

In Mark's Gospel, the baptism serves as the second scene in a three-part introduction to Jesus' ministry. The first scene is John's ministry, and the third is the temptation. Mark uses each to offer distinctive insights into the work Jesus will do.

In this scene, explicit connection is made between Jesus' work and the Holy Spirit's leading; implicit connection is made with the generations of faith who, at the right time and at the leading of the Spirit, will take their own place in line to do God's will. (*Thomas R. Steagald*)

JANUARY 19, 1997

Second Sunday After Epiphany

Worship Theme: We are called to be faithful witnesses to Christ's love.

Readings: 1 Samuel 3:1-10 (11-20); 1 Corinthians 6:12-20; John 1:43-51

Call to Worship (Psalm 139:1-6, 13-14):

Leader: O LORD, you have searched me and known me. You know when I sit down and when I rise up; you discern my thoughts from far away.

People: **You search out my path and my lying down, and are acquainted with all my ways.**

Leader: Even before a word is on my tongue, O LORD, you know it completely. You hem me in, behind and before, and lay your hand upon me.

People: **Such knowledge is too wonderful for me; it is so high that I cannot attain it.**

Leader: For it was you who formed my inward parts; you knit me together in my mother's womb. I praise you, for I am fearfully and wonderfully made.

All: **Wonderful are your works; that I know very well.**

Pastoral Prayer:

Our Creator and Redeemer, we praise you for your mighty works. You have created the cosmos, yet you also create each of our lives. Even in the earliest moments of life, while we were too tiny to even be seen, your awesome hand was crafting us, preparing us, loving us. Such is too great to be hidden or ignored—yet how often we have done just that to your love. We who have been the recipients of your grace have refused to share the good news with others. Forgive us, O Lord, for our reckless disregard of your love. Help us, O Lord, to become faithful witnesses—allowing your love to over-flow our lives and touch the lives of those around us. Make us instruments of your grace, as we proclaim the love of the One in whose name we are privileged to pray. Amen.

SERMON BRIEFS

SEEING THE VISION

1 SAMUEL 3:1-10

As we near the end of the twentieth century, think back to the persons who made the most different in the way we live. Chances are, the list won't include many politicians or political leaders. It would, however, include names like Thomas Edison, Henry Ford, Wilbur and Orville Wright, Jonas Salk. These were the visionaries—men and women who looked beyond their present to see what might be possible in the future.

In every area of life, visionaries help us look beyond where we are to where we might be. Average people see limits; visionaries see possibilities.

That is also true in the life of faith. God gives some people unique insights. An example of such visionaries in the Old Testament would be the prophets—those who received a word from the Lord and pro-claimed it to the people. In the New Testament, Paul was a visionary, he envisioned a church that included both Jews and Gentiles. In our own generation, Mother Teresa has been a visionary, raising the aware-ness of all Christians to the plight of the poorest among us.

God's visions come to people of authentic faith. Are you seeking to know God's purpose and direction for your life, your family, your career? Do you need a vision from the Lord? Our text offers insight into the kind of faith that visionaries have.

I. God Gives Visions to Those with Obedient Hearts

One of the most poignant verses in all of Scripture is found in verse 1: "The word of the LORD was rare in those days; visions were not widespread." Visions were rare because sin had corrupted the

46

house of Eli, the chief priest. His sons were evil in their actions, but rather than control or even punish them, Eli stood by and allowed them to corrupt Israel with their sin. The result was that God did not give his visions to Eli—sin was the obstacle.

By contrast, young Samuel was dedicated to God's service. Influenced by his godly mother, Hannah, Samuel was devoted to doing God's will. And because he had a heart for the Lord, Samuel was able to receive the visions that Eli could not receive.

As you seek to know God's vision for your own life, there is a critical lesson here: God will not give his visions where sin abounds. God's visions are given to men and women whose hearts are obedient toward the Lord.

II. God Gives Visions to Those with Open Hearts

Recall the story in our text. Once Samuel knew God was calling, he was open to the message. God gives his visions to those who are willing to receive them.

A salesman called on a farmer one day and began making a presentation about a new book on farming. The salesman assured the farmer that the book contained a wealth of new techniques that would make him a better farmer.

"I don't need any new book," answered the farmer. "I already know more about farming than I'm willing to do now."

Sometimes we say we want to know God's will for our lives when the fact is we are not willing to follow through on what we already know. Our hearts are not truly open to God's leadership.

It is as if God has given us part of a map and directed us to follow the designated path. "Where is the rest of the map?" we ask, and God responds, "I'll give you that part when you get to the end of this part."

Are you open to God's leadership in your life? Are you willing to follow his vision—even before you know the whole story? If so, then God can use you as a visionary, to achieve new vistas of faith in his name. (*Michael Duduit*)

PRECIOUS EARTHEN VESSELS

1 CORINTHIANS 6:12-20

Paul insisted on his freedom, through love's higher calling, from the law. But then he had the ongoing challenge to constantly clarify that this is freedom to exceed the law's limitations, not to violate them. Yes, he could do as he pleased. No, it did not please him to do any and all things—only what was to the glory of God.

Especially regarding the body, Paul wanted to be very clear that although humbly "we have this treasure in earthen vessels" (2 Cor. 4:7 NKJV), the vessels themselves are not to sneeze at. Indeed, the body is a most precious, if temporary, "temple of the Holy Spirit" (v. 19).

I. The Body Previously

Interestingly enough, the church has not always picked up on either the close link between the earthly and the spiritual or the respect for the proper care and feeding of the body to which Paul admonishes us. But the ancient Hebrews knew. In Genesis, the loss of perfection means first and foremost the loss of perfect unity with the body. Bodily shame—disruption of the natural state of perfect unity with one's body—was the telltale sign to God that Adam and Eve had sinned.

The church has too often trivialized sin. Instead of the loss of perfection and paradise, sin becomes a few bad things we do—drinking, smoking, gambling—and we can eliminate sin by eliminating these types of behaviors. This view is just too simpleminded for the Hebrews and for Paul. Their guilt was not over a lie here or a theft there. It was a guilt that went to their heart of hearts, to their involvement in the loss of the potential they had seen for perfect realization of God's whole creation.

It's an endless battle to try to get rid of sin by cutting it out piece by piece. You cast out one demon and seven others enter the empty space. You stop biting your nails and you start smoking. You stop smoking and you start yelling at your kids, taking tranquilizers, and overeating. You can't get rid of the bad until you find the good that it's filling in for.

When we lose touch with the great goodness of our creation we are in pain and in sin. People in this country spend billions of dollars a year on alcohol to help forget this loss. So many of the things we do are the desperate, self-destructive acts of people trying to again feel *something* and forget a lot.

II. The Body Politic

God's investment in material creation was costly from the start. And the "dust to dust" process does not mean that what is put into the stomach is not significant (v. 13). Furthermore, acts that defile the body have spiritual consequences (v. 18). Paul solemnly bows before the mysterious but awesome power and ramifications of the connection between body and spirit.

We don't want to underestimate the insatiable destructive bent of those who have already betrayed their own bodies and spirits. For them, these things are without value. You don't stop smoking or polluting or plundering unless the alternative is something very good. That's why the fight of conservationists is endless. You can save the rain forests this year, but they'll be on the market again next year because lots of people don't know that their own lives really are more important than making money.

III. The Body Glorious

The kingdom of God, in which all "sins" become obsolete, was postponed because it was seen as coming from outside. Saint Augustine ruefully commented: "Too late I loved you! And behold, you were within me, and I out of myself, and *there* I searched for you" (*Confessions,* X, 27).

The kingdom of God is not simply in the future; we are to seek it here and now, even in our earthly bodies. We *all* are members of that glorious body, in, as well as out, of the flesh. *(Kathleen Peterson)*

COME AND SEE

JOHN 1:43-51

Fred Craddock has observed that the "biblical word central to the Season of Epiphany is 'revelation,' for this is the time we celebrate the revealing of the Son of God. But the companion word to revelation is 'witness,' for revelation in the biblical sense is never open and obvious to everyone, interested or not, believer or not" (*Preaching Through the Christian Year, B* [Valley Forge: Trinity Press International, 1993], 81).

These words seem especially pertinent to the text for the day: Philip's witness to Nathanael. Philip is unable to prove what he believed he had found in Jesus, but he is able to say at least: "Come and see." What Philip sees moves him to help others to see—to want to help them, anyway, whether they do or do not see.

As Epiphany is the "moment" of God's self-revelation to the world, the season following prompts us to ask: How will we witness? How will we reveal that which has been revealed to us? We are concerned here with the style and substance of our evangelism.

I. Witness Is Not Technique, but Touch

In our denominations these days there is much discussion about church growth. Much of the discussion is framed in such a way to make it sound evangelistic; but I must confess that most often it sounds more like marketing. Direct mailings, telephone blitzes, the packaging of worship in alternative forms—you know the routine. And it may be great stuff, really, for this age in which we live—quick, efficient, impersonal.

My fear, however, is that our media will affect our message. "The media is the message," some will say, and more's the pity if our sales pitch so shapes our "product" that the church and its ministries will themselves become too quick (saving souls is a long and laborious process), too efficient (grace seems to me to imply a certain inefficient extravagance), and too impersonal (when God in Christ is anything but).

My suspicion is that when the excitement over this latest trend of techniques fades, we will be left with the time-honored and tested example we have before us today. If we really want to be evangelistic, if we want to be real evangelists, we may need to get off the phone, find a friend or stranger, and say, "Come and see."

II. Witness Is Faithfulness

This little vignette seems to radiate obscurity. Who is Nathanael that Philip, or Jesus, wants to have him along? After all, he seems somewhat bigoted, ready to condemn Jesus on account of his address and accent. And he isn't listed in the other Gospels and Acts as one of the Twelve. So what's the purpose of this story?

Perhaps it is a paradigm—a "go and do thou likewise" kind of story. Perhaps it is an exhortation to those of us who are believers to begin witnessing: not by coercing or arguing, lampooning or belittling.

Rather, as Philip was called and then went calling, the text is a summons to us to witness, to invite, to speak the truth of our faith's experience even to those for whom the invitation may sound strange. If we are faithful as Philip was faithful, God can claim the incredulous, even as Nathanael was claimed.

And perhaps it is a reminder, too, that even we who now believe once did not, that at one time we were no better off than Nathanael. But as he heard and believed, so others have heard and believed through him. So too will our faith be shared with others if we hear and believe.

III. Witness to the Overflow of Transformed Lives

Jesus called Philip, and Philip responded by witnessing to Nathanael. When we hear the authentic word of God, God's summons to discipleship, we will want to take others with us. If we haven't heard that first call, all the direct mail in the world won't help. But if we have heard the word, then we will be not only like Philip, but also like Peter, James, and John, who in Acts 4:20 say, "we cannot keep from speaking about what we have seen and heard." When people ask us, "What's going on with you people at the church?" we can answer, "Come and see." (*Thomas R. Steagald*)

JANUARY 26, 1997

❧

Third Sunday After Epiphany

Worship Theme: God's forgiveness comes in response to our repentance and faith.

Readings: Jonah 3:1-5, 10; 1 Corinthians 7:29-31; Mark 1:14-20

Call to Worship (Psalm 62:5-8):

Leader: For God alone my soul waits in silence,

***People:* for my hope is from him.**

Leader: He alone is my rock and my salvation, my fortress;

***People:* I shall not be shaken.**

Leader: On God rests my deliverance and my honor;

***People:* my mighty rock, my refuge is in God.**

Leader: Trust in him at all times, O people; pour out your heart before him;

***All:* God is a refuge for us.**

Pastoral Prayer:

Our Father and our God, we praise you. We lift up praise in response to your creative power, that fashioned earth and outer space and all that we are and have. We lift up praise for your awesome holiness, that draws us even as it forces us to recognize our own unworthiness. We lift up praise for your mercy and grace, that reached out to us while we were still consumed by sin and rebellion against your will. You alone are our deliverance and honor; you alone are our rock and salvation. And even as you extended your love toward us, make us instruments of your love in a lost and hurting world. Help us to boldly and compassionately go forth to proclaim your good news and to call people to decision. Equip us to be messengers of the kingdom, and help us to recognize that the time is short. For we ask it in the name of the One who announced your kingdom's coming even as he inaugurated it in our midst. Amen.

SERMON BRIEFS

WHEN REVIVAL COMES

JONAH 3:1-5, 10

Every Sunday school student knows the story of Jonah and the great fish. One of my favorite childhood songs comes from that story: "This is the fish that swallowed Jonah . . . gulp, gulp, gulp!"

But the story of Jonah being swallowed, then spit up by the great fish, is not the biggest miracle in this small Old Testament book. The greatest miracle is the revival that takes place in the evil city of Nineveh, when Jonah finally arrives and shares God's message with the city.

The revival that takes place in Nineveh clearly demonstrates that God desires to forgive those who truly repent and turn to him. Jonah knew that; in fact, that's why he wanted to avoid this prophetic assignment. He wanted the people of Nineveh punished for their sins, and he was afraid that if they heard God's words they would repent and God would forgive! He was a reluctant prophet if there ever was one—ample evidence that true revival does not come from the skill of the messenger but from God alone.

One of the great needs of the church in our own day is a divinely given revival—a spiritual awakening that will transform the church and society. What does it take for revival to come?

I. Revival Comes When God's Truth Is Proclaimed

Jonah didn't preach a revival sermon—there wasn't even an invitation and six verses of "Just As I Am"! Jonah didn't want these foreign people to repent; he wanted God to destroy them.

But what amazing power exists in the simple, authentic proclamation of God's word, accompanied by the power of the Holy Spirit! Even a reluctant prophet like Jonah can't stop God's work in this place, and the entire city was transformed.

God does not ask you or me to produce revival—he does tell us to be faithful in sharing his love and truth. If we will simply be obedient in sharing God's truth, God will take care of the revival. God will produce the transformation.

It doesn't matter if you are not a trained theologian; Jonah's message had just eight words! If you are willing to share what Jesus Christ has done in your life, then God can use you to bring revival.

II. Revival Comes When God's Message Is Believed

To Jonah's horror, people not only heard God's message but they also believed it! They took it to heart—they put on their mourning garments, demonstrating their grief over their sin.

It is not enough simply to hear God's message; we must also accept God's truth and respond to it in faith. That's what the people of Nineveh did, and it transformed their lives and their city.

Is God speaking to you now? Is there a word from the Lord for you? It won't make any difference in your life until you open your heart and mind to the Lord—until you are willing to receive God's truth into your heart.

III. Revival Comes When God's Truth Is Applied

Notice the king's proclamation (vv. 7-9); the people are to give up their evil ways and their violence. Already the people had put on their outer garments to reflect an inner transformation. Hearing the word is not enough; even professing faith is not enough in itself. Authentic faith results in positive action.

Revival is not a matter of hearing only. When we truly believe— when we are willing to make Christ Lord and Savior of our lives— there will be a transforming difference in our lives. (*Michael Duduit*)

MONITORING YOUR INVESTMENTS

1 CORINTHIANS 7:29-31

It is much to Paul's credit that he somewhat mitigates his advice in this passage by saying directly that it is *his* advice. On these matters, he says, "I have no command of the Lord, but I give my opinion" (v. 25). He also sets his advice in a particular context, saying,

"I think that, in view of the impending [present] crisis" (v. 26). So what we have here is a contextual opinion.

Yet even though Paul has clearly set forth the limits of his counsel here, it is clear that there is much timeless wisdom in this passage.

I. Counsel for the Moment

For the time and people on Paul's heart here, this is his best thought. He saw his world about to be transformed and naturally wanted everyone to focus on that reality. If the kingdom of God in its fullness may be arriving momentarily, it makes sense not to let yourself be distracted by lesser, mundane things.

So it seemed unwise to Paul, under those circumstances, for anyone to take on long-term and even problematic responsibilities like those involved in marriage (v. 28). If one was already married, however, Paul says, "Do not seek to be free" (v. 27). His basic advice is, at this moment in history, it was "well for you to remain as you are," whatever that status might have been (v. 26).

II. Counsel for the Long Term

Beginning with verse 29, Paul gets to the more radical application of this imminence orientation. He stresses again that the "appointed time has grown short." One should not allow even family responsibilities to distract from one's highest calling in the Lord. Even deep emotions of the moment, like grief and joy, cannot hold sway now. One cannot allow possessions, business dealings, and other things of this world to dominate one's attention, because they are all "passing away" (v. 31).

These insights are not limited to a specific time or place in Paul's ministry. Rather, out of his clear understanding of the illusory nature of the things of this world, Paul offers us the perspective from "higher ground" that is appropriate for all times and places. This new orientation doesn't mean we cannot cherish the present moment. In fact, it is meant to enhance our ability to experience life in its fullness, for in our present awareness we will also be open to the change that is emerging.

So Paul is not saying, "Don't be involved in your life and in how it can be developed now." He is saying, "Don't cling to your life as it is now; don't insist on plans that could distract you from what God is trying to do in your life." It is foolish to needlessly expend energy on the ephemeral and secondary when those things distract us from what is truly important. Don't worry about circumcision (v. 19), or whether the erasers are all back in line on the blackboard. Don't focus on the secondary and miss what God is trying to do.

III. Finding Your Place in God's Time

Paul states the key issue in verse 17: "Let each of you lead the life that the Lord has assigned, to which God called you." Don't let peripheral issues and things consume your life and keep you from God's purpose for your life. Don't spend all your time watching the stock market and miss the eternal investments God has in store for you.

Here is wisdom: Do less and accomplish more. It is the focus of mind and heart that moves mountains, not spinning your wheels around tasks that are not at the center of your highest calling.

Jesus appeared on a donkey outside Vatican City one day, and messengers ran in to tell the pope. With great excitement they cried out, "Jesus is outside. What shall we do?" The pope answered, "Look busy!"

Paul says it isn't busyness that makes the difference, but availability to what God wants to do in our lives. (*Kathleen Peterson*)

SCREAMS AND CALLS

MARK 1:14-20

I grew up in the time of tent revivals, and sometimes now, in the same way I miss the circus and the Saturday doubleheader, I miss the hot summer nights and the big canvas tabernacles. Dad preached in a tent once, and I can still recall the smell of burlap and hay. I heard my first electric guitar at a "tent meeting," and later—in the late sixties and early seventies when I began to think of myself as a preacher—I rather liked the idea of being backed up by a rock-and-roll band. Those were the days, weren't they?

I've been thinking about tents and revivals and Dad and stuff because the other day a tent revival preacher rolled into our town. The tent is small, the Winnebago is beginning to rust, but it seems like the real thing. In fact, maybe the tents of my childhood were not that much bigger, the cars not that much flashier—maybe it just seemed so.

Although I haven't attended the tent revival, I have rolled the car window down a couple of times as I was passing by. This guy is a screamer. Just hearing him sort of chilled my enthusiasm. In my nostalgia for the tents and the bands and the smells, I had forgotten exactly how these guys often preached—yelling, lots of anger and bile, veins bulging and indignation dripping like sweat. The new guy on the vacant lot is pretty typical, I guess. If you were categorizing the tent preachers under biblical precursors, you'd have to put the screamers in the camp with John the Baptist.

I figure that if you went to hear John, you were sure to get hellfire and brimstone every time. He didn't have a tent or a band, but I bet his veins bulged and his raiment probably smelled like sulphur. And he got results. There's no doubt about it. So you can't blame a lot of preachers for taking their cues from John, whose message was "Repent, for God's kingdom is coming." You still hear that message.

How different is the example of Jesus, whose message turns John's on its head. "The kingdom *has* come," Jesus says. "Now repent." And if, when the message was John's it was pretty much bad news—that folk are sinners and vipers and all—with Jesus there is self-avowed good news: "In spite of it all, you are chosen. So follow!"

Jesus calls, and rather quietly it would seem. Simon and Andrew, James and John—fishermen all, and none of them able to catch a fish in all the Gospels without Jesus' help. Jesus' presence enabled them to be fishers of people. It is Jesus' initiative that prompts faithful response.

Of course, with John and Jesus all that's necessary eventually gets preached. John will find his way to forgiveness, and Jesus will assuredly get around to judgment. The gospel circle remains unbroken. To me, however, the way they begin is significant. For John, the kingdom's coming ultimately depends on our obedience. For Jesus, our obedience ultimately depends on the kingdom's coming.

The difference could hardly be more telling; the telling could hardly be more different. And in both cases, the message is true: the kingdom is coming, the kingdom has come. Now repent. (*Thomas R. Steagald*)

FEBRUARY

❧

Mending the Net, Sharpening the Hoe

Symbol: Vine

The vine is one of the most vivid symbols in the Bible, and is used to explore the relationship between God and his people.

Texts:

> "The vineyard of the LORD Almighty
>   is the house of Israel,
> and the men of Judah
>   are the garden of his delight.
> And he looked for justice, but saw
>   bloodshed;
>   for righteousness, but heard cries of
>   distress. (Isa. 5:7 NIV)"

"I am the true vine, and my Father is the gardener. . . . I am the vine, you are the branches. If a man remains in me and I in him, he will bear much fruit; apart from me you can do nothing. . . . This is to my Father's glory, that you bear much fruit, showing yourselves to be my disciples" (John 15:1, 5, 8 NIV).

Invocation:

O Jesus, you have promised never to forsake or leave us. Teach us day by day the deep rewards of faithful ministry, and most of all help us to know always the reward of being near you. In the name of Jesus. Amen. (Paraphrased from Reuben P. Job and Norman Shawchuck, *A Guide to Prayer*)

Scripture Focus:

- The vine is also used as the emblem of Christ. It follows from his words expressing a new relationship between God and man through him (John 15:1, 5, 8).
- The vineyard is the protective place where the children of God (vines) flourish under the tender care of God (the Keeper of the vineyard) (Isa. 5:7).

- The vine is used as the symbol of the church in which alone this relationship exists. (Consider John 15, Isa. 5, Heb. 10:23-25, and Gal. 5:13-15.)

Prayer Focus:

- Pray for the church you serve, the staff, leaders, and potential leaders.
- Pray for protection from the powers of evil that will thwart her growth.
- Pray for the mission of the church in her community and the world.
- Pray for the church and her witness to individuals and systems.
- Pray that the church you serve may always maintain a strong connection to the vine.
- Pray that you as the pastor may encourage that connection to the vine.
- Pray that the church you serve may do her work as a result of the strong connection to the vine.
- Pray for your family (by name).

Prayer:

O Lord, in whose hands are life and death, by whose power I am sustained, and by whose mercy I am spared, look down upon me with pity. Forgive me that I have until now so much neglected the duty which thou has assigned me, and suffer the days and hours of which I must account to pass away without any endeavor to accomplish thy will. Make me to surrender, O God, that every day is thy gift, and ought to be used according to thy command. Grant me, therefore, so to repent to my negligence, that I may obtain mercy from thee, and to pass the time which thou shalt yet allow me in diligent performance of thy command, through Jesus Christ. Amen. (Samuel Johnson, 1709–1784) *(Bill Self)*

FEBRUARY 2, 1997

❧

Fourth Sunday After Epiphany

Worship Theme: Jesus reveals God's love to us.

Readings: Deuteronomy 18:15-20; 1 Corinthians 8:1-13; Mark 1:21-28

Call to Worship (Psalm 111):

Leader: Praise the LORD! I will give thanks to the LORD with my whole heart, in the company of the upright, in the congregation.

People: Great are the works of the LORD, studied by all who delight in them.

Leader: Full of honor and majesty is his work,

People: and his righteousness endures forever.

Leader: He has gained renown by his wonderful deeds;

People: the LORD is gracious and merciful.

Leader: He provides food for those who fear him;

People: he is ever mindful of his covenant.

Leader: He has shown his people the power of his works, in giving them the heritage of the nations.

People: The works of his hands are faithful and just; and his precepts are trustworthy.

Leader: They are established forever and ever, to be performed with faithfulness and uprightness. He sent redemption to his people; he has commanded his covenant forever.

People: Holy and awesome is his name.

Leader: The fear of the LORD is the beginning of wisdom; all those who practice it have a good understanding.

All: His praise endures forever.

Pastoral Prayer:

God of grace and glory, we join all of creation in giving praise to your name. You alone are worthy of praise and honor. Though we are unworthy to be in your presence, yet we praise you for the love which you expressed through Jesus Christ, your Son, which enables us to come boldly before the heavenly throne. We thank you, O Lord, for your revelation in the wonders of nature, in the beauty of the world around us. But even more, Lord, we thank you for the revelation of yourself through your Son, which has enabled us to know you as a God not only of power but of love, not only of judgment but of compassion. Help us to yield ourselves to your Spirit's gentle touch, that we might day by day know you better and serve you more faithfully. For we ask it in the name of the One who gave himself in order that we might pray these words. Amen.

SERMON BRIEFS

THE PROMISE OF GOD'S PROPHET

DEUTERONOMY 18:15-20

Is there any word from the Lord? We want to know God's expectations of us and his will for us. When we are in crisis or face a decision we long for divine guidance and grace—a word from beyond.

This is why we worship, to thank and glorify God and to enjoy his divine presence. Worship is from an Anglo–Saxon word, *worthship*. It means to ascribe supreme worth to God. When we worship we come to

- hear a transcendent word from beyond.
- catch a glimpse of the divine Presence.
- discover heaven's will and grace for our lives.

Just as Israel sought to know God's will, so do we. Even as we come to worship, we hope to gain insight into God's work and will in our lives. God responded to Israel's need with a unique gift: the prophets, who were messengers of God to his people.

Although today we have the advantage of having God's Word, the Scriptures, God still provides a prophetic ministry to his church today.

I. The Promise of a Prophet (v. 15)

The Israelites were forbidden to consult fortune-tellers and spiritualists (a la the New Age Movement). They were to avoid pagan religious practices, which included child sacrifice (v. 10). How would they know the will of God or hear his word? The Lord promised to provide a prophetic spokesman like Moses—the prototype of the prophets.

God has his spokespersons in each generation. He is not playing hide-and-seek. God wants us to know and do his will, made known to us by his prophets. Although they often did point to future events, biblical prophets were not so much fore-tellers as "forth-tellers"— inspired preachers of the divine word.

II. The Power of a Prophet (v. 18)

God promised to raise up his prophets and to put his word in their mouths, enabling them to speak all he commands. Any power the prophets possessed derived from their divine calling and the continuing presence of God in their lives.

Even today, God's messengers are called to declare the gospel with both its offer and its demand. We are not called to preach our opinions but the gospel of the Lord Jesus Christ. Authentic prophets proclaim the life, teaching, death, and resurrection of Jesus.

III. The Test of a Prophet (v. 20)

It is dangerous to presume on God and think too highly of oneself. That is the mark of a false prophet (see Jer. 28:8f.). The test of a true prophet is the fulfillment of God's purpose. The proof of the prophet is the authenticity of his or her preaching.

God speaks in many ways. He reveals himself in the beauty and dependability of the natural world, his creation. God also speaks in the human conscience giving us a sense of right and wrong. He communicates in history as well. God's will and purpose are discovered in the Holy Scriptures. The clearest word from God is heard in the person of his Son, Jesus (Heb. 1:1-2).

Someone has observed, "Jesus is the best picture God ever had taken." Yes, there is a word from the Lord. Are you listening for it? *(Alton H. McEachern)*

WHEN FREEDOM IS DANGEROUS

1 CORINTHIANS 8:1-13

Someone called me recently to tell me something they thought I, as pastor, should know. They had been at a local theater to watch a G-rated movie, and had seen one of our church leaders going into an R-rated movie. The caller asked: "What would the youth of your church think if they saw this person's example?"

The shopping mall in Corinth did not have an eight-screen theater; but Corinth did have situations where a Christian's freedom could lead to a dangerous influence on someone else.

I. The PRACTICE of the People in Corinth

Corinth had pagan temples where animal sacrifices were offered to idols. People would bring an animal, the priests would kill it, and some of the meat would be burnt in offering. But the rest of the meat became the property of the temple or the priests and was often sold at public market.

Many of these temples rented their facilities for private functions, just like churches today rent fellowship halls for wedding receptions. Thus the temples were centers of pagan worship and community social life.

II. The PROBLEMS Generated for the Christians

The questions arose: Could a Christian eat meat that had once been offered to the idols? Could a Christian attend a feast in a pagan temple? Even to purchase the meat could be seen as supporting the temple financially. And what would a Christian do at a wedding party if thanks were offered to a pagan deity?

These same questions can come up today when Christians are invited to a wedding in a non-Christian place of worship, pressured at their jobs to give to a charity they find unbiblical, or support a community festival that promotes unchristian values.

The more mature Christians knew the idols did not represent true gods; eating meat that had been offered to a stone idol was no more bowing to that idol than eating devil's food cake is Satan worship today. But weaker Christians were confused. They feared any acknowledgment of the pagan deity would be a slippery slope to idolatry.

III. The PRINCIPLES Paul Applied

Paul applied two principles. First, "knowledge puffs up." Sometimes spiritually knowledgeable Christians become impressed with their own level of learning. I once knew a man who memorized scriptures by the book, not by the verse. He could quote more passages than anyone I knew. But he did not go to church anywhere because he could not find a pastor who had "a heart for the Word." He was a "super-Christian," and he knew it!

Second, Paul said, "Love edifies." The old preachers' saying is: "Nobody cares how much you know 'til they know how much you care." This advice is good for all leaders. Paul makes this point in 1 Corinthians 13:2, where he says even if he had all knowledge but did not have love, he would be nothing.

The word translated "love" or "charity" simply means to prefer another; to put the other person's needs ahead of your own. Though the mature Christian had a right to eat the meat, the needs of the weaker Christian to not be tempted take priority. "Sometimes we have to give up our right to be right in order to get right with God."

IV. The PARALLELS We Face Today

We don't have to worry about the origin of the meat we purchase at the market. Still there are many activities in which mature Christians can participate without harming their faith, but which hurt their witness. How many can you name? *(Bill Groover)*

EMPOWERED AUTHORITY!

MARK 1:21-28

Authority is somewhat suspect in American culture today. Dr. Diane Komp, author of the book *A Window to Heaven*, identifies her own such suspicion in particular to God's authority and reliability.

In the foreword to her book, Dr. Paul Brand cites her suspicion concerning God when he writes, "Schooled by medical mentors who told her to set aside her personal feelings as she treated young cancer patients, Dr. Komp's almost non-existent faith slipped away until she could no longer believe." In her own words, Dr. Komp shares, "If I were to believe, it would require the testimony of reliable witnesses."

The issue of a reliable and authoritative witness of faith provides the context of the story from Mark. It seems not all that much has changed in terms of God's witness to a suspicious world.

For Dr. Komp, that reliable witness of God's love came through the very children for whom she provided treatment. Their dreams, their stories, their undoubting trust of this God who loved them provided the needed reliable witness, the authoritative witness, to create an abiding trust in God.

Mark's Gospel seeks to provide a reliable and authoritative witness to the reality of God's present, in-breaking kingdom through Jesus Christ.

I. The Life of Jesus Is a Reliable Witness

As the children's faith was an effective witness for Dr. Komp, the words and deeds of Jesus most powerfully testify to the authority of the source empowering such words and works. God empowers the authority of Jesus, and that empowerment becomes evident in the words and works of Jesus.

This is the difference between Jesus and the scribes. The words and deeds of the scribes lack something. The something they lack is the empowerment of God. Mark intends to show the difference between the empowered authority of Jesus and the kingdom he seeks to bring and the unempowered authority of the scribes.

II. Transformed Believers Are a Reliable Witness

In the business world today there seems to be a plethora of literature concerning empowerment in the workplace. The idea is that a good leader empowers others to productivity. According to Mark's Gospel, God is empowering a new kingdom of love and grace through Jesus Christ and those who would seek to follow him. Word and deed receive their authority from God.

Jesus has come to proclaim such a kingdom empowered with the authority of God. People who witness this authoritative witness can tell the difference. In such a kingdom, such authority is even granted to dying children whose testimony can be so effective. So empowered are they by God that one doctor will never be the same because of their words and deeds. Such is the authority of God's witness in a kingdom that will have no end.

The church needs to be reminded of the source of her authority and witness. It becomes easy to know the words and to mimic the work of Christianity. However, people know the difference between what is authoritative and what is not. In the long haul the false or unempowered witness will be found out.

The question this text poses for the church today is who is the source of its ministry and witness? Mark wants to make it clear to those who will listen that the words and deeds of Jesus are connected to God, who empowers them with authority in a kingdom that is here, now, and forever. If the church today is to preach, witness, or minister to the needs of a hurting world, it must do so with an empowered authority, thus ensuring the consistency between what it says and what it does. According to Mark, people will know the difference! (*Travis Franklin*)

FEBRUARY 9, 1997

❧

Fifth Sunday After Epiphany

Worship Theme: God has given us the privilege of sharing the gospel with others.

Readings: Isaiah 40:21-31; 1 Corinthians 9:16-23; Mark 1:29-39

Call to Worship (Psalm 147:1-11, 20c):

Leader: Praise the LORD! How good it is to sing praises to our God; for he is gracious, and a song of praise is fitting.

***People:* The LORD builds up Jerusalem; he gathers the outcasts of Israel.**

Leader: He heals the brokenhearted, and binds up their wounds.

***People:* He determines the number of the stars; he gives to all of them their names.**

Leader: Great is our LORD, and abundant in power; his understanding is beyond measure.

***People:* The LORD lifts up the downtrodden; he casts the wicked to the ground.**

Leader: Sing to the LORD with thanksgiving; make melody to our God on the lyre.

***People:* He covers the heavens with clouds, prepares rain for the earth, makes grass grow on the hills.**

Leader: He gives to the animals their food, and to the young ravens when they cry.

***People:* His delight is not in the strength of the horse, nor his pleasure in the speed of a runner;**

Leader: but the LORD takes pleasure in those who fear him, in those who hope in his steadfast love.

***All:* Praise the LORD!**

Pastoral Prayer:

Our great and loving Father, we rejoice in your power and your love. You created the heavens, the force of wind and wave; yet you also demonstrate love toward your smallest and weakest creatures. We marvel at your power, and we give thanks for your grace, which reached out to us in the midst of our sin and restored us to fellowship with you. How can we fail to sing your praise for such love; how can we fail to share your greatness with a lost world? We are grateful that you have chosen us to be a part of your kingdom; help us to be more than mere occupants of your kingdom, but to be ambassadors—proclaiming your truth and demonstrating your love. We ask it in the name of our Savior; who is the greatest evidence of your love and power. Amen.

SERMON BRIEFS

THE HIGH KING OF HEAVEN

ISAIAH 40:21-31

Chapter 40 was written concerning the close of Israel's exile in Babylon. It is filled with hope as the prophet is instructed to "comfort my people, says your God" (vv. 1-2). Prophets normally confront people with the Lord's demands and call for their repentance. Here he is told to "speak tenderly" (literally "speak to the heart"). This is a message of encouragement and reassurance.

The focal passage shows God to be great—incomparable. As the songwriter exclaimed, "How great thou art."

I. God Is Creator and Lord of History (vv. 21-24)

The Lord is the High King of heaven "who sits above the circle of the earth" (v. 22). The circle is the vault of the heavens above the earth. It appeared to be a dome on which the stars were fixed. (See Job 22:12-14.) God "walks on the dome of heaven." In Genesis 1 it is called "the firmament" (v. 6). The sky looked to be a dome above the earth to ancient people. They envisioned God living above his creation.

The prophet ridiculed the mighty pagan rulers. He probably had King Cyrus in mind. To God the inhabitants of the earth appear no bigger than grasshoppers—and their princes amount to nothing (v. 23). They are like plants withered and blown away by the hot desert wind (the sirocco). The storm carries them away like stubble (v. 24). The Lord is King of kings.

II. God Is Incomparable (vv. 25-26)

To whom can God be compared? Certainly not to a pagan idol (vv. 18-20). Babylon was a center of star worship or astrology. They believed the stars to be gods. That ancient pagan myth is still very much alive—and still pagan. The prophet contends that the stars are part of God's creation that line up in the heavens like soldiers on a parade ground and "not one is missing" (v. 26). Don't worship the stars but the God who created them.

III. God Cares for Us (vv. 27-31)

Captive Israel had grown faint and weary. They had long been a people without a land and they had grown bitter. In verse 27 they accused God of ignoring their plight. The prophet assures them of the heavenly Father's care. This eternal Creator does not grow weary and there is no limit to his understanding (v. 28). This Almighty God gives power and strength to those who trust in him (v. 29). As J. B. Phillips would say, "Their God was too small." The prophet shows God to be great and the believer's source of strength.

Verse 31—portraying eagle wings of faith—is a magnificent climax to the passage. When even the young are exhausted, those who wait on the Lord are empowered. Eagles molted and grew new feathers. Ancient people saw this as a symbol of spiritual renewal: "your youth is renewed like the eagle's" (Ps. 103:5). To wait on the Lord literally means to cling to him as a vine entwines itself around a tree (wisteria). It is a metaphor for trust and dependence on the Lord.

In crisis he delivers us—we mount up with wings like eagles.

In busy times he delivers us—we run and do not grow weary.

In routine times he delivers us—we walk and do not faint.

Faith is tough-minded trust in the Eternal. And faith is what results in victory in our lives. *(Alton H. McEachern)*

69

THE JOY OF PERSONAL EVANGELISM

1 CORINTHIANS 9:16-23

God has chosen people to be the only means of spreading the gospel. Why?

God is glorified in accomplishing the task using the simplest tools. Think of the pyramids of Egypt. People flock to them and stand amazed as they behold them. Because of their size? Hardly. They were built using only the most primitive technology and human labor. The fact that the Egyptians accomplished so much with so little amazes us.

Look around at the Body of Christ today. There are Christians in every nation, among every major language group. Billions of them. Because of angels? No. Because God has used people often no more willing, no more trained, no more gifted than any of us.

Paul recognizes three possibilities regarding our acceptance of our evangelistic mandate.

I. Some Will Never Share the Good News

Paul says the least about this possibility: "Woe to me if I do not." What does he mean?

First, the person who fails to share the good news will lose the blessings he would have gained by having been a part of God's work. I quit asking God why he used people the first time he used me to lead someone to Christ.

Paul knew that if he did not share, he would lose the blessing of seeing those he had won to Christ. He would lose the joy of knowing he had done for someone else what had been done for him. He also could be referring to the sorrow he would feel if he saw those left behind he could have helped.

II. Some Will Share the Good News, but Unwillingly

The idea of a reluctant witness is an amazing concept. It could describe some people who really don't want new people to come into their church, but they allow it. Or perhaps they share unwillingly because they will feel guilty if they don't.

Still, sharing the gospel unwillingly is a foreign concept to Paul. He doesn't say much about it, except that there is no reward for sharing strictly out of a sense of obligation.

III. God's Plan Is for Us to Share the Good News Joyfully

The greatest reward and joy is simply to share the good news freely with everyone. Paul doesn't have to find out first if someone can afford the gospel, or if they deserve an opportunity.

Paul remembers just how special were the people God used to witness to him, and he delights in being that special to others. We all can remember people who helped us develop and grow: teachers, friends, relatives, and, of course, parents. And we appreciate these people. But the people I appreciate most are those who "risked offending me" by sharing their faith with me. There were several who witnessed to me, invited me to church, and tried to help me. To know someone else feels this way about me makes me feel rather special.

One last thing Paul says in verse 22b: "I have become all things to all people, that I might by all means save some." A multitude of means exist by which we can reach people. Some friends witnessed to me directly. My wife's mother didn't think she could, so she offered me Sunday lunch if I would go to church with her. It was her prayers, and her unique approach to "lunchtime evangelism," that helped me become Christian.

You may have neighbors who will not come to church, but they would come to a Bible study in your home. Maybe they would read a Christian book if you gave them one. If you do not like one method, keep looking for a method that fits you. But whatever the method, share with others what God has done for you! *(Bill Groover)*

WHAT'S OUR PERSPECTIVE?

MARK 1:29-39

In recording the early part of Jesus' ministry, Mark seeks to emphasize the multidimensional nature of who he is and what he has come to do. The healing of Simon's mother-in-law, the casting out of demons, his teaching, and his statement concerning his preaching ministry all spotlight activities that will become the signposts of his ministry. From the beginning of his portrayal of Jesus, Mark seeks to define the many ways in which Jesus will proclaim and witness to the kingdom of God. Mark also reveals the source of his empowerment as he has Jesus rising early to be alone with God in prayer.

While these passages don't carry the drama of the feeding of the five thousand or Jesus walking on the water, they do share in a subtle way the connection between the works Jesus does and the source that empowers such work. This is an important connection for Mark, because he wants us to realize that the kingdom that Jesus has been sent to express is a direct revelation of God and God's activity in a hurting and sinful world. In all of these ways Jesus embodies and proclaims the presence of the kingdom of God.

I. The Kingdom Is Revealed in His Power Over Nature

As Jesus heals Simon's mother-in-law, then others who are ill, one sees the power of God's kingdom erupting into everyday life through the person of Jesus. In this Epiphany text, we see how God's kingdom becomes manifest in the routine and ordinary lives of people.

The miracles of Jesus are not important because of their value as spectacle but because they symbolize the presence of the kingdom in human life. As Jesus moved into lives, so did the kingdom.

II. The Kingdom Is Revealed in His Power Over the Supernatural

Jesus demonstrates power over not just natural phenomena but also supernatural, represented by the demons who possessed people. He held utter authority over them, even to the point of forbidding their speech. They recognized that when Jesus spoke, he did so with the full authority and power of God's kingdom.

III. The Kingdom Is Revealed in His Presence in Individual Lives

It is interesting to note the response of the people who experience that abiding presence. A woman rises from her illness to serve in a common way. Demons recognize Jesus for who he is when everyone else seems duped. His disciples, who should have trusted him most, act exasperated when they find him alone: they exclaim, "Everyone is searching for you" (v. 37). How strange to hear these stories and the stranger-still responses of those who experience the reality of God's kingdom.

Jesus seems to stand out in these stories as the one who seems sure, trusting, and empowered to authoritatively and authentically manifest the difference God's presence makes in the midst of all kinds of life experiences. Although subtle, these passages express the mystery of how God's kingdom will manifest itself, and the mixed response of those who experience it.

What will be our response as we encounter the manifestation of God's kingdom in the everyday? Moses at the burning bush; Isaiah in the temple; fisherman by the sea; a woman at a well; Paul on a road to Damascus—all serve to remind us of how God's manifestation meets us where we are. As a pastor, I can recall haunting, yet powerful moments in ministry when in a hospital room, a nursing home, or in visiting a prospect, God encountered me and those around me and invited us to respond.

In such moments what will be our response? *(Travis Franklin)*

FEBRUARY 16, 1997

❧

First Sunday in Lent

Worship Theme: Through Jesus Christ, God's kingdom has become a reality in our world.

Readings: Genesis 9:8-17; 1 Peter 3:18-22; Mark 1:9-15

Call to Worship (Psalm 25:1-10):

Leader: To you, O LORD, I lift up my soul. O my God, in you I trust;

People: **do not let me be put to shame; do not let my enemies exult over me.**

Leader: Do not let those who wait for you be put to shame; let them be ashamed who are wantonly treacherous.

People: **Make me to know your ways, O LORD; teach me your paths.**

Leader: Lead me in your truth, and teach me, for you are the God of my salvation;

People: **for you I wait all day long.**

Leader: Be mindful of your mercy, O LORD, and of your steadfast love, for they have been from of old.

People: **Do not remember the sins of my youth or my transgressions; according to your steadfast love remember me, for your goodness' sake, O LORD!**

Leader: Good and upright is the LORD; therefore he instructs sinners in the way.

People: **He leads the humble in what is right, and teaches the humble his way.**

Leader: All the paths of the LORD are steadfast love and faithfulness,

All: for those who keep his covenant and his decrees.

Pastoral Prayer:

O Lord, we enter this special season in a spirit of preparation and anticipation. We know it is a time of preparation—preparing our lives as we recognize the sin that is in us; preparing our hearts to receive the gift of life made possible by Christ on the cross; preparing our church to proclaim your kingdom with power and boldness. And even as we prepare, we live in anticipation—anticipation of Good Friday, with its awesome darkness; anticipation of Easter; with its explosion of light; and anticipation of Christ's return, when the kingdom that has already begun will be fulfilled—when every knee will bow and every tongue confess that Jesus Christ is Lord. We live in anticipation of that day; prepare us to be faithful witnesses of the cross, of the empty tomb, and of the kingdom yet to come. Amen.

SERMON BRIEFS

OUR COVENANT GOD

GENESIS 9:8-17

The idea of our covenant relationship with God is a major motif in the Scriptures.

- God made a covenant with Abraham in Genesis 17.
- God made a covenant with Israel at Mount Sinai, where he gave them the Ten Commandments in Exodus 20.
- God had his prophet Jeremiah promise a new covenant (31:31).
- God in Christ said, "This cup is the new covenant in my blood" when he instituted the Lord's Supper in the Upper Room (1 Cor. 11:25).

I. God's Covenant with Noah (vv. 8-11)

Noah lived in an evil time that brought divine judgment on the human race. The forty-day flood was sent to punish evil and destroy all flesh. (See Gen. 6:5-8.) Noah and his family found favor with the Lord and were spared by building the ark. In this passage we see

75

God taking the divine initiative to establish a covenant with Noah, his descendants "and with every living creature" (v. 10).

Basically, a covenant is an agreement between two parties. It may take the form of a contract or treaty. In the case of covenants with God, God is the superior party and takes the initiative to establish the agreement. God made a covenant with Noah, not the other way around.

God promised Noah that "never again shall there be a flood to destroy the earth" (v. 11). God initiates our salvation and covenant relationship with him. We do not find God—he finds, calls, and saves us. We are saved by divine grace, not by our human initiative.

II. The Sign of God's Covenant (vv. 12-17)

Ancient people thought the rainbow was God's weapon from which his lightning arrows were shot. (See Ps. 7:12-13.) The rainbow in the sky after a storm was a fearful sight—a symbol of fiery destruction.

God made the rainbow a symbol not of destruction but of deliverance. It was to be a reminder of his gracious covenant with Noah and with us. The rainbow reminds us of divine mercy: "When the bow is in the clouds, I will see it and remember the everlasting covenant between God and every living creature of all flesh that is on the earth" (v. 16).

The rescue of Noah's family from the flood was an act of divine grace. God saved a family and the ark became a symbol of divine mercy and salvation.

The early church did not initially use the cross as a symbol of their faith. The humiliation of Jesus' public execution was too fresh in their memories. Instead, early Christian art often depicted the ark. It stood for the church and salvation for those within it, by faith. By the ark God gave the human race a second chance, even as the gospel gives us the opportunity for redemption. As Lent begins, let the rainbow and Noah's ark symbolize our gracious God and his covenant promises. (*Alton H. McEachern*)

THAT HE MIGHT BRING US TO GOD

1 PETER 3:18-22

Some people think they cannot come to God. One man committed sins in the past for which he was sure God would never forgive him. He had been involved with some atrocities in wartime. I can see how such people, who are having trouble forgiving themselves, could wonder if God could ever forgive them.

Another person was an older man who was dying. All his life he had rejected God's will for his life. Toward the end of his life, I offered him God's gifts of forgiveness and eternal life. He refused, saying it just would not be right to wait until the end.

As logical as what these people said appears, look at what Jesus did in order to bring people just like them to God.

I. Jesus Suffered That He Might Bring Us to God

If we could grade sins on a scale of 1 to 10, could we then say Christ died for sins that rank 7 or less, but not 8 or more? Murderers, rapists, and such would not be included? Only those with lesser sins, such as lying or stealing, could be forgiven?

The Bible knows no such grading. Jesus says that to look at another person with lust in your eye is no different than committing adultery. Calling a person a fool is as sinful as killing them. All sins rank 10. Thus, if the murderer cannot be drawn to God, neither can the liar.

Through what Jesus did on the cross—through his sacrifice and death—he has overcome the power of sin: any sin. Nothing stands between us and God, because Jesus has bridged the gap.

II. Jesus Preached the Message of Deliverance for the Captives

Who are the spirits in prison? Some say they are people who died before Jesus lived. Jesus preached to them and gave them the opportunity they had not had in life. Others say they are fallen angels, the spirits cast out of heaven with Lucifer when he rebelled against God. Jesus preached to them and simply told them what he said on the cross: "It is finished!" God's plan of redemption is accomplished.

Possibly. But I know some other spirits who were formerly disobedient and were imprisoned in bonds of slavery to their sin. Paul was one, according to his testimony in the Bible, and I was another. Jesus preached to me, and told me, "It is true. I suffered for your sins that I might bring you to God. Now, will you come?" Fortunately, I did!

Whatever holds you captive, Jesus Christ is ready to loose the bonds and free you to experience new life.

III. Jesus Gave Us Baptism as a Sign We Can Be Brought to Him

We receive that "good conscience" when we begin with a bad conscience, or conviction for our sinfulness. By faith we desire to turn away from sin and live for God. We desire to see the old sinful self crucified as Christ was, and buried. By faith we desire to see God create in us new hearts and a new spirit, and be raised from the dead to live for him. Then by faith we act out this spiritual drama in water, burying the old and being raised anew. The entire process, everything baptism means—repentance, believing, trusting, obeying, and hoping—is the faith that saves us.

IV. Christ Now Calls to Us from a Position of Supreme Authority

Can you come to God? Can your sins be forgiven? Only if you have heard the preaching of Jesus. Only if you admit being oppressed by your own sinfulness. Only if you want to be set free to follow Christ.

You may know Jesus suffered that he might bring you to God, he preached to you, he has given you baptism for a sign, and his call has come with authority. *(Bill Groover)*

KNOWING THE SON

MARK 1:9-15

It is important to Mark for the reader to know that Jesus is indeed the Son of God. This is one of the major themes running throughout Mark's Gospel. That identity is proclaimed boldly in the events surrounding the baptism of Jesus.

These events signify the beginning of something radically new and different in terms of God's self-revelation to the world. Mark wants to make it clear that through the life of Jesus, God is seeking to bring a new kingdom into the reality of the world.

I. We See Who Jesus Is Through His Baptism

The powerful image of the heavens being torn apart and the descending dove provide for the reader bold, authoritative proof that Jesus is no less than the Son of God.

This text lends itself to a powerful dialogue of all the encompassing claims that are made upon one's life by God through the church at baptism. According to Mark, baptism identifies who we are as God's children. Mark's story of baptism and of what it means describes vividly a life identified and led by God.

II. We See Who Jesus Is Through His Temptation

Immediately following his baptism, Jesus faced a time of temptation in the wilderness. Despite the harshness of the surroundings and the seductive nature of the temptations, Jesus withstood the experience.

It is important to recall that Jesus was led into the wilderness to be tempted by the spirit of God. Many times in the church we emphasize the justifying grace of God in baptism, but forget the sanctifying grace of God in baptism. Mark seems to be saying that it is not enough just to know to whom we belong; we must realize that such a claim has far-reaching implications as to what we do and where we are willing to be led. Jesus' life and authority in the kingdom were expressions of how and where God was leading.

III. We See Who Jesus Is Through His Proclamation

Jesus not only lived in the reality of the kingdom's presence, he also proclaimed the kingdom's arrival. In announcing the kingdom's arrival, he challenged his listeners to respond in repentance and faith.

The kingdom of God is here in the person and identity of Jesus Christ, the Son of God. Following the time of temptation, Jesus lays out the formula for how one comes to such saving and life-giving knowledge. The kingdom is here, Jesus proclaims; repent, and follow where the kingdom of God is seeking to lead. This proclamation becomes the heart and soul of all that Jesus is and does.

Lent is a time of soul-searching in light of the truth of the gospel. It is all about knowing whose we are and allowing that knowledge expression in all that we do.

Catherine Ann Powers is the student who was an accomplice in a bank robbery in Boston in 1970, when a policeman was murdered. For twenty-three years she was a fugitive from justice. In 1993, after all those years of running, she turned herself in to the authorities. What makes her story interesting is she had put together an enviable life. She was married, had a daughter, and held a good job. All the ingredients of happiness were there, except one: she was not whom she appeared to be.

In answer to why she turned herself in, she responded, "Because I had to reclaim my past in order to live with full authenticity in this moment—in openness and truth instead of hiddenness and shame."

In this passage, Mark reminds us who Jesus is—through his baptism, temptation, and proclamation. And because of who he is, we can be all God wants for us—to experience life at its best and most meaningful! (*Travis Franklin*)

FEBRUARY 23, 1997

Second Sunday in Lent

Worship Theme: Authentic discipleship requires following Christ to the cross.

Readings: Genesis 17:1-7, 15-16; Romans 4:13-25; Mark 8:31-38

Call to Worship (Psalm 22:25-28):

Leader: From you comes my praise in the great congregation;

People: **my vows I will pay before those who fear him.**

Leader: The poor shall eat and be satisfied;

People: **those who seek him shall praise the LORD. May your hearts live forever!**

Leader: All the ends of the earth shall remember and turn to the LORD; and all the families of the nations shall worship before him.

All: **For dominion belongs to the LORD, and he rules over the nations.**

Pastoral Prayer:

Eternal Father, we come before you this day with praise on our lips and repentance in our hearts. We praise your greatness, your gifts of life and love, your holiness and your compassion. You alone are worthy of praise, O Lord. Yet we come also in repentance, for we have too often ignored your greatness and foolishly pretended that we were the ones who deserved praise. You have called us to a cross, but all too often we have only been willing to look for a crown. As we approach the time when we celebrate the death and resurrection of our Lord Jesus Christ, stir us afresh, with a vision of your love and our limits. Give us courage to carry the cross in discipleship and obedience, and wisdom to recognize that it is not our strength that enables us, but yours. Amen.

SERMON BRIEFS

A COVENANT OF FAITH

GENESIS 17:1-7, 15-16

In Genesis 9, God made a covenant with Noah, his descendants, and "all flesh" to remind us of divine mercy. Its symbol is the rainbow. In this chapter, God established a covenant with Abraham, the man of faith, and his descendants. Notice that God promised to make Abraham "the ancestor of a multitude of nations" (v. 4). By faith in the God of Abraham this has literally come to pass. The symbol of this covenant for the Hebrews was circumcision. For Christians, Abraham's children by faith, the symbol of the new covenant is baptism and the Lord's Supper. (These are signs of our membership in the covenant community.)

I. God Promised an Everlasting Covenant (vv. 1-7)

As we look back from the perspective of history, the most important person of ancient times was not a king or conqueror, not an Egyptian pharaoh or Persian king. He was not a brilliant Greek philosopher or Phoenician mathematician, but a man of faith— Abraham. He accepted the call of God and believed the divine promise. Abraham became the father of nations and forefather of the Messiah. Today, three world religions look to Abraham as the example of faith: Jews, Christians, and Muslims. The patriarch was called to have faith in the future. He became a knight of faith. (See Heb. 11:1-3, 8-12, 17-19.) The language of this passage is as majestic as the creation account (Gen. 1:28). Abraham is considered "the new creation" by Paul in Romans 8:23. Notice that God's promise to Abraham is an eternal one (v. 7).

The covenant is one of dual relationship. The Lord promised Abraham's descendants, "I will be their God" (v. 8). We believe that promise to be true not only for the Hebrews but also for Abraham's children by faith, all believers. We belong to God, and he is our God.

II. God Makes All Things New (vv. 5, 15-16)

God changed Abram's name to Abraham, which means "the ancestor of a multitude." He was destined to become the father of nations. Sarai, Abraham's wife, had her name changed to Sarah, which means "princess." Their new names symbolized their new relationship with God, in response to his covenant promises.

In Revelation, we are told that believers will receive a new name (3:12). We will also be given a new song (5:9). God will make a new heaven and a new earth (21:1), and at the end of time he will make all things new (21:5).

The life and faith of Abraham show us that one person plus God can make a great difference. Abraham believed God's promises and entered into a covenant relationship with him. The world is different 4,000 years later because of one man's faith!

The faith journey is one of growth in our understanding of God and growth in his likeness. The life of a believer is one of pilgrimage with a new name and a new goal. God keeps his covenant promised.

God is still calling people to faith and to follow. The word *church* in Greek literally means "the called out" people of God—in covenant relationship and on mission. *(Alton H. McEachern)*

THE REASONABLENESS OF FAITH

ROMANS 4:13-25

H. L. Mencken said: "Faith may be defined as an illogical belief in the occurrence of the improbable."

John Stott said: "Faith is believing or trusting a person, and its reasonableness depends on the reliability of the person being trusted."

From our human perspective, God has made some rather improbable promises. Is it reasonable or illogical for us to trust God's promises?

I. How Improbable Are God's Promises?

God promised Abraham, at age 100, a baby. This promise appears no more improbable than promises made to us. Karl Barth quoted John Calvin, saying: "Everything by which we are surrounded conflicts with the promise of God. He promises us immortality, but we are encompassed with mortality and corruption. He pronounces that we are righteous in his sight, but we are engulfed in sin. He declares his favour and goodwill towards us, but we are threatened by the tokens of his wrath."

II. Can God Possibly Keep His Promises?

Paul says Abraham was "fully convinced that God was able to do what he had promised" (v. 21). Why? Abraham believed the God "who gives life to the dead and calls into existence the things that do not exist" (v. 17). If, prior to making promises with Abraham, God had raised any dead person, it isn't recorded in Genesis. But God can "call into existence the things that do not exist." This second statement refers to creation out of nothing. Abraham believed God created everything, and in particular, life. If God can form Adam and Eve from the dust of the ground, he can form a child from the dust of an old man's seed.

We have more reason to believe. In addition to the understanding Abraham had, when Paul said, "God gives life to the dead," we can also think of the miracles of Jesus raising Lazarus, and especially the resurrection of Jesus.

III. But Does God Want to Keep His Promise?

Abraham certainly believed God did. God had come to Abraham on a couple of occasions to tell him. God desired to have a chosen people, and having a chosen people would glorify God. If I said a person desired glory, that statement would be an insult. But to say God desires glory is not an insult. It must be understood God only desires a fraction of the glory due him. We easily can give a person more glory than is deserved, but never will we be able to recognize even a fraction of the glory that already belongs to God! Verse 20*b* says that when Abraham realized keeping this promise would give glory to God, Abraham's faith was strengthened because he knew God would keep his promise.

Likewise, we know God will be glorified by keeping his promises to us. But we have even more reason to believe than Abraham. God has made us a promise just as improbable as the one he made to Abraham. He has promised us eternal life. And to prove he can keep his promise, he has raised Jesus. To prove he desires to keep his promise, he sent Jesus to the cross. Verse 25 says, "[Jesus] was delivered up because of our offenses, and was raised because of our justification" (NKJV).

Placing your faith in a God who has all the power necessary to keep his promises and who has paid the ultimate price of sending his only begotten Son to the cross is not "an illogical belief in the occurrence of the improbable." It is the only reasonable response an intelligent person can make. *(Bill Groover)*

FOLLOWING THE LEADER

MARK 8:31-38

Following the inspirational confession of faith by Peter, the disciples receive a startling new definition of Jesus and discipleship in light of the impending passion. These passages mark a significant shift in terms of how Jesus now defines himself, his role, and the role of those who would seek to be his followers.

Jesus now wants to move from the fact of his messiahship to its meaning. That identification is now coined in his use of the term Son of Man. Only Jesus uses this term to refer to his role. The term seems to symbolize Jesus' freedom to define himself in light of much speculation as to who he really is. Such freedom on Jesus' behalf is exercised subject only to the will of God. This is the second time we hear Jesus predict his passion. The cross is the reason why Jesus has come and the nature of the kingdom he seeks to proclaim.

I. The Cross Is Not What We Have in Mind

We see how uneasy such proclamation is in our own lives as we hear Peter's response to such a pronouncement. Jesus' messiahship to this point has been well received by the disciples. However, now the reality of why Jesus has come is just too much to bear, and Peter attempts to keep him from such a future. Peter's humanity in light of such kingdom realities reveals how fickle people can become when it comes to discipleship.

Most of the time, like Peter, we want to follow as long as the terms are acceptable and not too costly. Peter's admonition contrasted to Jesus' prediction reveals such a stark disparity as to the claims and demands of God's kingdom and our conditional response.

THE ABINGDON PREACHING ANNUAL 1997

II. Discipleship Means Following—Even a Cross

Jesus models powerfully what true following means as he denies self, takes up the cross, and follows God's lead. Jesus' response to Peter so clearly relates that Peter needs to get behind him. Such is the only place a true disciple can ever be if one is to follow. Jesus then uses this opportunity to define once again the true nature of what following him means. In light of Jesus' prediction, the message is all too real. Ultimately, discipleship means giving up everything. Dietrich Bonhoeffer said it best in his book, *The Cost of Discipleship*: "When Jesus calls a man he bids him come and die."

The message of this story is not any easier to hear today than it was then. Most of us, if we are honest, find ourselves in Peter's camp. But Jesus is deadly serious. In this season of self-denial, we must recognize anew what it means to follow Christ. In a world obsessed with instant gratification, this text clearly presents the gospel alternative.

In *Disciple Bible Study of The United Methodist Church*, I ran across a quote that defines what must be our response to this Jesus who calls us: "Faith is not belief without proof. Faith is obedience without reservation!" As uneasy as it is for us to hear this story of true discipleship, we too must trust where Jesus leads without reservation!

An image that might be helpful in sharing this text is the kid's game, Follow the Leader. As a kid, I remember everyone could hardly wait to be the leader. Such is the way of our culture. Everyone wants to lead, but few want to follow. When is the last time we saw a best-seller on *How to Be a Great Follower*? We seem to be preoccupied with leading, but Jesus clearly points out that being a good disciple is all about how one follows. *(Travis Franklin)*

86

MARCH

ॐ

Mending the Net, Sharpening the Hoe

Symbol: Towel

Jesus washing his disciples' feet and drying them was an act of humility and service. He turned the flow of power from top down to bottom up.

Text:

"So he got up from the meal, took off his outer clothing, and wrapped a towel around his waist. After that, he poured water into a basin and began to wash his disciples' feet, drying them with the towel that was wrapped around him" (John 13:4-5 NIV).

Invocation:

"Almighty God, by the power of your Holy Spirit open our eyes, ears, hearts, and very lives to your presence so that today we may worship and serve you in faithfulness, be blessing and healing reminders of your love to all whose lives we touch. We offer our prayers in the name of Christ. Amen." (Reuben P. Job and Norman Shawchuck, *A Guide to Prayer*)

Scripture Focus:
- John 13:4-5
- Hebrews 12:1-3
- 2 Timothy 4:6-8
- 2 Thessalonians 3:7-13

Prayer Focus:
- Remember gratefully the acts of kindness that have blessed you personally in the past.
- Visualize acts of mercy you may have performed.
- See future leaders with towels in their hands.
- Pray for opportunities for your church to serve the poor and the disadvantaged in your community.

Prayer:

"Accept the work of this day, O Lord, as we lay it at thy feet. Thou knowest its imperfections, and we know of the brave purposes of the morning only if you have found their fulfillment. We bless thee that thou art no hard taskmaster watching grimly the stint of work we bring, but the Father and Teacher of men who rejoices with us as we learn to work. We have not to boast there before thee, but we do not fear thy face. Thou knowest all things and thou art love. Accept every right intention, however brokenly fulfilled, but grant that ere our life is done we may under thy tuition become true master workmen, who know the art of a just and valiant life. Amen." (Walter Rauschenbusch, as quoted in Harry Emerson Fosdick, *The Meaning of Service*) *(Bill Self)*

MARCH 2, 1997

❧

Third Sunday in Lent

Worship Theme: The cross is the means by which God has brought us from death to life.

Readings: Exodus 20:1-17; 1 Corinthians 1:18-23; John 2:13-22

Call to Worship (Psalm 19:7-10, 14):

Leader: The law of the LORD is perfect, reviving the soul;

People: **the decrees of the LORD are sure, making wise the simple;**

Leader: the precepts of the LORD are right, rejoicing the heart;

People: **the commandment of the LORD is clear, enlightening the eyes;**

Leader: the fear of the LORD is pure, enduring forever;

People: **the ordinances of the LORD are true and righteous altogether.**

Leader: More to be desired are they than gold, even much fine gold; sweeter also than honey, and drippings of the honeycomb.

All: **Let the words of my mouth and the meditation of my heart be acceptable to you, O LORD, my rock and my redeemer.**

Pastoral Prayer:

Unto you, O Lord, we lift up our hearts in joyous thanksgiving, for you have forgiven us, redeemed us, and adopted us into your heavenly family. Though we rebelled against you, you reached out to us, though we sinned against you, you gave your only begotten Son in our behalf; though we put him to death on a cruel cross, you transformed that instrument of execution into a lifeline. We praise you, O God, for your remarkable grace, that forgives to the uttermost, that saves the most vile sinner, that transforms hate into love, anger into acceptance, rebellion into repentance and forgiveness. Thank you, Lord, for the power of the cross. May that power give us a new boldness to share your good news with all we encounter. For we ask it in the name of the One who gave himself on that cross so that we need never die. Amen.

SERMON BRIEFS

PRINCIPLES FOR QUALITY LIVING

EXODUS 20:1-17

These timeless commandments were given to Moses on Mount Sinai en route to the Promised Land. They have never lost their relevance. Embedded in the Ten Commandments are two great principles that God has given to enable us to live life with quality and direction.

I. We Are to Honor God Above All Else (vv. 3-11)

How do we give God the honor that is rightfully his?

We recognize that *God comes first* (v. 3). This is the foundational commandment—the priority of God. God is eternal and he is unique—"you shall have no other gods before me." A Scottish clan chieftain was told to deny his loyalty to the Stuart king or die. He said, "You may take my head from my shoulders but you cannot take my king from my heart." God is to have priority in our hearts and our lives.

We put *nothing in God's place* (vv. 4-6). God said there were to be no graven images. We may feel safe on the second commandment—after all, not many of us have a little carving of Baal in the family room! But anything that we put before our loyalty to God becomes our idol. It can be our home, family, work, sports, or car. What shape is your idol? Let nothing come between your soul and the Savior.

We *honor God's name* (v. 7). The command to not take God's name in vain is more than simply a prohibition of cursing, which is really a terrible form of prayer. Profanity not only reflects a heart darkened with hate, but it shows an utter disrespect for a holy God. The commandment also means that we are not to take God's name and then fail to live up to our profession.

We *worship God faithfully* (vv. 8-11). As Christians—who do not live by ceremonial Jewish law—what does it mean for us to keep the Sabbath day holy? Because Christ arose the first day of the week, most Christians worship on the Lord's Day—the first day of the week, when Jesus rose from the grave—instead of on Saturday. The word *holy* means different or set apart. The Sabbath principle is valid. We are to observe a weekly day of rest and gladness, worship and study.

II. We Are Also to Honor One Another (vv. 12-17)

First we are told to *honor parents* (v. 12). This is a commandment to show respect for those who reared us. It holds the promise of long life. It is equally important for parents to be worthy of their children's respect. Shakespeare wrote, "How sharper than a serpent's tooth is a thankless child."

Then we are reminded that *life is sacred* (v. 13). This is not a prohibition against all killing, such as the killing of animals, capital punishment, warfare, or police action. It may be translated, "You shall do no murder." All life is the gift of God and therefore is sacred.

Further, we see that *sexuality is sacred* (v. 14). Adultery violates one of God's good gifts and violates other persons. Sex is sacred within the context of marriage, love, and commitment. Outside that context it is demeaning to human personality and a deliberate violation of the known will of God. Let us determine to be pure.

We must also recognize that *property is to be respected* (v. 15). This commandment prohibits stealing, a universal problem. We may be outright thieves, or we may steal indirectly. Honest work is right, and stealing violates another person and his or her property rights. Let us determine to be honest in all our dealings.

Truth is to be protected (v. 16). Words are powerful and important. Once spoken they cannot be taken back. Words can incite to violence or inspire to faith. Words can hurt or help and, therefore, truth is essential. Satan is "the father of lies" (John 8:44). God hates a lie (Prov. 6). The New Testament teaches us to speak the truth in love. Read 1 Corinthians 13 in the New English Bible translation.

We must also recognize that *attitudes can be destructive* (v. 17). "You shall not covet" is not simply an external commandment, but a very internal one. Covetousness is wrong desire. It relates to our inner motives, setting our heart on the wrong thing or person. We have more things to covet than earlier generations. Ours is an acquisitive society. The Quakers teach that "it is a gift to be simple." Covetousness kills our contentment and leads to greed. Let us learn to be magnanimous.

As Christians, we find in these Ten Commandments a set of profound guidelines that demonstrate the kind of life God wants us to live. (*Alton H. McEachern*)

THE POWER OF THE CROSS

1 CORINTHIANS 1:18-23

God has taken the cross and made a symbol of life from a symbol of death, a symbol of morality from a symbol of immorality, a thing of pride from an embarrassment. He has displayed strength in weakness, and wisdom in foolishness.

I. To Some the Cross Appears Foolish or Weak

The Jews looked for a sign. God would send his King and defeat their enemy, the Romans. Yet Jesus didn't defeat the Romans; they defeated him, didn't they?

The Greeks sought wisdom and logic. They wanted a religion any reasonable person could accept. Who can blame them? But after thousands of years, humanity has not developed one logical religion that all intelligent people have heard, understood, and embraced. We never will. The Greeks also rejected the notion of a god who hurt. If your sins could hurt God, you would have to have some power over God. To the Greek, this concept was foolish.

The sign, however, was given. Numerous prophecies had been fulfilled. The victory had been won, but against a far more dangerous enemy than Rome: sin. And the cross was not foolish; its wisdom was just deeper than the Greeks could fathom. They had omitted one crucial fact: "God is love."

Are contemporary people any different? No. Some seek signs and miracles. Some are still looking for answers for all the world's political and economic problems. We want to conquer violence, drugs, and crime. But we have a bigger enemy about which no one wants to talk: sin. We are just like the Jews who thought their biggest enemy was Rome.

Other modern people are seeking wisdom. New Age seekers are constantly trying to market some intelligent-sounding, spiritualized philosophy whereby they make themselves god. They think we are foolish to submit to the authority of a God who loves all the way to a cross and who speaks through a Bible. "Christ may have died on the cross, but he didn't have to. You can conquer sin by reading a self-help book, meditating, or easiest yet, just by redefining sin."

Personally, I want an authority in my life who loves me, who feels my pain when I hurt, and who has a plan by which all my failures can be turned into victories. In other words, I need the cross.

II. The Cross Is a Symbol of Wisdom and Strength

The cross is a symbol of wisdom because it is God's plan. It amazes me when people who cannot understand how to cure the common cold, much less design life, can think we are as intelligent as God and are suitable authorities.

I have often compared the cross to a rock. A rock the size of my fist can prevent a car from beginning to roll down a hill. But let the same car start rolling and get to that rock, and the car will keep going with only a slight bump. It would take a much bigger rock to stop the car, and something more than a rock to turn the car around and get it going in the other direction. Sinful humanity is going downhill, fast. Only the cross can stop us, turn us around, and get us going in an upward direction. That's power!

God has taken a cross, a means of capital punishment, and made it a thing of beauty. That's power. If God can change the cross into strength, wisdom, beauty, morality, and life, just think what he can do with us! *(Bill Groover)*

A DANGEROUS MAN!

JOHN 2:13-22

This is a disturbing passage for some Christians. Seeing Jesus angry to the point of violence offers a somewhat awkward picture in relation to the Jesus so many people want to see. John is not afraid to depict the humanity of Jesus. John also seeks to portray Jesus sharing the message of the kingdom with a sense of urgency that demands a decision from those he encounters now! This scene hinges on the question of Jesus' authority. A new day has come to human history initiated by God in Jesus. This new revelation as authoritative truth demands that people decide.

What is the source of Jesus' authority? In this story, we observe two different sources.

I. Jesus' Authority Emerges from His Holiness

The temple was to be a place of prayer, but it had been turned into a flea market! Perhaps it was not only the merchandising that offended Jesus but also the exploitation of the poorer worshipers. Jesus knew that a holy and righteous God was not honored by such a display. And his own holiness gave Jesus an authority with which to stand against the powerful people who misused the temple.

Jesus fashions a whip of cords and drives the money changers out, overturning their tables, spilling their coins. The kingdom Jesus brings will divide those who have an authentic faith from those who do not. This story certainly illustrates that disparity in the reaction of those Jesus encounters. John is not afraid to show an angry Jesus because, in John's eyes, Jesus has every reason to be angry in reaction to the apathetic faith of those he encounters in, of all places, his Father's house.

Our own lives help to determine our credibility in standing for the things of God. If our lives do not match our witness, there is no authority to our words.

II. Jesus' Authority Emerges from His Confidence in God

Jesus could demonstrate such boldness because he knew that his life was in God's hands. Even though he knew he was only a few days from the cross, nevertheless, he had absolute trust in the Father that he would be raised from the grave in power and glory!

The disclosure of his passion in answer to the question of authority is Jesus' way of revealing the cosmic nature of the authority on which he is acting. It was only after the Resurrection that the disciples understood the meaning of that authority and the ultimate difference it would make in terms of the salvation of the world.

Martin Bell, in his book *The Way of the Wolf,* describes the issue present in this story from John when he writes: "to live is to decide, to risk being wrong, to bet your life. . . . It is not enough to be interested in this man, or fascinated by him or drawn to him. Either we stand ready to commit our deaths to him or we don't. No one ever knows the Christ and then commits himself. Commitment is the one and only way by which we may know the Christ."

There is no in-between when it comes to a person's response to the authority with which Jesus communicates the gospel. The response of the Jewish religious leaders, expressed through their question concerning the authority by which Jesus does such things, only demonstrates their lack of authentic faith. They frankly do not know who Jesus is.

In this Lenten season, the church must proclaim the gospel with a sense of urgency that is inherent to its proclamation. The connection of Jesus' passion to his anger and outrage illustrates the passion and the authority with which Jesus acted. Such a response must be characteristic of our response to who Jesus is, lest we preach a watered-down gospel that demands nothing of anyone.

As the community of faith, we must recognize the danger of Jesus in the authoritative word he speaks, for it demands nothing less than all we are. Such a word was dangerous in the first century and is no less dangerous today! *(Travis Franklin)*

MARCH 9, 1997

Fourth Sunday in Lent

Worship Theme: The resurrection of Jesus Christ is our source of hope.

Readings: Numbers 21:4-9; Ephesians 2:1-10; John 3:14-21

Call to Worship (Psalm 107:1-3, 21-22):

Leader: O give thanks to the LORD, for he is good;

***People:* for his steadfast love endures forever.**

Leader: Let the redeemed of the LORD say so, those he redeemed from trouble and gathered in from the lands, from the east and from the west, from the north and from the south.

***People:* Let them thank the LORD for his steadfast love, for his wonderful works to humankind.**

Leader: And let them offer thanksgiving sacrifices,

***All:* and tell of his deeds with songs of joy.**

Pastoral Prayer:

In this season of repentance, O Lord, we seek your presence. Though we are undeserving of your love, yet we praise you and thank you for that love, so marvelously revealed on the cross. So often, Lord, we have fallen short of your will for our lives—and still you love us! So many times, Lord, we have turned away from your truth and chased foolish notions—and still you keep us in your care! What awesome love you offer to so unworthy a people. Come to us, we pray, and transform our lives into useful instruments of your divine purpose. May the power of the Resurrection anoint our hearts and empower our service, that we may be your true and faithful servants. Amen.

SERMON BRIEFS

PATIENCE FOR THE WAY

NUMBERS 21:4-9

We are inching our way toward Easter. We are impatient and want to get there now! In some respects we are like God's people in today's scripture text. The Jews are moving from Mount Hor to the Red Sea. They are still very much a pilgrim people, not sure of their destination but anxious about the journey. Their grumbling is treated as a serious problem. Impatience breeds distrust and mutiny. As we wait during this Easter season we can learn needed lessons.

I. Waiting on God Takes Special Patience

Our whole society seems to be waiting for something significant. What significant event are we waiting for? It varies with different people. For some it is more money or a better job. For others the hunger is for meaning in life. Henri Nouwen has written: "Beneath all the great accomplishments of our time there is a deep current of despair. While efficiency and control are the great aspirations of our society, the loneliness, isolation, lack of friendship and intimacy . . . and a deep sense of uselessness fill the hearts of millions of people in our success-oriented world."

Like the ancient Jews, we are "on the way" also. But to where? Often we do not know, and that lack of knowledge requires open hearts and patience. Our journey takes patience and grace. We cannot put life on fast-forward. What we can do is to rely on God to help us develop patience. It is listed as part of the fruit of the spirit of God in Galatians 5:22-23.

II. God's Good Gifts Are Not to Be Ignored

The people "spoke against God and against Moses" (v. 5). That sounds so typical! They had a better plan! Their question was extremely sarcastic. They wanted to know why they were led out into the desert to die of hunger and thirst. The rest of the complaint is summed up by these words: "There is no food and no water, and we detest this miserable food." The people hated the manna, the special food given by God.

97

The liberty they had and the food they consumed were not enough for them. They wanted more! But what really matters in life? Is it not some worthwhile work to be engaged in?

Albert Schweitzer left a promising career in medicine and music to pursue his sense of calling in Africa. He served as overseer of the laborers who cleared vegetation on the site and worked on the buildings. One of the most educated and gifted men of his age, Schweitzer was foreman of a group of workers hewing down trees! He wrote in his book *Out of My Life and Thoughts:* "As soon as the building site had been cleared, I started making the land near it ready for cultivation. What a joy it was to win fields from the jungle!"

One of the gifts of God is a sense of work to accomplish. Patience is required to find that work and to accomplish it.

III. God Takes Care of Our Most Pressing Problems

The Jews were bitten by poisonous snakes because of their grumbling. God provided a remedy for their dilemma. A snake of bronze was made and placed on a pole. Whenever someone was bitten he had only to look at the bronze serpent and he would live. We learn from 2 Kings 18:4 that the bronze snake later became a pagan symbol and lost its original meaning.

Jesus took the image of a healing pole and applied it to himself in John 3:14-15. He said he was to be lifted up. Anyone who looked to him for life would find it. Most people want to cling to life at all costs and will do almost anything to escape death.

We will do well to consider an ancient Persian story about a rich man who was walking in his garden with one of his servants. The servant cried out that he had just encountered Death who threatened him. The servant begged his master for the use of his fastest horse so he could flee to Teheran, which he could reach that night. The master consented and the servant galloped off at full speed. On returning to the house, the master himself met Death and questioned him: "Why did you terrify and threaten my servant like that?" Death said, "I did not threaten him. I only showed surprise in finding him here when I had planned to meet him in Teheran tonight."

We have a sin problem and a mortality problem. God, through Christ, provides a way to be redeemed from sin and to have eternal life. *(Don M. Aycock)*

TO SEE GOD'S POWER

EPHESIANS 2:1-10

If in this Easter season you would see the greatness of God's power, look not to creation with its awesome mountain grandeur; look not to the dark secret of the seashore at night, mind-boggling as the unfolding universe is; look not to the accounts of Jesus healing and teaching, as out of step with this world as they are. Rather, look to the power of God revealed in the two resurrections—the resurrection of Jesus, and the resurrection of each and every saint from the unredeemed life.

I. The Resurrection of Jesus Demonstrates His Lordship

God's power is demonstrated first and foremost in raising Jesus. This was no public event; there was no news conference, no brass band or TV coverage. Yet in the stillness of that resurrection dawn, a new world was born. God's re-creation of the world began in earnest.

The significance of the Resurrection is that the outcome of the struggle with Satan is settled; planning on the new world and the new race of men and women like Jesus can begin. God made this Jesus, his beloved son, lord of all the universe. His name is above all authority, all power, all rule, and all lordship. And Jesus is lord of the church, the re-created people of God.

II. The Resurrection of Jesus Confirms Our New Life

This unique, unparalleled demonstration of God's power in raising Jesus is also shown in the raising of every follower of Jesus from the dark kingdom of Satan into the kingdom of light, the kingdom of the Son of God.

As we look at this account of the Christian's resurrection to new life, *have you experienced it?* Paul packages the thrilling theology of Jesus' resurrection in chapter 1 with a grim anthropology (2:1-5), a sketch in satanology (2:1-5), and the importance of walking in good works (2:6-10).

In verses 1-5 we have a dark study of humankind—a condensation of Romans 1:18 through chapter 3. We see the saga of the living dead, those who are dead and know it not. It speaks of a common captivity of humankind; we were all dead, deluded, dominated, disobedient. We walked in trespasses and sins.

We did not stroll absently nor stumble accidentally into this deadly walk; it was a deliberate choice of steps in a chosen direction (v. 2). We walked according to the *aeon* (the god Aion, worshiped two centuries before Christ, was a personification of this world) or course of this world. By our very nature we were children of wrath; children filled with wrath and children destined to experience the wrath of God unless by some miracle we were saved. We were children with a tendency toward the will of the flesh and the imaginations of an evil heart.

Paul acknowledges the sinister, unexplainable operation of an evil force, both within us and outside us, acting upon us. The living dead, those spiritually still under the spell of the devil, know not that they are dead. It is only after we have been raised, made alive in Christ, tasted the eternal cup of God's grace, that we know we were dead in our sins and trespasses. Thus the Christian hates with a holy hatred the dead man's walk of pride, self-justification, and immorality.

In verse 5 we see Paul ringing the changes on the theology of grace expressed in the resurrection we share with Jesus Christ. God's great love sent Jesus to cancel the powers of evil and to plead with our deadened spirits. Through the Holy Spirit we are made aware of our sin, moved to repentance, our desires are changed and a new vision is planted in our souls. Our spiritual resurrection in Christ is proof to all the powers in the universe that God blesses his people.

III. The Resurrection of Jesus Challenges Us to a New Walk

We are raised to walk in a new path, not in the old darkness where our feet never ceased to stray, but in a path strewn with good works that God has provided for us before we even knew him.

There are three kinds of work mentioned in verses 8-10. There is *God's work*, a work of salvation springing from his eternal decision to love us, to pour out his grace through Jesus, to reveal the secret of the gospel through us, to appoint Christ as ruler over all, to create a new race of people like Jesus. Then there are the *human works* mentioned in verses 8-9. However commendable a man's kindness, generosity, moral outlook, rule keeping—"All for sin could not atone; thou must save, and thou alone" ("Rock of Ages, Cleft for Me, Augustus M. Toplady). The long and the short of it is simply that we cannot be saved by anything we do; but only by what God has done in Christ.

The third category of works is the *good works of the Christian* seen in verse 10. There are several references in the Bible to an examination of our works at Judgment Day. These works are not the works of the merely moral person, but the works spoken of in this verse. God's mercy in Christ gives a foundation and basis for the good works of a Christian. His good works are a result, not a cause, of his salvation.

In eternity, God prepared good works, like mystery packages, and put them in the life path of each Christian, that we should find them and carry them out in our daily life. In this way we show forth to an unbelieving world by our very nature, outlook, and deeds what the power of God really is. *(Earl C. Davis)*

SIN AND SNAKEBITES

JOHN 3:14-21

Weaving images of Christ within the context of human sinfulness, the Gospel of John helps one to feel a part of the tapestry that began even before the New Testament. When the people of Israel encountered venomous snakes in the wilderness (Num. 21), God offered a way of salvation. God still offers a solution to our need for salvation: Jesus Christ.

I. We Must First Recognize Our Need

If our own sin was as obvious as a snakebite, comprehending our need for salvation would be easier. One obstacle to overcoming sin is denial. We deny our brokenness and our need for God's mercy. The Bible repeatedly reveals God's pattern of offering solutions to the crises of the human condition. God's grace and mercy are ready to respond to human need. The stumbling block arises in our failure to accept the gift.

Questions of denial are the signs of alarm. "Why do I need to be saved?" we may ask, or "From what do I need to be saved?" "Why do I need Jesus Christ?" We are like alcoholics who must first own up to their alcoholism, or addicts who must confess their helplessness. We are all sinners who must recognize our sinfulness.

Some have accused the church of ego-bashing and negativity when we talk of sin. This is missing the point and adding to the denial of the human condition. Christ does not say that we are to live in misery because we are sinful. Christ offers abundant life to those who acknowledge their sin and their need for salvation. The Bible says that we are guilty of sin. The Bible does not say that we are to spend our lives feeling guilty, but living as forgiven people.

II. God Offers a Means of Salvation

God does not remove evil. God offers a solution to the crisis of evil, a means of salvation. God did not save the Israelites by taking the serpents away. The Israelites were saved by faith in God's ability to save them. Some people face enormous hardship in life. It is faith that sees them through such struggles.

History records that when Abraham Lincoln was seven years old, his family was forced out of their home on a legal technicality, and he had to work to help support them. At age nine, his mother died. At age twenty-two, he lost his job as a store clerk. He wanted to go to law school, but his education was lacking. At twenty-three, he went into debt to become a partner in a small store. At twenty-six, his business partner died, leaving him a huge debt that took years to repay. At twenty-eight, after courting a young woman for four years, he asked her to marry him but she said no. At thirty-seven, on his third try, he was elected to Congress, but two years later, he lost re-election. At forty-one, his four-year-old son died. At forty-five, he ran for the Senate and lost. At forty-seven, he failed as the vice-presidential candidate. At forty-nine, he ran for the Senate again, and lost. At fifty-one, he was elected president of the United States and became one of the greatest leaders of this nation.

When someone asked Lincoln what enabled him to endure a life of hardship, he replied, "Faith in God."

III. God's Grace Overcomes Our Sin

Offering judgment has always been easier than offering grace. Certainly there are consequences for sin. The awesome message of this passage is that God offers grace to a world deserving of condemnation. Though the world did not believe in God, God believed in the world. That is still the message today. Undeserved grace is the foundation of salvation.

Such extravagant grace calls for a radical response. We accept God's gift of grace when we commit ourselves to follow Christ through faith. God calls to a sinful world. Our response echoes God's call of love, devotion, and forgiveness. The motto "Jesus Saves" is not just a slogan; it is a life-transforming reality. *(Gary G. Kindley)*

MARCH 16, 1997

Fifth Sunday in Lent

Worship Theme: God used the cross to overcome the power of evil.

Readings: Jeremiah 31:31-34; Hebrews 5:5-10; John 12:20-33

Call to Worship (Psalm 51:1-12):

Leader: Have mercy on me, O God, according to your steadfast love; according to your abundant mercy blot out my transgressions.

People: **Wash me thoroughly from my iniquity, and cleanse me from my sin.**

Leader: For I know my transgressions, and my sin is ever before me.

People: **Against you, you alone, have I sinned, and done what is evil in your sight, so that you are justified in your sentence and blameless when you pass judgment.**

Leader: Indeed, I was born guilty, a sinner when my mother conceived me.

People: **You desire truth in the inward being; therefore teach me wisdom in my secret heart.**

Leader: Purge me with hyssop, and I shall be clean; wash me, and I shall be whiter than snow.

People: **Let me hear joy and gladness; let the bones that you have crushed rejoice.**

Leader: Hide your face from my sins, and blot out all my iniquities.

People: **Create in me a clean heart, O God, and put a new and right spirit within me.**

Leader: Do not cast me away from your presence, and do not take your holy spirit from me.

All: **Restore to me the joy of your salvation, and sustain in me a willing spirit.**

Pastoral Prayer:

O God of mercy, we have taken your good creation and turned it into a merciless land. Our sin has corrupted all we have touched. We are without hope until we find our hope in you. Yet as Easter approaches, we are reminded again that the cross has changed everything. We who were lost are now found; we who were blind can now see. Though we are unworthy, yet because of what Christ has accomplished you have washed our sins away, you have blotted out all our iniquities. Can there be any greater miracle than your grace and its transforming power in our lives? As your cross has overcome evil, so let us be representatives of the power of the cross, standing against evil wherever we encounter it, and announcing the overcoming power of Christ's love. For we ask it in the name of the One who hung on that cross, and made all the difference. Amen.

SERMON BRIEFS

A FORWARD-LOOKING FAITH

JEREMIAH 31:31-34

Real faith looks forward. While the people of God are told to remember what he has done for them in the past, no real progress can be made by staring into the rearview mirror. Jeremiah tells his contemporaries "a time is coming." He helped them look forward to a time in the future when their condition would improve. Jeremiah promised a new covenant. The new covenant would face the people forward and help them live life as it came toward them.

In the book *Unfinished Business*, Halford Luccock told a story of the little town of Flagstaff, Maine. The town was to be flooded as part of a large lake for which a dam was being built. All improvements and repairs in the whole town were stopped. What was the use of painting a house if it was to be covered with water in six months? Why repair anything when the whole village was to be wiped out? So, week by week, the whole town became more and more bedraggled, more gone to seed, more woebegone. Then Luccock added by way of explanation, "Where there is no faith in the future, there is no power in the present."

I. Forward-Looking Faith Is Based on the Nearness of God

Jeremiah's description is arresting. God would set aside the old covenant. In its place God would give his people a new covenant. Its foundation would not be on written laws and regulations. The Lord would put his spirit directly into the hearts of people. It would be based on his nearness.

How do we think about that new covenant? A baby bird was heard to ask its mother, "Mother, what is air?" To this she made no reply, but spread her wings and flew. A baby fish asked its mother, "Mother, what is water?" She made no reply, but swished her tail and swam. A baby ant asked its mother, "Mother, what is dirt?" She made no reply, but stretched her legs and dug the burrow a little deeper. A child in a nursery asked her mother, "Mother, what is love?" She made no reply, but picked up the child and hugged her.

Like water to a fish; like air to a bird; like dirt to an ant; like love to a child—such is the presence of God to those who love him.

II. Forward-Looking Faith Comes Naturally

The covenant described by Jeremiah was natural and internal. People were not forced to learn of God. Instead, they knew God naturally. This does not mean that disciplined study of religious matters is useless. It simply means that God wants to be known by people everywhere. God has given knowledge of himself to everyone, as we can see from Romans 1:20.

This comes about as we give ourselves to God through Christ. Knowing God this way establishes us and strengthens us. In times of trouble we will already have a relationship with God that we can count on.

Aesop told this old story. A wild boar was busily whetting his tusks against a tree in the forest when a fox came by. "Why are you wasting your time in this manner?" asked the fox. "Neither a hunter nor a hound is in sight, and no danger is at hand." "True enough," replied the boar, "but when the danger does arise, I shall have something else to do than to sharpen my weapons."

III. Forward-Looking Faith Results in Forgiveness

Jeremiah 31:34 is a most comforting passage: "For I will forgive their wickedness and will remember their sins no more" (NIV). Gaining God's forgiveness is not a matter of following minute rules or loathsome regulations. It is knowing and trusting God. That trust can help us walk through incredible times.

Christ calls us to a faith that looks forward. Which way are you facing? *(Don M. Aycock)*

THE PRIEST LIKE MELCHIZEDEK

HEBREWS 5:5-10

The fifth chapter of Hebrews compares the human high priest of the Jews with Jesus Christ, the high priest of the Christians. The early verses of the chapter point out that the office of high priest calls for one with the following two qualifications: he must be from among men; and he must be by divine appointment. Verses 5-8 show us how Jesus meets these qualifications.

I. Melchizedek Modeled Priesthood

The story of Melchizedek, king of Salem and priest of the most high God, is a fascinating story. He is a shadowy figure, appearing suddenly without any parentage mentioned. He appears once and is gone. His bringing forth wine and bread is seen as symbolic. Chapter 7 of Hebrews states his case most poetically: "Without father, without mother, without genealogy, having neither beginning of days nor end of life, but resembling the Son of God, he remains a priest forever" (v. 3).

Melchizedek was the first priest of Almighty God, and his priesthood was the model for that of Christ "a priest forever after the order of Melchizedek." (For more references, see Gen. 14:17-20; Ps. 110:4; Heb. 5, 6, and 7.)

II. Jesus Is a Priest After the Order of Melchizedek

Our sermon passage is bracketed by the tantalizing phrase describing Christ as a priest after the order of Melchizedek. In what way is Jesus like this priest? It is true that Aaron was also a priest by divine appointment, so what was the distinctiveness of this early priest? The ancient commentary presents Melchizedek as a one-of-a-kind priest; that is why the enigmatic reference of his lack of a father or mother. His was a divine appointment in a time and in a place when men scarcely knew what to make of the God he served. There was no priest before him; there was no priest of his line after him; he was a one-of-a-kind priest.

In like manner was Jesus a priest; no priest like him before or after, while Aaron founded a line of priests stretching centuries. There is another aspect of similarity between Melchizedek and Jesus: the nature of their priesthood. The priesthood of Aaron was for the offering of animal sacrifice, the fulfilling of the legal system of atonement. Melchizedek's priesthood was a ministry of encouragement and the offering of the bread and wine, symbols of the sacrifice of Christ, the perfect, complete, and final atonement for sin. Now the system of animal sacrifice presided over by Aaron ceased, but the ministry of the bread and wine, the sacrifice of Christ, shall never cease. Thus, while Aaron and Melchizedek were both priests appointed by the Lord, the priesthood of Melchizedek is lasting, while that of Aaron is not.

One further aspect of the priesthood of Melchizedek worthy of comment is this: Melchizedek combined both the kingly and the priestly functions; he was king of Salem, king of *peace,* as well as the priest of the Most High.

III. Jesus Is Our Eternal High Priest

In verses 7 and 8, the humanity of Jesus is emphasized. The priest was a representative of the people; he was among the people and one of them. Indeed, when he offered sacrifice, he first offered sacrifice for his own sins. Such was his identification with humanity. The writer of Hebrews said that Jesus "was in all points tempted like as we are, yet without sin" (4:15 NKJV). The full experience of humanity, including temptation, was tasted by Jesus.

In these verses we are told that Jesus offered up *prayers* and *supplications* (pleas for help in calamity and prayers for definite requests). An old Jewish saying on ascending levels of prayer tells us that there is, first, the level of silent prayer, then crying out in prayer with raised voice, and finally prayer with tears, against which no door can be barred. We see Jesus at all these levels of prayer as we reflect on the all-night vigils and the experience in Gethsemane.

In a phrase hard to understand, this passage also tells us that Jesus learned obedience by the things that he suffered. Jesus, in his humanity, gradually learned the full extent of the Father's will, and put his will in subjection to that will, as we are told in Gethsemane.

So Jesus is the great High Priest forever. High Priest by divine appointment, with a higher and more noble ministry of bread and wine, spilt blood and mangled body, than Aaron ever dreamed. Jesus is the High Priest who, in his link with humanity, gains the victory over death for all, and is able to sympathize with us all. He understands our struggles and trials, because he has been there. *(Earl C. Davis)*

HOPE FOR THE TROUBLED SOUL

JOHN 12:20-33

Jesus concludes his public ministry and announces that his hour has come. Even Gentiles seek this rabbi, perplexing his followers. Jesus' explanation is to announce his death as a part of God's greater plan. What could be gained by dying? Jesus' answer: the conquering of evil and the salvation of the world! Even now, in retrospect, the significance of what Christ did, and what Christ does, staggers our understanding.

I. The World Is Slow to Recognize the Need for God

This text precedes the betrayal and crucifixion of Christ. The world is poised to nail Jesus to a tree. Both the religious leaders and Jesus' followers will conclude that his ministry ends at the cross. They will think him finished, but God is not finished.

By Christ's death God's power is revealed. The world of Christ's day needed Jesus as does the world today. The irony of the crucifixion is that a world that quickly judges and condemns discovers its own salvation is at risk. The One who seemed powerless was the one power on whom the world depended. The world is slow to recognize its need for God.

II. The World Is Slow to Recognize the Power of God

Evil has met its match in the power of the Christ. John's Gospel emphasizes that "the ruler of this world will be driven out" (v. 31). Christ's power comes in his obedience unto death. As is true with one seed that falls to the ground and brings forth abundant life, Christ's death yields abundant living for those who follow the Way.

What a paradox is the power of God! God's Spirit brings life to the womb of an unassuming virgin. God's Son is revealed in the humility of a lowly manger. Christ's power over death is revealed through the agony of the crucifixion. The Resurrection is announced to the least likely group of witnesses, female followers who were not apostles. At the Ascension, Jesus announces the gospel mission to the world in the presence of an enormous crowd: eleven disciples.

God, in power and wisdom, chooses those whom the world would ignore. Through the least likely of persons, the sacred mystery of God's love is revealed.

III. There Is Hope for the Troubled of Soul

Jesus was willing to take up his cross. He did not succumb to self-satisfaction, personal desire, or his own long-range goals.

Wanting to avoid suffering is human nature. Christ has shown that suffering can be redemptive. "Now my soul is troubled. And what should I say—'Father save me from this hour'? No, it is for this reason that I have come to this hour" (v. 27). The glory of God is revealed through the life yielded to God's purpose. This truth is so significant and yet so elusive.

There is blessing and joy in stepping out in faith through generous giving and gracious living. There is hope for those who despair. There is hope for those who are faithful and yet see no fruit of their labor. There is hope for those who truly want to be freed from addiction. There is hope for those who follow the way of Christ without visible reward.

A plaque by an anonymous author hangs in the office of a friend. It reads: "When you stand at the edge of all the light you have and step off into the darkness, you can be certain that one of two things will happen. You will be given a solid ledge on which to stand, or you will be taught to fly." (*Gary G. Kindley*)

MARCH 23, 1997

୨

Palm/Passion Sunday

Worship Theme: Authentic discipleship carries a great cost but offers an eternal reward.

Readings: Isaiah 50:4-9*a*; Philippians 2:5-11; Mark 14:1–15:47

Call to Worship (Psalm 118:1-2, 19-24, 28-29):

Leader: O give thanks to the LORD, for he is good; his steadfast love endures forever!

***People:* Let Israel say, "His steadfast love endures forever."**

Leader: Open to me the gates of righteousness, that I may enter through them and give thanks to the LORD.

***People:* This is the gate of the LORD; the righteous shall enter through it.**

Leader: I thank you that you have answered me and have become my salvation.

***People:* The stone that the builders rejected has become the chief cornerstone.**

Leader: This is the LORD's doing; it is marvelous in our eyes.

***People:* This is the day that the LORD has made; let us rejoice and be glad in it.**

Leader: You are my God, and I will give thanks to you; you are my God, I will extol you.

***All:* O give thanks to the LORD, for he is good, for his steadfast love endures forever.**

Pastoral Prayer:

On this day when we remember the joyous procession of the palms that greeted Jesus on his entrance to Jerusalem, so we celebrate your presence among us this day, O Lord. As they praised Jesus that day, so let our hearts praise you on this special day. As they proclaimed his greatness, so we honor your majesty. And yet, Lord, we recognize that much of the crowd which praised him on Sunday would curse him only days later. And too often, Father, we see ourselves in that picture—not that we curse Jesus, but that we turn our backs on him. And it may be Lord, that apathy is more painful to you than outright opposition. So help us, Lord, as we celebrate this season of the year, to be consistent in our praise, faithful in our discipleship, and steadfast in our love, just as you have been steadfast in your love to us. We ask these things in the name of Christ, who loves us no matter what. Amen.

SERMON BRIEFS

THE COST OF DISCIPLESHIP

ISAIAH 50:4-9*a*

On this Palm Sunday we remember the ride Jesus took into Jerusalem on the last week of his life. But we remember more than that. We remember a prophet who lived before Jesus and who laid out his life as a testimony to God. Isaiah wrote about a servant of the Lord who was willing to pay any price in the cost of discipleship. Discipleship is costly because of what it requires from us. Here are some qualities that characterize true disciples.

I. A Teachable Nature

Being open to the truth is a quality needed for all disciples. How can we learn if we are closed-minded? Like Isaiah's servant, we can remain receptive to whatever God has for us. The servant has an "instructed tongue."

But this matter can go awry if we are not careful. Right after the Civil War, a host of people became teachers because they thought teaching was an easy way of making a living. In his autobiography, *Up From Slavery,* Booker T. Washington told about one of these fellows. This man went from village to village teaching a little and receiving pay for it. In one town the people asked if he taught that the earth is round or flat. The teacher replied that he was prepared to teach that the earth was either flat or round, according to the preference of a majority of his patrons. Truth by survey!

A true disciple is teachable but not gullible.

II. A God-Formed Conscience

The servant in Isaiah has his ears opened by the sovereign Lord. He has not been rebellious, nor has he drawn back from the task. Even physical violence did not deter him. The description in verse 6 of the abuse is appalling. But the servant did not run. Disciples have their consciences formed by the Lord himself.

Our consciences inform us that we humans have a fatal flaw. We are lost and cannot save ourselves. We simply cannot pay the price. Even if we could, who would be willing? We are like a slave in the antebellum South named Tom. His owner allowed him to take jobs off the plantation at night, on holidays, and on weekends. He worked hard for his owner and then would walk fifteen miles into town, work there, and return home. After two hours of sleep he would repeat the action. This went on for years, and he saved every penny. He refused to marry but spent every waking hour working.

After he saved a thousand dollars he went to his owner and asked how much he was worth. The man said that most slaves brought from between eight to twelve hundred dollars. However, since Tom was getting old and did not have any children, if he wanted to buy himself, the owner would let him go for six hundred dollars. Tom thanked his owner and went back to his cabin and dug up his money. He fondled the cash and remembered how long it took to get it. He put it back into its hiding place, went back to his owner, and said, "Freedom is a little too high right now. I'm going to wait till the price comes down."

III. An Assurance of God's Vindication

Discipleship is not up to us alone, thankfully. Following the Lord is not a do-it-yourself project. It is living with the awareness that God

113

will bring all things together under his control in the end. Waiting is difficult, but the wait will be worth the effort.

In Carl Sandburg's books on the life of Abraham Lincoln there is a chapter entitled, "Palm Sunday '65." It was about April 9, 1865, when Robert E. Lee surrendered to Ulysses S. Grant at Appomattox Court House in Virginia. On that Palm Sunday the war ended and peace began to reign. A few skirmishes flared up here and there until everyone finally got the word, but the war really was over.

That is not a bad definition for Palm Sunday. God was ready to present his peace plans to men. There would be no compromise. A skirmish broke out on Friday, but men did not yet realize that the battle was over.

Palm Sunday is the day when Christ proclaimed his victory over the hostile forces opposed to him. He faced these forces armed only with power of self-giving love, but that was enough. God is still seeking to let everyone know the battle is over and that Christ has won. His life was the treaty. Discipleship is the honor of signing the peace treaty with God. (*Don M. Aycock*)

PALM SUNDAY FROM THE INSIDE

PHILIPPIANS 2:5-11

Palm Sunday is such a joyful occasion! The decorations are festive, and we eagerly look forward to the coming Easter celebration! Yet there are times when I feel kinship to the Pharisees who urged Jesus to quiet the chants of the people crowding the way that Sunday as he came down the Mount of Olives riding on a donkey: "Hosanna to the Son of David! Blessed is the one who comes in the name of the Lord!" (Matt 21:9) That was fiery stuff; the sort of thing rebellions are made of!

Jesus' response was startling and firm: *If the crowd ceased to proclaim his glory, the very stones of the streets would take up the chant!* Still, somehow I see the rider of that donkey, the object of this adoration and celebration, looking rather sadly at the crowd, mindful of where this road will lead before the week is out, and equally mindful of the contrast between this charade and his previous existence. And I think it took a mind and heart full of love and determination to stay the course that day.

Paul dares to speculate on the thinking and heartbeat of Christ. "Have the mind of Christ," he tells his beloved church. What was the mind-set of Christ as he rode the donkey that day? What is the mind of Christ which we are to have?

I. It Is a Mind-Set of Self-Renunciation

Can you picture in your mind's eye the leave-taking of Christ from heaven to come to earth? I see Christ preparing to leave heaven, looking around at what he is about to leave. All the unspeakable glories of that place! He leaves all the beauty; he leaves the exalted position he has in heaven as the Son; he leaves the equality he has with the Father.

As he stands at the portals of heaven and looks downward, he is thinking of how incredible it is that he who created this universe should place himself into the body of a man, the mind of a man, the knowledge of a man; confined in time and space to the backwaters of history, to the tiny country of Palestine, and to the care of the young girl Mary. But it goes further. In his divinity as he takes leave of heaven, Christ sees the ordeal ahead when, experiencing all a man can experience of hatred and pain and suffering and evil, he will endure the cross because of the goal ahead.

II. It Is a Mind-Set of Humility and Obedience

It is a mind-set of commitment to a descent from glory, round by round descending into the domain of the devil, into the territory claimed by the spiritual powers who had rebelled from the Father. In verse 5 we are told that Jesus, having the nature *(morphe)* of the Father, having the inner character, essential and permanent, laid it aside, not seeing equality with the Father a thing to be held to, but rather, emptying himself, and taking on the nature of a servant, a slave. He humbled himself, taking on the *skema*—that which is changeable about one's self—of a man. And not just a man, but a servant. And as a servant, he became obedient even to death. Executed as a common criminal, as one who plotted against the good of the people, as one who would foment rebellion against Rome.

III. It Is a Mind-Set Honored by the Father

In answer to this self-renunciation, this humility and obedience, the Father has raised him from the dead, says Paul. And not just that, but God has given to Jesus a name that is above every name. God has declared that at the name of Jesus every knee shall bow and every tongue shall confess that Jesus is Lord! That was the earliest Christian confession, and still the only one that counts: *Jesus is Lord!*

This paragraph, nestled in the middle of Paul's Letter, is no mere exercise in academic theology; it is a basis for daily living. I heard a talk radio host call a group fanatics because they believe that if they lose their life in an act dedicated to their faith (not Christian), they will go to heaven and be much better off. He thought it ridiculous that the prospect of how one will spend eternity beyond this life should dictate one's actions and lifestyle here. He is the deluded one, the fanatic about this world.

Paul knew that Jesus was able to go through the garden and face the cross because he trusted in the Father, and trusted him to make all well beyond the cross. We must have this same mind-set, the mind of Christ, enabling us to look beyond this world and live in a way that will glorify Christ. As Charles Wesley said, "Mild he lays his glory by . . . Veiled in flesh the Godhead see" ("Hark the Herald Angels Sing"). (*Earl C. Davis*)

WHICH ONE ARE YOU?

MARK 14:1–15:47

This Gospel text of Jesus' passion is a moving narrative with all of the elements of powerful drama. Jesus is the object of a sinister plot involving betrayal and murder. The woman who anoints him at Bethany demonstrates the devotion of his disciples. Jesus transforms the traditional Passover meal into the sacred mystery of the Lord's Supper. Christ is the only character in this drama who fully understands the plot and has already anticipated the ending.

It is a drama in which you might find yourself. The question is, which one are you?

I. There Are Those Who Deny Their Faith Because of Fear

Peter thought that he would never betray Jesus, but he discounted his own fear. His actions betrayed his true belief. Peter feared judgment by the Sanhedrin or the Romans more than judgment by God.

Fear is our greatest enemy. It keeps us from sharing fully of what we have. We are afraid that we will not have enough if we give some away.

Fear robs us of the power God brings to our life. When we live by faith, we can do all things through Christ. When we live in fear, our timidity robs us and others of the blessing of faithful living.

II. There Are Those Who Will Only Accept God on Their Terms

Fear is involved here, as well. Fear of change. Fear of God acting in new and different ways. Fear of things not being the way they have always been. Fear of life not being predictable. Fear of being challenged to grow and mature. Fear of being moved outside our comfort zone.

Judas had other expectations of Jesus. Judas' frustration and disappointment led him to betray the one for whom he had been waiting. Judas wanted the messiah to come on his own terms.

Most of the Pharisees, Sadducees, and those of the Sanhedrin (the Jewish Council) looked for a messiah who believed as they did. They expected God to meet their criteria. God's kingdom needed to fit their mold of what was law. Though convinced that they were right, they would prudently wait until after the festival to make their move. After all, they did not want a riot on their hands (14:2).

III. There Are Those Unwilling to Accept the Radical Nature of the Kingdom of God

Christianity can never be faith on our own terms. It is not about building the church as we like it, but building the kingdom as God desires. When we insist on being in control, we are unable to give God the control.

Some people saw Jesus as someone to save them from tyranny and oppression. For them he was a miracle worker and a mystical prophet. He awed them, and they shouted, *"Hosanna!"*

Some people saw Jesus as a threat to established religion, a manipulator of men and women, and a purveyor of trickery. They shouted, *"Crucify him!"*

117

Today, some people see Jesus the way they see the church: with skepticism. Some folks wonder if Jesus can really do anything to save them from injustice, poverty, or a lifestyle of unhappiness.

Some people see Jesus as a good-luck charm. Christ is a "Saint Christopher medal," which not only protects, but saves us from sin.

Some people see Jesus as a demanding Lord whose expectations are great and whose love we must earn. The notion of grace is foreign to these folks.

Some people see Jesus as a friend and companion, a Savior and a Lord who is worthy of a lifetime of commitment.

The question is: Which one are you? *(Gary G. Kindley)*

MARCH 28, 1997

❧

Good Friday

Worship Theme: The cross is God's ultimate demonstration of his love for us.

Readings: Isaiah 52:13–53:12; Hebrews 10:16-25; John 18:1–19:42

Call to Worship (Psalm 22:21-27):

Leader: Save me from the mouth of the Lion! From the horns of the wild oxen you have rescued me.

People: **I will tell of your name to my brothers and sisters; in the midst of the congregation I will praise you:**

Leader: You who fear the LORD, praise him! All you offspring of Jacob, glorify him; stand in awe of him, all you offspring of Israel!

People: **For he did not despise or abhor the affliction of the afflicted; he did not hide his face from me, but heard when I cried to him.**

Leader: From you comes my praise in the great congregation;

People: **my vows I will pay before those who fear him.**

Leader: The poor shall eat and be satisfied; those who seek him shall praise the LORD.

People: **May your hearts live forever!**

Leader: All the ends of the earth shall remember and turn to the LORD;

All: **And all the families of the nations shall worship before him.**

Pastoral Prayer:

On this Good Friday, O Lord, we recognize all that is not good about our lives, because it stands in such contrast to all that is good about you. We seem so concerned about our own comfort, but you sent your Son to a land where he had no place to call his home, no place to lay his head. We are consumed by advancing our own cause, but you sent your Son to become a sacrifice for others. We love ourselves most of all, but you so loved the world that you gave your only Son. This day is good, Lord, not because of anything we have done but because of what you have done for us. And because of your love and its incredible demonstration on the cross, we gather this day to confess our sins, to recommit our lives, and to praise your holy name. May the days ahead also be good ones, as your Holy Spirit works through our lives to demonstrate your love and power to a lost world. For we ask it in the name of the One who gave himself for us. Amen.

SERMON BRIEF

THE BETRAYAL OF GOD

JOHN 18:1–19:42

There is a sign that I have often seen in gardens. It is a verse that concludes, "One is closer to God in a garden than anywhere else on earth." Both Genesis and John's Gospel share important accounts of the betrayal of God in a garden. Both accounts remind us that sin and evil can often be found in the most beautiful and serene places.

I. Jesus Was Betrayed by Those Who Feared Him

After a meal and much conversation concerning what was about to occur, Jesus leaves Jerusalem and crosses the Kidron valley. He takes the disciples to Gethsemane on the Mount of Olives. Judas knows it well, for he has gone there often. Judas goes there again, but this time he brings soldiers.

Betrayal means to abandon, to forsake, or to deny. Judas abandoned his commitment to Christ to hold fast to his ideals of national loyalty. His hope for Israel followed one path: power. The power that Judas sought would overthrow Rome and restore Israel. He waited for the day when Jesus would demonstrate his power as messiah, but God's idea of power is found in humility. Christ emptied himself, and was filled with God's power.

Jesus' power was recognized, if misunderstood. His power to influence people, to change lives, to alter custom was a threat to religious and political leaders alike. Jerusalem was already a hotbed of turmoil. They would tolerate no further factions. Out of their own fear of the unknown, they betrayed Jesus.

II. Jesus Was Betrayed by Those Who Loved Him

Peter followed the soldiers who took Jesus to the high priest. He was warming himself against the chill of the night when they recognized him. "Did I not see you in the garden with him?" asks a slave of the priest (18:26). Fear begins to swell in Peter. He has not yet received the courage of the Holy Spirit. Peter denies knowing Jesus, and the rooster crows to mark the moment. Betrayal hurts most when it comes from those dearest. Guilt also carries greater pain when the betrayer knows how devastating his action is.

Perhaps this truth is what brought Joseph of Arimathea and Nicodemus to the cross to claim Jesus' broken body. Joseph, who secretly followed the Christ, and Nicodemus, who came to him in the cover of darkness, now make a public appearance. Their own fear had also led to their betrayal of Jesus. Their voices were not heard speaking up for him to the Sanhedrin. Only after Jesus' death did Joseph talk to Pilate, and then only about Jesus' corpse.

III. We Betray God When We Place Our Trust Elsewhere

Genesis reminds us that the entrance of sin into the world came from misplaced trust. Rather than obeying God and trusting in God's guidance, Eve yields to the serpent and Adam follows suit. Fear follows: as God walks in the garden, Adam and Eve scurry for cover. The passion of Christ also points to misplaced trust and betrayal of faith. Money and power sway Judas, weariness has fallen the disciples ("Could you not stay awake with me?"), and all are fearful.

The truth of Good Friday is that Jesus bridged the gap between humanity's sin and God's goodness. God exhibits the remarkable power of grace for all the world to see. There are those who question who Jesus was and is. The truth is in the power of the Resurrection. Death still holds no power over those who believe. Hope is eternal and comes from placing trust and faith in the God who revealed amazing grace through Jesus Christ. How appropriate that the demonstration of God's grace was also in a garden—the resurrection of Jesus from the garden tomb. Betrayal is forgiven. Death and sin are no more. (*Gary G. Kindley*)

MARCH 30, 1997

❧

Easter Sunday

Worship Theme: The Resurrection is evidence that in Christ we have the assurance of eternal life.

Readings: Isaiah 25:6-9; 1 Corinthians 15:1-11; Mark 16:1-8

Call to Worship (Psalm 118:1-2, 14-24):

Leader: O give thanks to the LORD, for he is good; his steadfast love endures forever!

People: **Let Israel say, "His steadfast love endures forever."**

Leader: The LORD is my strength and my might; he has become my salvation.

People: **There are glad songs of victory in the tents of the righteous:**

Leader: "The right hand of the LORD does valiantly; the right hand of the LORD is exalted;

People: **the right hand of the LORD does valiantly."**

Leader: I shall not die, but I shall live, and recount the deeds of the LORD.

People: **The LORD has punished me severely, but he did not give me over to death.**

Leader: Open to me the gates of righteousness, that I may enter through them and give thanks to the LORD.

People: **This is the gate of the LORD; the righteous shall enter through it.**

Leader: I thank you that you have answered me and have become my salvation.

People: **The stone that the builders rejected has become the chief cornerstone.**

Leader: This is the LORD's doing; it is marvelous in our eyes.

All: **This is the day that the LORD has made; let us rejoice and be glad in it.**

Pastoral Prayer:

O God of life and redemption, we bring our abundant praises to you on this wonderful Easter Sunday. We marvel at your love and celebrate your mercy, which were demonstrated so vividly in the death and resurrection of our Lord Jesus Christ. We celebrate this day because of what you have done. Where we sowed sin, you reaped salvation; where we sowed rebellion, you reaped redemption; where we sowed death, you reaped life. On Good Friday, humanity offered you its cruelty and rejection; on Easter Sunday, you answered with grace and acceptance. How do we respond to such an awesome love? Help us, O Lord, to respond with faithfulness to the cause of Christ, who loved us all the way to the cross. Help us, O Lord, to respond with obedience to the One who was obedient to you no matter what the cost. Help us, O Lord, to respond with boldness as we proclaim the name that is above every name, the name that angels shout in triumph and that causes demons to flee in terror, the name that transforms and delivers, even the name of Jesus Christ, who rose on Easter Day. It is in his name we pray. Amen.

SERMON BRIEFS

EASTER IS HERE!

ISAIAH 25:6-9

From the earliest times men and women have looked beyond their present sorrows to a hoped-for future. Death and despair just did not seem right as the final word. The prophet Isaiah looked at such a time. He painted a picture of a future in which a banquet would be spread by the Lord. All who sorrowed would be invited. What a spread it would be!

We Christians gather today, Easter Sunday, and remember that death and despair are not the last words. Good Friday and silent

Saturday seemed to be the end. But as Tony Campolo puts its: "It was Friday. The cynics were lookin' at the world and sayin', 'as things have been so they shall be. You can't change anything in this world, you can't change anything.' But those cynics didn't know that it was only Friday. Sunday's comin'!"

I. Easter Is the Sign That Life Is Greater Than Death

Isaiah spoke of a banquet for all of those who love God. The past, present, and future all come together in that moment. Life, through Christ, is more enduring than death. The "shroud" will be destroyed. He will "swallow up death."

On Easter Sunday, Christ broke out of the seeming permanence of death. That breakthrough was a sign of what lies in store for any who will come to Christ as a follower. It was also a sign of the ability of God to break through every form of barrier, hindrance, and grave that stands in his way. This happens in our lives when we accept him. It happens when God gets "under the skin" of even the most outward pagan.

When George Bush was vice president of the United States, one of his official duties was to represent our country at the funeral of Soviet leader Leonid Brezhnev. The entire funeral procession was marked by its military precision. There was a coldness and hollowness that enveloped it. Since the Soviet Union was officially atheistic, no comforting prayers or spiritual hymns were sung. Only the marching soldiers, steel helmets, and Marxist rhetoric were offered. There was no mention of God. Mr. Bush was close to the casket when Mrs. Brezhnev came for her last good-bye. Bush said, "She walked up, took one last look at her husband and there—in the cold, gray center of that totalitarian state—she traced the design of the cross on her husband's chest. I was stunned. In that simple act, God had broken through the core of the communist system" (*Christianity Today,* October 16, 1986, p. 37).

II. Easter Is the Sign That God Was Willing
to Sacrifice on Our Behalf

Isaiah rejoiced in the fact that we could "trust in him" and he "saved us." We are his because he gave his Son to save us from our sins. That called for incredible sacrifice.

Humans can hardly imagine that sort of sacrifice. We get it confused. For example, in 1977 a man named Jean Bedel Bokassa, a former French paratrooper, proclaimed himself emperor of the Central African Republic. This new nation was founded in 1960 and had a population of two million people. It is listed among the twenty-five poorest nations. The average annual income was $155 when Bokassa took over, yet he held a $30 million inaugural gala! He had a six-foot diamond-encrusted scepter and a two-ton gold-plated throne. His 2,000 guests were served hundreds of pounds of caviar and 24,000 bottles of champagne, all flown in by chartered plane from France. Despite the poverty of "his people" and the extravagance of his coronation, Bokassa was quoted as saying, "One cannot create a great history without sacrifices." True enough, but who made the sacrifice?

III. Easter Is a Day of Celebrating the Triumph of Christ

"Let us be glad and rejoice in his salvation." That is Isaiah's conclusion. And why not? The light has come to scatter the darkness. We need no longer live in fear and dread.

Robert Louis Stevenson looked out of his window one evening many years ago. Those were the days before electric lights. Stevenson saw the town lamplighter coming along. As this lamplighter lit the street lamps in succession, Stevenson was impressed at the sight. He wrote about the lamplighter who went along "punching holes in the darkness." Jesus Christ came into this world as a light, and he punched holes in the darkness.

That is reason for celebrating. Easter is here! *(Don M. Aycock)*

THE PROBLEM WITH EASTER

1 CORINTHIANS 15:1-11

Paul writes to a troubled church at Corinth. He has already dealt with questions of marriage, morality, Christians taking each other to court, factions within the church, misuse of the Lord's Supper, and now he addresses the most devastating question the troublemakers in that congregation can possibly raise: the reality of the Resurrection. This is the bedrock of his gospel, for we are the Easter people;

Jesus is the firstfruits of the Easter harvest from the dead, and we are the rest of that glorious harvest.

The gospel, the good news, is this: Christ died for our sins, was buried and rose on the third day. Such a gospel may seem too good to be true, and so Paul marshals not only his own experience but also that of other Christians in Christ before him to deal with the unbelievable nature of Easter.

I. Paul Didn't Make It Up

Paul reminds them he didn't make this gospel up. First, he stressed that "This is what I received." He says the same thing when he is discussing the misuse of the Lord's Supper. Paul doesn't claim he was the first or only one to receive the revelation of the gospel; there were those in Christ before him. Paul was merely the first to put the Resurrection on paper; he had heard it often, passed down in the preaching of men like Peter, reaffirmed in the teaching ministry of the church, and marvelled upon around the table in humble homes of those "of the Way." Second, Paul says the amazing facts of the gospel—the death and resurrection of Jesus—are "in accordance with the scriptures" (vv. 3, 4).

II. The Witnesses Didn't Make It Up

Not only does Paul pass along the gospel handed down to him by those who were eyewitnesses to those things, and the truth according to the Scriptures, he also appeals to the testimonies of those who saw the resurrected Lord. These early Christians didn't make that experience up; they *saw him* after the Resurrection.

First, says Paul, Cephas (Hebrew for Peter) saw him. According to the Gospels, Mary Magdalene was the first witness to the Resurrection, but Paul passes on the testimony known to him about the witnesses. Jesus appeared to Peter first and in a private way, possibly because Peter needed forgiveness and reassurance after the heartbreaking denial. Then Jesus was seen by all the Twelve; obviously, literally, the eleven, since Judas has taken his life and no replacement had been made.

Lest anyone think this little band of disciples fabricated the whole Resurrection story, Paul goes further—Jesus was seen alive after his crucifixion by a crowd of more than 500 at one time, most of whom were still alive when Paul penned these words! What an honored group; and how they must have treasured the sight of the resurrected Jesus all their lives!

Last of all, says Paul, Jesus appeared to him. Unworthy, unexpected, in the blinding light of the Damascus road, Jesus granted this mercy to Paul (v. 8). And with that blessing, Paul felt he was elevated into the original band of disciples.

The good news of Easter comes on the wings of grace. The gospel—the death and resurrection of Jesus and the appropriation of the grace provided there—is the result of God's grace; it is nothing we deserve. We are unworthy people, sinners who deserve death, not life. Paul, even in this context of the proclamation of Easter, cannot get away from his feelings of guilt and sin. God's grace brought about Easter, God's grace preaches Easter, and God's grace alone is able to stir human hearts to believe and accept the good news of the Resurrection. *(Earl C. Davis)*

MAKING SENSE OF IT ALL

MARK 16:1-8

Being confused about life's events is easy. A family struggles with broken relationships, yet the situation does not seem to get much better. A couple wrestles with chronic illness, knowing that the future holds more health problems. Victimized by crime, a family strives to overcome the haunting feelings that linger after the incident. How does one make sense of it all?

If years of familiarity have dulled the sense of awe at Easter, read again Mark's account of that incredible morning. The Easter story reminds us:

I. God's Ways Are Different from Our Ways

The Pharisees did not understand this truth, and neither did the apostles. They waited for the messiah to come on their terms. When Jesus entered their lives, even those who called him "Lord" were not certain who this Christ was. Judas apparently wanted a military leader, or at least someone who could lead them out from under Roman domination.

After Jesus' death, the apostles were hidden, shaking in their sandals behind bolted doors and shuttered windows. The faithful women, rising early that first dawn of what would become the new Sabbath, went to a cemetery expecting to find a corpse. What they found was a messenger of God. Grief turned to fear and wonder. Could it be that Jesus was alive? Is that what he had meant when he spoke of rising on the third day?

II. We Begin to Make Sense of Life When We Ask, "Who?"

Perhaps our pattern has been to ask, "How?" or "Why?" Most often, however, the Bible addresses the question, "Who?" The creation accounts of Genesis are not intended to give the formula for *how* God created the universe. Genesis tells *who* created everything and whose we are. The Gospels do not detail the method of Mary's conception of Jesus. They simply state that the Holy Spirit came upon her and she conceived. The message of the Gospels emphasizes whose son Jesus is and who Christ is for us.

Scripture does not describe the physiology of Christ's resurrection. Not one human witness was present at that precise moment. We do not have a clue as to the details of how it occurred. What we have are witnesses to the empty tomb and to the risen Christ. *Who* is risen is what matters! Christ arose!

III. It Is Our Acceptance of God's Grace That Helps Us to Make Sense of It All

The Rev. Kelly Clem and the congregation of Goshen United Methodist Church in Piedmont, Alabama, will never forget Palm Sunday 1994. A tornado destroyed their sanctuary during the worship services on that day, injuring ninety people and killing twenty. Six of the dead were children, including the pastor's four-year-old daughter. At the time the storm hit, the children were singing "The Lord Will Provide."

We cannot say that God's will causes everything that happens. The God revealed through Christ does not send tornadoes to kill young children who are singing God's praises. The same God behind the creation of the universe is at work even now, wherever there is crisis or sorrow or pain. God is at work bringing comfort, hope, and resurrection.

129

It is faith that bridges the gap. Faith steps in when we cannot understand yet choose to believe in the gracious God who is about the work of redemption. Only God can take the tragedy of the cross and turn it into an Easter celebration. The church dares not forget the incredible grace we have to celebrate. It is grace that rolls away the stones from the tombs of our existence and helps to make sense of it all. *(Gary G. Kindley)*

APRIL

❧

Mending the Net, Sharpening the Hoe

Symbol: Cloud

The clouds in the heaven are the natural veil of the blue sky and are used as a symbol of the unseen God. It is the visible token of God's presence.

Text:

"By day the LORD went ahead of them in a pillar of cloud to guide them on their way and by night in a pillar of fire to give them light, so that they could travel by day or night. Neither the pillar of cloud by day nor the pillar of fire by night left its place in front of the people" (Exod. 13:21-22 NIV).

Invocation:

"O God our Father, renew our spirits and draw our hearts to thyself that our work may not be to us a burden but a delight; and give us each love to thee as we sweeten all our obedience. Help us that we may serve thee with the cheerfulness and gladness of children, delighting ourselves in thee and rejoicing in all that is to the honor of thy name; through Jesus Christ our Lord. Amen." (From *The Book of Worship*)

Scripture Focus:
- Exodus 16:10-13
- 1 Kings 8:10-13
- Matthew 17:5-8
- Ezekiel 10:4-5

Prayer Focus:
- Focus on your need for God's presence in your ministry. Remember the process God used in calling you to ministry. Recall periods of clear and definite divine leadership in your ministry. Think of times in the immediate future in which you will need reaffirmation of this leadership.

- Recall the names of persons in the church you serve who need to serve effectively.
- Pray for your official church body that they may be servants and fellow ministers of the towel.

Prayer:

"O Thou Who art the Light of the Mindset to know Thee, the Light of the souls that love Thee, and the Strength of the thoughts that seek Thee; help us so to know Thee that we may truly love Thee, so to love Thee that we may fully serve Thee, whose service is perfect freedom; through Jesus Christ our Lord. Amen. (Gelasian Sacramentary, A.D. 494) *(Bill Self)*

APRIL 6, 1997

❧

Second Sunday of Easter

Worship Theme: Forgiveness is available to those who confess sin and turn to Christ.

Readings: Acts 4:32-35; 1 John 1:1–2:2; John 20:19-31

Call to Worship (Psalm 133):

Leader: How very good and pleasant it is when kindred live together in unity!

People: **Give thanks to the Lord, and praise him forever.**

Leader: It is like the precious oil on the head, running down upon the beard, on the beard of Aaron, running down over the collar of his robes.

People: **Give thanks to the Lord, and praise him forever.**

Leader: It is like the dew of Hermon, which falls on the mountains of Zion.

People: **Give thanks to the Lord, and praise him forever.**

Leader: For there the LORD ordained his blessing, life forever-more.

All: **Give thanks to the Lord, and praise him forever.**

Pastoral Prayer:

We praise you, O God, for you are the Lord of springtime, the Lord of new life, the Lord of resurrection. Even as we bask in the glory of the Easter season just passed, we continue to marvel at your glorious deeds among us. The first flower of spring is a miracle of your love, O Lord, for which we are grateful. And just as the change of seasons replaces the harshness of winter with the newness of spring, so your gracious love takes our sinful, rebellious lives and transforms them into new creations in Christ. We confess our sins before you, O Lord, and ask for your forgiveness. Remake us, day by day, that we might honor you in our actions, our attitudes, our words, and our thoughts. For we ask it in Jesus' name. Amen.

SERMON BRIEFS

THE PRISTINE CHURCH

ACTS 4:32-35

The text from Acts depicts a church that is almost too good to be true. It describes a group of people of "one heart and soul" (v. 32). The church's love and trust are reflected by the phrase "everything they owned was held in common." This is how the Christian faith ought to look, but in practice some of what we see in the church is ugly by comparison to this pristine picture of primal Christianity.

I. Money Can Corrupt

Economics and materialism tear at the fabric of our nation as few things do. Economics and materialism are not strangers to the church either, as the story of Ananias and Sapphira will soon brutally demonstrate (Acts 5:1-11). Economics and materialism seem at the root of many conflicts. This is why 1 Timothy 6:10 states plainly, "the love of money is a root of all kinds of evil, and in their eagerness to be rich some have wandered away from the faith."

Most pastors can nod in agreement with my Liberian friend's assessment of pastoral care in the African context. He quipped, "Most of my counseling has to do with business—woman business or money business." I would guess that my friend speaks for many pastors in the United States, too.

II. Competition Can Kill

We all are familiar with the parable of the laborers in the vineyard. Some workers go out at sun-up, others at three-hour intervals throughout the day. A few work about an hour. Yet at the moment of payment, all workers—the early and the late—receive the same wage. It seems unfair to our way of understanding equity! The prodigal son is the same way. Where is the justice in the way the owner of the vineyard or the prodigal's father deals with those who do less than their share? And from our point of view, we surely understand the grumbling.

In our families, in our places of work, in our schools, in our neighborhoods—even in our churches—our tendency as groups of people is to compare ourselves with one another. One of the most accurate and devastating measures happens to be cash. We all know how to quantify someone's hourly or annual wage quickly to size up the person. Unfortunately, this proclivity to compare also puts us at odds with one another. Most of us are geared for competition, not cooperation.

III. The Church Can Transform

Verse 33 says it all: "With great power the apostles gave their testimony to the resurrection of the Lord Jesus, and great grace was upon them all." This community of early disciples was empowered by a vision of power that was virtually unknown. Neither jail time, nor fear of the government, nor fear of the religious authorities made these early disciples afraid. They were so overwhelmed by the spirit of Jesus' resurrection, that no longer were money or competition the driving forces in their lives; serving the Lord cooperatively was. Each contributed what he had and took only what he needed. What made the difference? The transforming power of Christ in their lives!

About a year ago my two little boys were discovering the trials and tribulations of a seesaw. The younger kept yelling at his mother to make his older brother get off, but he soon discovered that one person riding a seesaw was less than satisfying. When a four-year-old realizes he cannot play the game alone, but he needs a cooperative partner, there is a seed for the kingdom of God. (*David N. Mosser*)

THE PATH TO SALVATION

1 JOHN 1:1–2:2

Do you know what it's like to desperately want to shower? You've been working in the garden or on the car on a hot day. You're

135

dripping with sweat and coated with grime. Just thinking about it makes you want to go wash up, doesn't it?

But I've seen little boys and girls who are covered with nearly their weight in dirt and grime, and it doesn't seem to bother them. No matter what their dirt quotient, they still don't want a bath!

People can be the same way when it comes to sin. Sin corrupts, pollutes, makes a life filthy, but often we don't even see it—like children merrily playing away while they become progressively dirtier. But we are not children, and sin cannot be washed away from our lives like dirt from a child's body. How can we deal with sin in our lives?

Jesus Christ came to reveal God to us, and to provide for us a means to be reconciled to the Father—to overcome the barrier our sin has created between us and God. In these verses, we receive insight into how Jesus Christ can transform our lives.

I. Recognition of Sin Leads to Confession (vv. 8-9a)

Doctors tell us that some forms of pain are actually beneficial, because they alert us to medical conditions we might otherwise overlook. A problem is rarely solved before it is recognized as a problem. That is why the Holy Spirit convicts us of sin—so that we realize our own need and will be open to a solution.

And the solution to the sin problem begins with confession—acknowledging our own sin, our own weakness. Confession requires laying aside pride and recognizing our own unworthiness next to God's holiness.

II. Confession of Sin Leads to Forgiveness (v. 9)

God is eager for us to confess our sins because he is eager to forgive. Jesus gave us a wonderful picture of God's forgiving nature when he told the parable of the prodigal son. The watching, waiting father stands ready to receive and forgive the wandering son, if only the young man will take that first step back home.

When we acknowledge our sin and confess it, God is ready to forgive our sin and transform our lives.

III. Forgiveness of Sin Leads to Cleansing (v. 9)

No matter what your sin, no matter how great or small, God is willing to forgive you and to cleanse your life. God's cleansing is not superficial but complete. If you have surrendered your life to Christ as Lord and Savior, from that point forward when God looks at you, he does not see the sinful acts you have done, but he sees the sinless purity of Jesus Christ who stands in your place.

Christ removes the power of sin. Before sin held us in bondage, but Christ has freed us from that slavery. Sin has no dominion over us, except what we allow it to have. And as we walk day by day with Christ, sin has less and less place and influence in our lives.

Christ removes the penalty of sin. In the Letter to the Romans, Paul wrote, "the wages of sin is death"—utter and total separation from God. But through the power of Christ, we have been released from that inevitable penalty, and have been set on a new path that leads to the eternal presence of God.

Here is one of the great promises in all of Scripture, but it demands a response. Are you willing to reach out in faith and allow Christ to transform your life? *(Michael Duduit)*

FACT AND FAITH

JOHN 20:19-31

It's commonly understood that the church began at Pentecost. But as I see it, that's when the church was empowered by the Holy Spirit for its life and ministry (see Acts 1–2). I contend the church was born when Jesus rose from the dead.

The resurrection of Jesus is the cornerstone of the church. Or as Paul wrote, "If Christ has not been raised, our preaching is useless and so is your faith" (1 Cor. 15:14 NIV).

Christian apologetics (the theological discipline of highlighting the credibility of Christianity's claims) has provided an intellectually irrefutable case for the Resurrection. The existence of the church, the shift of the worship calendar from the Jewish sabbath (seventh day of the week) to Sunday (first day of the week), the New Testament, the transformation of the disciples from cowards at Jesus' arrest and crucifixion into crusaders in less than three days, and the continuing testimonies of people who claim a personal relationship with him have been cited as overwhelming witnesses to the resurrection of Jesus. It has even been said there is more evidence for the resurrection of Jesus than the birth of George Washington.

John 20:31 makes the connection between the fact of the Resurrection ("these are written so that you may come to believe that Jesus is the Messiah") and the saving *faith* inspired by the Resurrection ("and that through believing you may have life in his name").

I. The Fact of the Resurrection

Belief *(pisteuo)* in the resurrection of Jesus is more than two feet planted firmly in the air. It is the conviction and confidence enabled by the fact of the Resurrection.

John refers to the resurrected appearances of Jesus to Mary Magdalene (vv. 10-18), the disciples (vv. 19-23), and Thomas (vv. 24-29) as "written so that you may come to believe" (v. 31*a*). They provide proof for the profession.

II. The Saving Faith Inspired by the Resurrection

When the Philippian jailer asked Paul and Silas how he could be saved, they replied, "Believe on the Lord Jesus, and you will be saved" (see Acts 16:30-31). The resurrection of Jesus inspired the belief in Jesus, which enables salvation through Jesus.

John's understanding of salvation includes existential and eternal dimensions. Existentially, Christians are happy, whole, joyful, and secure. Eternally, Christians say with David A. Redding, "Anyone who feels sorry for a dead Christian, as though the poor chap were missing something, is himself missing the transfiguring promotion involved" (*Getting Through the Night*, 1972).

Of course, the greatest apologetic proof for Jesus' resurrection is not what we *say* about it but rather how we *look* as a result of it. Referring to John's Gospel, Rudolf Bultmann noted: "Its purpose is to awaken the faith that Jesus is the Messiah, the Son of God" (*John*, 1964). In other words, the fact of Jesus' resurrection inspires *animated* faith.

The only gospel that some folks will ever hear or see is the gospel according to you. Do you *look* saved?

That's the connection between fact and faith. Or as the song goes, "If you're happy and you know it, then you really ought to show it." *(Robert R. Kopp)*

APRIL 13, 1997

❧

Third Sunday of Easter

Worship Theme: The Resurrection has power to transform our lives.

Readings: Acts 3:12-19; 1 John 3:1-7; Luke 24:36*b*-48

Call to Worship (Psalm 4:3-5):

Leader: The LORD has set apart the faithful for himself;

People: **the LORD hears when I call to him.**

Leader: When you are disturbed, do not sin; ponder it on your beds, and be silent.

All: **Offer right sacrifices, and put your trust in the LORD.**

Pastoral Prayer:

O holy and righteous God, who nourishes all creation with your light and makes joyful all that lives on earth and in the heavens. We confess our sins before you. Where you offered light, we have chased after darkness; when you offered peace, we have created confusion; while you offered hope, we clung to false gods of vanity and pride. Forgive us, O Lord, and restore us that we might again bask in the warmth of your presence. Help us to claim the power of Christ's resurrection in our lives day by day—power to love, power to forgive, power to overcome sin and live in your righteousness. Satisfy our restless hearts by bringing them to rest in the fullness of your love. For we ask it in the powerful name of the Resurrected One. Amen.

SERMON BRIEFS

WHAT MAKES THE DIFFERENCE?

ACTS 3:12-19

On the heels of Peter's healing of a man lame from birth is one of several sermons Peter preaches in the early part of Acts. There is nothing quite like a miraculous healing to get people's attention, and

Peter certainly had got their attention! The text says, "they were filled with wonder and amazement at what had happened" (Acts 3:10).

The content of Peter's sermon is like many sermons in Acts. First, the sermon addresses the historical reality of how people who should have received Jesus as messiah, instead handed him over to the authorities to have him murdered. Second, Peter's sermon addresses the question: "[W]hy do you stare at us, as though by our own power or piety we had made him walk?" (v. 12).

How is it that ordinary people like Peter or John—or even us—can do miraculous works? It is a good question, and one that haunts people who, aside from following Christ, are about as ordinary as anyone else.

I. The Resurrection Makes the Difference in Our Lives

At the end of Luke's Gospel, Peter and the other disciples are discouraged and feel alienated, abandoned by Jesus. Peter knows all too well that he denied Jesus three times, just as Jesus predicted he would. In Luke 23:49, the scene is summarized like this: "But all his acquaintances, including the women who had followed him from Galilee, stood at a distance." Jesus was entirely alone—all had fled, or at least had kept their distance out of fear and shame. Yet, from the empty tomb of Jesus' resurrection the church was born at Pentecost.

The book of Acts is filled with stories of the disciples being, in a sense, reborn and becoming more Christlike than they could have ever imagined. Acts 5 tells us: "Yet more than ever believers were added to the Lord, great numbers of both men and women, so that they even carried out the sick into the streets, and laid them on cots and mats, in order that Peter's shadow might fall on some of them as he came by" (vv. 14-15). Clearly, Peter has come out of the shadows of denial to cast a healing shadow of his own.

II. The Resurrection Can Make a Difference in Your Life

Peter's sermon urges others to partake of this same grace that dramatically changed his own life. This is the primal call of the gospel, calling us into a relationship with Christ, which recreates us in God's own image. Peter exhorts the people to "repent therefore, and turn to God so that your sins may be wiped out" (v. 19), and this will give new life—whole and complete in God.

Max Dupree tells a powerful story about people's identity. A young physician had a patient who owned a small business. The doctor had gone beyond normal expectations in helping this businessman, and in gratitude the man invited the physician and his wife to dinner and a symphony concert. During the concert, the orchestra presented a premier performance of a new composition. After the piece was performed and the audience applauded, the conductor turned to the young businessman and introduced him to the audience as the composer—much to the shock of the physician, who had not known of his patient's musical talents.

The physician wondered whether his patient was an amateur composer whose primary identity was running a business, or whether he was actually a professional composer who also operated a business for the sheer enjoyment of it. "Did his experience with balance sheets help his orchestration? Or did his knowledge of harmony enable him to listen for the music in a well-run organization?" (Max Dupree, *Leadership Jazz* [Dell, 1992], 186-87).

Each of us has the choice, by God's grace, to become a Peter of Acts rather than a Peter of the gospel, because Christ can and does work in human life. *(David N. Mosser)*

BECOMING HIS CHILDREN

1 JOHN 3:1-7

The famous writer George Bernard Shaw received a unique proposal from dancer Isadora Duncan. She believed that the two of them should have a child together. As she explained it: "Think what a child it would be, with my body and your brain!"

Shaw declined the offer, sending this response: "Think how unfortunate it would be if the child were to have my body and your brain!"

Parents are justly proud of their children, and often point to physical or emotional characteristics in their children that correspond to similar characteristics in themselves. That's what we mean when we call little Junior a "chip off the old block."

But what if your father is God? John says that in Christ we have become children of God. What does it mean for you and me to be children of God?

I. Being a Child of God Produces a New Lifestyle

When we become part of the family of God, we experience a transformation that produces a new lifestyle.

Purity becomes a priority (v. 3). We live in a culture in which purity is not so much an asset as a liability! For example, a generation ago, the loss of one's sexual innocence before marriage carried a stigma; today, many of our young people try to hide the fact of their virginity because their peers will look down on them for it. What a devastating indictment of a society, when purity is not honored but ridiculed!

For the child of God, however, purity is a priority to be sought. We want to be fashioned in the image of God—to share in his holiness and righteousness. That does not mean we will achieve such purity in this life; but for the children of God, purity is the desire of their hearts.

Sin no longer dominates (vv. 4-7). Before we knew Christ, we were controlled by sin. The apostle Paul says we were "slaves" to sin—it held us in bondage, it dominated our lives. But Christ has freed us from bondage to sin, and we no longer allow sin to dominate our lives as it once did.

Does that mean Christians don't sin anymore? Not at all. The difference is that once Christ has come to reside in your life, sin is now an unwelcome visitor. You are no longer "at home" in a sinful lifestyle. And as you grow in your Christian walk—through prayer, studying God's Word, sharing your faith with others—then sin has less and less influence in your life.

One of the ways we recognize the child of God is through a transformed lifestyle. There is another important characteristic John cites here:

II. Being a Child of God Produces a New Hope

Have you attended the funeral of someone who is not a Christian? It is altogether different than the funeral of a child of God. For the non-Christian, the funeral service is really an ending, a ceremony marked by tragedy and loss. For the Christian, however, the funeral ought to be in some sense a celebration. For the child of God, death is not a tragic ending but an incredible beginning of an eternity with God.

We do not know all that we would like to know about that future, but we know that it is filled with hope and expectancy. As John says, "What we will be has not yet been revealed," but we do have the promise of something special. "What we do know is this: when he is revealed, we will be like him, for we will see him as he is" (v. 2). We will one day have the privilege of seeing Almighty God in all his glory and power, and we will have the even greater privilege of in some way sharing in that divine experience with the Father.

What a hope! What a Savior! (*Michael Duduit*)

GETTING UP BY LOOKING AROUND

LUKE 24:36*b*-48

Trust in our Lord is *inspired* when we look around; Psalm 121 says, "I lift up my eyes." Trust in our Lord is *completed* when we look up to him; in the scripture text from Luke we read, "Look at my hands and my feet. . . . Touch me and see . . . ."

I. Getting Up by Looking Around

I'll never forget a scene from an episode of "The Three Stooges." Curly cried, "Moe! Moe! I can't see!" Moe asked, "What's the matter?" And Curly replied, "I've got my eyes closed."

God's handiwork is all around us "from sea to shining sea." All we have to do is look around—*open our eyes*—and we'll see Someone very sovereign is running the show. Only the emotionally, intellectually, and spiritually blind of this world cannot see our Lord is in control and will ultimately prevail.

The psalmist was being rhetorical when he asked, "I lift up my eyes to the hills—from where will my help come?" He knew God is in control. He quickly sang out, "My help comes from the LORD, who made heaven and earth." Therefore, he concluded, "The LORD . . . will keep your life" (Ps. 121).

The psalmist was saying that if God can create a world, he can most certainly conserve us here and now and hereafter.

Are you down? Look around!

II. Looking Around Doesn't Always Work

Unfortunately, there's always enough pain and suffering in our world to keep us down. There are *intentional* tragedies precipitated by nasty people. There are *natural* tragedies like fire, floods, earthquakes, disease, and so on.

Looking around doesn't always inspire us. Sometimes it gets us down to look around.

III. Staying Up by Looking Up

When the resurrected Jesus appeared to the disciples, their trust was completed as their potential for confident living and eternal life was assured. That's why Jesus said, "Look at my hands and feet . . . Touch me and see." Getting in touch with Jesus—entering into holy communion with him through the spiritual disciplines of worship, prayer, fasting, Bible study, sacrament, and fellowship—enables a person to live triumphantly amid the meanness, madness, and misery of life in the modern world.

When Larry King asked Chuck Colson how he has avoided the pitfalls of so many church leaders who can never live up to human expectations, Colson said, "I tell people, 'Don't follow me! Follow Jesus!' "

That's why our church has rearranged the chancel furniture. Our pastors don't sit in the kingly high-backed seat. We've reserved it for our Lord. Only Christ is king! We've even put a sign on it: "This seat reserved for the King of kings and Lord of lords. Jesus!"

It's like we read in Hebrews: "Let us fix our eyes on Jesus, the author and perfecter of our faith" (12:2 NIV). To put it another way, the only way to stay up is to look up to Jesus.

When we're getting down, we must remember the gospel. We must remember Jesus. We must remember how he conquered death and assured the same for you and me through faith. We must remember his resurrected greeting to the disciples, which is the experience of all who trust in him: "Peace be with you" (Luke 24:36*b*).

That's how we stay up: we look up to Jesus. (*Robert R. Kopp*)

APRIL 20, 1997

❧

Fourth Sunday of Easter

Worship Theme: Jesus is the Good Shepherd who provides for our needs.

Readings: Acts 4:5-12; 1 John 3:16-24; John 10:11-18

Call to Worship (Psalm 23):

Leader: The LORD is my shepherd, I shall not want.

People: He makes me lie down in green pastures;

Leader: he leads me beside still waters; he restores my soul.

People: He leads me in right paths for his name's sake.

Leader: Even though I walk through the darkest valley, I fear no evil;

People: for you are with me; your rod and your staff—they comfort me.

Leader: You prepare a table before me in the presence of my enemies;

People: you anoint my head with oil; my cup overflows.

Leader: Surely goodness and mercy shall follow me all the days of my life,

All: and I shall dwell in the house of the LORD my whole life long.

Pastoral Prayer:

Like sheep before the shepherd, O Lord, we gather in your presence. Like sheep, we have wandered our own way, oblivious to the danger that surrounds us. Yet with a loving hand, you have restored us to the safety and security of the fold. Like a shepherd, you provide for our needs. Like a shepherd, you guide and direct our paths. Help us to understand, O Lord, what an enormous gift you have given us. And help us to minister with love and compassion to one another, even as you have ministered to us. Grant us grace that our lips will praise you, our lives honor you, and our love model your supreme example. In the name of the Good Shepherd, who gave his life for his sheep. Amen.

SERMON BRIEFS

NO OTHER NAME

ACTS 4:5-12

Peter and John are in a predicament familiar to persons in public life—teachers, preachers, government officials. These persons often have to defend their actions that produce change.

Peter and John had previously healed a man lame from birth—in fact, they had dramatically changed his life. The crowd was amazed by what they had seen and wanted to know how all this had happened. Peter recounts the many and various things God had done for the people by the teachers of the law and the prophets, who had urged the people to change their relationship with God.

In the midst of the sermon, Peter and John are interrupted by a group of religious authorities who are annoyed by what they believe is false teaching. What may be more at stake was their perception that these two were urging a change in the status quo. These religious authorities had the two arrested and put into custody of the civil authorities. In spite of the religious and civil authorities, however, "many of those who heard the word believed; and they numbered about five thousand" (Acts 4:4).

The leaders asked, "By what power or by what name did you do this?" (v. 7). The Holy Spirit fills Peter and he begins to address those in authority in what looks to us like a courtroom scene. Peter tells those assembled that it was not his power that restored the lame man, but rather the life-giving power found in the name of Jesus Christ of Nazareth. Peter is determined not to take the credit for the healing, but rather credit the power of God at work in the one whom the people had crucified. It is God and God's Christ that has the power to heal, make whole, and give salvation. And only in God can these blessings be acquired by mortals. In a sense, Peter shares deeply the gospel's conviction that only God can raise up what people have struck down.

What is interesting about Peter's speech is his connection of both the physical and the spiritual aspects of healing. Not only is the lame man healed of his affliction, but also those who are lame or sick in the spiritual sense can also be healed. This is the ultimate hope that God holds out for God's people.

Herbert Spencer (1820–1903), an English philosopher, once said: "A living thing is distinguished from a dead thing by the multiplicity of the changes at any moment taking place in it." Change for the sake of change is not a worthy goal, but change that improves our effectiveness is what we seek.

This is true of the church as well. It is naive to believe that today's church can be just like the church depicted in Acts, though there is much to learn from the earliest church. In each generation, we as the church of Jesus Christ must learn how to take the gospel to a new group of persons who need to hear the good news. Our task is "to be wise as serpents and innocent as doves."

Three people had adjacent businesses in the same building. At one end of the building the businessperson put up a sign that read: "Year-End Clearance Sale." At the other end of the building, another merchant followed suit with a sign that read: "Closing-Out Sale." The store owner in the middle of the building knew he had to do something to keep his business from being hurt, so he put up a sign that read: "Main Entrance."

I'm not suggesting that Christians change their signage, but I am suggesting that believers in Christ are alert to a new generation of pagans, who have yet to hear the life-giving word of the gospel. This is because, as Peter told us all long ago, "There is salvation in no one else, for there is no other name under heaven given among mortals by which we must be saved." *(David N. Mosser)*

THE SECRET OF LOVE

1 JOHN 3:16-24

To his contemporaries, Jesus was a rabbi, a teacher of the law; such men were expected to spend their time interpreting the law.

No wonder he frustrated the Pharisees so much, for instead of discussing the law, Jesus kept talking about love.

"Rabbi, is it okay to pull an ox out of the ditch on the Sabbath . . . or to pay taxes to Rome . . . and can we stone a woman caught in the act of adultery?" And each time, Jesus challenged them to quit focusing their mental microscopes on the letter of the Law, and to see the divine spirit of the Law. Jesus wants us to understand that you can keep the law in detail without loving, but you cannot love without being obedient to God's law.

Jesus was motivated by love. It was the unifying principle of his earthly life. And the message of John's letter is that Christ's followers must also choose love as a life principle if we are to walk in his steps. If we are to share his life, we must share his love. What are the characteristics of such love?

I. Love Is of God

True love is not a human characteristic; its source is God. John talks about "God's love" (v. 17)—he is talking about God's kind of love. It is the love that has a divine author.

We use the word *love* too loosely in this culture. We love our wives, husbands, children; I love my cat, my dog, my new boat; I love my carpet, my new curtains, my furniture. What we refer to as love is often really infatuation, affection, lust, concern, or a bad case of heartburn!

Love is not something you learn in a seminar or from a book; it must be experienced in our own lives. That is why John says "we know love"—we know it because we have experienced it in Christ. The cross of Christ is the supreme expression of love; to know Christ's sacrificial love, and to accept that cross as our own, is to open our lives to truly experience love for the first time.

If our culture knows so little real love, it is because we know so little of God. He is a God of love, and if we wish to know him we must be willing to be loved and to love.

II. Love Is Action

Love goes beyond words. It is very practical—it must be applied in daily life, sometimes with people who are not very loving or lovable. Real love requires us to take our eyes off ourselves and see the needs of others.

We Christians can be guilty of talking about love but showing very little. One Christian author recalls his first encounter with a Christian. He was walking down a high school corridor when a young woman stepped into his path, held up a Bible to his face, and exclaimed, "You'd better get right with the Lord or he'll condemn you to hell!" For years, his impression of Christians was wild-eyed fanatics carrying thirty-pound Bibles in wheelbarrows and screaming at people. His impression of Christ wasn't one of love, but of anger.

What impression of Christ do we give? Loving, caring, concerned for people and their needs? Or is our Christ moody, distant, legalistic, disconnected from daily life? And is our love given freely, or does it carry expectations that must be met before we show our love?

Just as the source of love is God, the reality of love is action. As I demonstrate love, God makes himself more and more real in my own life.

III. Love Is Costly

Love is not cheap. God's love came at the expense of a cross—and we must also expect to pay a price if we are to show authentic love. There is risk—of vulnerability, of misunderstanding, of rejection. We must take a chance in order to love others. Some will reject it, others will misuse it, but there will be those who respond to it, and who experience Christ's presence in our love. Psychiatrist Karl Menninger said, "Love cures. It cures those who give it and it cures those who receive it."

The life of love is not an easy or a common one, but it is the road that leads to Christ, and to the abundance of fellowship with him. *(Michael Duduit)*

OUR LEADING AND LOVING LORD

JOHN 10:11-18

The good news of Christianity is God's unconditional love for us in Jesus. Regardless of who, what, where, or when, God loves us. He loves us no more and no less than he loves anybody else. He lived,

149

died, rose, and reigns in Jesus for us no more and no less than he lived, died, rose, and reigns for anybody else. His love is inclusive. Or as he said, "God so loved *the world.*"

Even people who are not yet in relationship with God through faith in Jesus are *wanted* by him. Jesus said, "I have other sheep that do not belong to this fold. *I must bring them also,* and they will listen to my voice. So there will be one flock, one shepherd" (v. 16). Our Lord does not want anyone left out of the wholeness, happiness, joy, and eternal security of life in the kingdom.

That's why he is the *Good Shepherd.* He leads and loves people into confident living and eternal life.

I. The Good Shepherd Leads

Shepherds don't follow sheep. That's especially true with our Lord. He knows who he is (sovereign God), who we are (people in need of his salvation), and what we need to be and do (exemplified in Jesus and explained in the Bible). *He is Lord!* We are his people. *He is the Good Shepherd!* We follow where he leads. He knows what we need and leads the way (John 10:14).

It's like the old song, "Trust and obey, for there's no other way to be happy in Jesus, but to trust and obey." He leads. We follow.

Shepherd is a metaphor for *king.* Jesus is the Shepherd-King. Describing the decision to become a disciple, Peter wrote, "You have returned to the Shepherd and Overseer of your souls" (1 Pet. 2:25 NIV).

Practically, it means our Lord doesn't solicit suggestions on how to run the kingdom. He doesn't ask if we'd like to feed the hungry, house the homeless, clothe the naked, visit the sick, and all of the rest (Matt. 25). He directs us into the social responsibilities of the gospel. He *leads* as Lord.

II. The Good Shepherd Loves

He is the *Good* Shepherd. Unlike a hired hand, who is paid to do a job, our Lord willingly, sacrificially, and selflessly *wants* to help (John 10:11-13). Jesus freely chooses to care (John 10:11, 14-18).

John Calvin wrote, "Christ declares that He is the Good Shepherd, who keeps His Church safe and sound, first, by Himself, and next, by His agents" (*John,* 1553).

He leads because he *loves,* and those who know him follow him. (*Robert R. Kopp*)

APRIL 27, 1997

≈

Fifth Sunday of Easter

Worship Theme: Love is the motivating factor for the Christian life.

Readings: Acts 8:26-40; 1 John 4:7-21; John 15:1-8

Call to Worship (Psalm 22:25-31):

Leader: From you comes my praise in the great congregation;

People: my vows I will pay before those who fear him.

Leader: The poor shall eat and be satisfied; those who seek him shall praise the LORD.

People: May your hearts live forever!

Leader: All the ends of the earth shall remember and turn to the LORD;

People: and all the families of the nations shall worship before him.

Leader: For dominion belongs to the LORD, and he rules over the nations.

People: To him, indeed, shall all who sleep in the earth bow down;

Leader: before him shall bow all who go down to the dust, and I shall live for him.

People: Posterity will serve him; future generations will be told about the LORD.

Leader: and proclaim his deliverance to a people yet unborn,

***All:* saying that he has done it.**

151

Pastoral Prayer:

Almighty God, whose love is beyond understanding, whose mercy is beyond comprehension—we lift up our hearts to you in prayer. Though we were captives of our sinful and rebellious ways, your love has released us. You have freed us to experience divine love in our own lives. Your atoning love has freed us from the penalty of sin, which was rightfully ours to pay. How can we express our thanksgiving, except to praise your name and to allow your love to be seen in us. Grant to us a determined faith and a fervent love, that we might be reflections of your divine grace. Hear our prayer, O Lord, as we offer our petitions in the name of the One who is love, even Jesus Christ our Lord. Amen.

SERMON BRIEFS

BECOMING ONE

ACTS 8:26-40

The story of Philip and the Ethiopian is full of surprises. We are dazzled by the speed and action of the account. The story functions mainly as a reminder that in God's new community—the church—old boundaries are not only smudged, they are being erased. The Ethiopian's conversion is one in a series of three conversions (the Ethiopian, Saul, and Cornelius), which redefine for Jewish-Christians the dimensions of the people of God.

All people have a built-in sense that observes life and makes judgments about life from each person's unique perspective. Quoting Thoreau, Eugene Peterson affirms this in his book *Working the Angles*: "I should not talk so much about myself if there is anybody else whom I knew as well. Unfortunately, I am confined to this theme by the narrowness of my experience." People can only assume truth from their angle of vision. Acts, however, changes all of that. God's gracious perceptions of persons make them fit and, therefore, God's realm keeps expanding.

One of many surprises in this story is that anyone would be traveling in the middle of the day in the Near Eastern heat. A friend who lived in Iraq said that often the daily temperature reached 135 degrees F. Thus, the question of why one would travel in the heat would naturally arise. We might also ask *how* Philip was transported to and from the Ethiopian, but the text is interested mainly in telling us something else. The text wants us to see God's grace in action.

This new community of the Spirit, seen in its ideal vestment at Pentecost in Acts 2, opens up the community of faith to even those who live at its very edges. Ethiopians in biblical times were generally thought of as persons of color, as well as foreigners who lived beyond the reaches of the African desert. Therefore, Ethiopians were viewed as marginal in a negative sense, but also in a positive sense as persons who engendered curiosity. They were often held in esteem and amazement. Since the Ethiopian was a minister for Queen Candace, we can only assume he was a person of high status. Whether he was a Jew or Gentile is still open for debate.

God, of course, created all people and created them to be in fellowship with one another. Sometimes, though, humans put limits on who is welcome and who is not in particular communities. As pastor in my first church, I was curious why the members seemed to be so open and warm toward me. I was young, inexperienced, single, a recent progressive seminary graduate, just returned from Africa and, on top of all that, I was from California. These, after all, were not particularly stellar pastoral credentials to bring to a small United Methodist church in rural central Texas! But the people seemed to respond to my ministry, making me all the more curious.

One morning before Sunday school I cornered two of my older members in the kitchen and asked them: "Why did you accept me so completely, since I am about as different from anyone here as we could imagine?" They merely replied, as if waiting months for the question, "You are one of us, now!"

When the church welcomes all persons as those for whom Christ has died, then we will be near the kingdom of God. *(David N. Mosser)*

LOVE AT THE CENTER

1 JOHN 4:7-21

The Roman army had subdued his kingdom, and now the king of Armenia stood before the conquering general. The king fell to his knees and pled with the Roman general: "Do whatever you wish with

me, but I beg you to spare the lives of my family." The general spared
the life of the king and his family.

Later, the king asked his wife what had been her impression of
the Roman conqueror, but she responded, "I never saw him."

"How could you have failed to see him?" asked the king. "He was
only a few feet away. What were you looking at?"

With tears welling up in her eyes, the queen replied, "I saw only
you, the one who was willing to die that I might live."

Each of us who has given his or her life to Christ can put ourselves
in the story, for we know what it is to have someone love us enough
to die for us. Such remarkable love is at the very center of the
character of God, and thus it is at the center of our walk with Christ.

I. God Demonstrates His Love to Us

God has shown his love to us through Jesus Christ (v. 9). Through
his death on the cross, Christ paid the price for our sin at the cost of
his own blood. God so loved us that he "sent his Son to be the atoning
sacrifice for our sins" (v. 10). Never has there been a more awesome
display of love than on Good Friday, when Jesus took our sin upon
himself and carried them to a cross. And never has there been a more
awesome display of the power of love than on Easter morning, when
Christ emerged victorious from the tomb.

God has also shown his love to us through the indwelling Holy
Spirit (v. 13). We have ongoing evidence of God's love in our lives,
through the presence of the Holy Spirit. Just as a wedding ring on
the finger is a constant reminder of the love of a husband or wife, so
the continuing presence of God's Spirit within us is a reminder of
God's love for each one of us.

II. Our Response to God's Love Is to Love One Another

The implication of God's amazing love is clear: "since God loved
us so much, we also ought to love one another" (v. 11). If we have
experienced God's atoning love through Christ, and if we continue
to experience God's love through the indwelling presence of the
Spirit, then we are compelled to become instruments of God's love
to others. Just as metal conducts electricity, we are to be "conduc-
tors" of divine love—allowing it to pass through us and touch a lost
and hurting world.

If God's love has really come to dwell in us, it makes a transforming difference. It is impossible to be a repository of divine love and, at the same time, be motivated by hatred for others. Love and hatred are like oil and water—they do not mix. If God's love is present, there is no room for hatred or bitterness.

Have you experienced God's love in your own life? As you yield your life to Christ's saving presence, you will come to understand authentic love as you have never known it before. Let love transform you! (*Michael Duduit*)

FORMULA FOR THE GOOD LIFE

JOHN 15:1-8

Every day is the first day of the rest of your life. What are you going to do with it? What are you doing today for tomorrow? What are you going to do today that will make you happy for the rest of your life?

The formula for the good life is incredibly simple: *Holiness = Happiness.*

Jesus explained, "Remain in me, and I will remain in you . . . I am the vine; you are the branches. If a man remains in me and I in him, he will bear much fruit; apart from me you can do nothing" (vv. 4-5 NIV).

The degree of happiness in a person's life is directly related to the degree of holiness in a person's life. As branches, our life and energy are linked to our connection to the vine, or God.

A man with a debilitating alcohol problem went to his doctor for help. The doctor said, "Now sit down and let me show you something." The doctor proceeded to fill one glass with whiskey and another glass with water. He put a worm into each glass. The worm in the whiskey quickly keeled over, while the worm in the water seemed to be getting along quite well. The doctor asked his struggling patient, "What does that tell you?" "Well," the man said, "I guess it means I won't get worms if I drink whiskey."

Some folks just don't get it. Some folks just don't get Jesus. They don't see the obvious. They don't see Jesus as the answer to all of their questions. They don't see Jesus as the way to the good life. Some folks, as Jesus said, just don't have eyes that see or ears that hear (Mark 8:18).

We can't do too much about the spiritually deaf and blind. They require God's intervention. But as the parable of the sower reminds us (Matt. 13:1-23), we still have the privilege and responsibility to work with our Lord for the salvation of the world. We can point people to Jesus as Lord and Savior. We can proclaim Jesus as the way to the good life.

Let me be direct. I have never met a person who has invited Jesus into her or his life and nurtures that relationship through the spiritual disciplines who isn't happy, whole, joyful, and secure.

Let me be even more direct. If a person isn't happy, whole, joyful, and secure, that person isn't close to Jesus (vv. 5, 7-8). If a person is holy, that person is happy. If a person isn't happy, that person isn't holy.

Today is the first day of the rest of your life. If you want to be happy, get closer to Jesus! If you want to be happier, get holier! (*Robert R. Kopp*)

MAY

੨ৡ

Mending the Net, Sharpening the Hoe

Symbol: Dove

The symbol of the dove is used both as messenger (Gen. 8:8-12) and Holy Spirit (John 1:32).

Texts:

"Then he sent out a dove to see if the water had receded from the surface of the ground. But the dove could find no place to set its feet because there was water over all the surface of the earth; so it returned to Noah in the ark. He reached out his hand and took the dove and brought it back to himself in the ark. He waited seven more days and again sent out the dove from the ark. When the dove returned to him in the evening, there in its beak was a freshly plucked olive leaf! Then Noah knew that the water had receded from the earth. He waited seven more days and sent the dove out again, but this time it did not return to him" (Gen. 8:8-12 NIV).

"Then John gave this testimony: 'I saw the Spirit come down from heaven as a dove and remain on him' " (John 1:32 NIV).

Invocation:

"Almighty God, you have called the church into being and have gathered us into one family. By the power of your Holy Spirit help us to live in unity and peace with all of your children. May our actions this day be fruit of our faith in your Kingdom. In the name of Christ. Amen." (Reuben P. Job and Norman Shawchuck, *A Guide to Prayer*)

Scripture Focus:
- Ephesians 4:1-6
- Genesis 8:8-12
- John 1:32
- Matthew 3:16-17
- Psalm 139:9-10
- Romans 8

157

Prayer Focus:
- Think of the baptism of Jesus.
- Visualize the dove coming upon him.
- Hear the blessing of God bestowed upon him.
- See the dove descending upon your congregation.
- See individuals who need to be blessed as the congregation meets. Call them by name.
- Recall projects that need to be energized.
- See the heavenly dove upon those projects.

Prayer:

O heavenly Father, may your Spirit be upon our people. May we realize that your Holy Spirit is the earthly presence of the glorified Lord. May Christ become Lord of his church by your Spirit, and of individuals, as well as the community. May the power of thy Spirit be more than the power of ecstasy and miracles. Let your Spirit truly produce a new creation. May your people, to whom I am a shepherd, truly walk and live by the Spirit. Amen. *(Bill Self)*

heart as personal Lord and Savior, it's the most essential ingredient of being a Christian. That's why it's the greatest sign of salvation.

It has been said, "You can be right about every area of theology and polity but wrong about Jesus and you're dead wrong and can lose your soul. You can be wrong about every area of theology and polity but right about Jesus and you will be saved." Being right about Jesus is proved by our love. As the song goes: "They'll know we are Christians by our love." *(Robert R. Kopp)*

MAY 11, 1997

੩**

Ascension Sunday

Worship Theme: We live in the light of Christ's ultimate victory.

Readings: Acts 1:1-11; Ephesians 1:15-23; Luke 24:44-53

Call to Worship (Psalm 47):

Leader: Clap your hands, all you peoples;

People: shout to God with loud songs of joy.

Leader: For the LORD, the Most High, is awesome,

People: a great king over all the earth.

Leader: He subdued peoples under us, and nations under our feet.

People: He chose our heritage for us, the pride of Jacob whom he loves.

Leader: God has gone up with a shout,

People: the LORD with the sound of a trumpet.

Leader: Sing praises to God, sing praises;

People: sing praises to our King, sing praises.

Leader: For God is the king of all the earth;

People: sing praises with a psalm.

Leader: God is king over the nations;

People: God sits on his holy throne.

Leader: The princes of the peoples gather as the people of the God of Abraham.

All: **For the shields of the earth belong to God; he is highly exalted.**

Pastoral Prayer:

Mighty and everlasting God, who has raised up our Lord Jesus Christ from the grave and who has set him at your right hand, we praise you for the victory that you have made available to us through Christ. We are grateful for the promise that just as Christ conquered sin and death and is even now in your divine presence, so you have enabled us to share in his resurrection, and one day we will be able to gather around the throne and sing your praises. Grant us boldness, O Lord, to share that good news with a lost world—help us to be ambassadors of your grace, proclaimers of your glory. Our eternal God, as Christ revealed your love in his own earthly life, so let us be reflections of your love in all that we do, that we might truly be more like the One in whose name we pray. Amen.

SERMON BRIEFS

TAKING CARE OF LAST MINUTE MATTERS

ACTS 1:1-11

Whenever we plan a trip, we have to take care of a lot of details. Plans have to be made for someone to take care of the pets, flowers, mail, and other matters. Hours before leaving on the trip, last minute details have to be done.

Jesus had been on earth thirty-three years. He had completed his earthly ministry with his death and resurrection. For forty days he felt he needed to take care of last minute details. We need to know some of what Jesus said and did in the days prior to his ascension.

I. Christ Assures the Reality of His Resurrection (vv. 1-3)

Jesus took time during the forty days prior to his ascension to prove to his disciples the reality of his resurrection. They had seen him die, and they needed to know that he was alive.

Modern disciples need to hear Christ's assurance about his resurrection. They would know that Jesus has the power over life and death. And, they would know that Christ is present with them today.

II. Christ Teaches About the Priority of His Kingdom (vv. 6-7)

Jesus taught constantly about the meaning of his kingdom. The disciples continued to misunderstand. Jesus wanted his followers to know that the kingdom meant a spiritual rule.

Christians need to keep kingdom priorities constantly before them. What are these priorities? Win the lost, edify the saved, gather in worship, minister to human needs, and live like kingdom people are the priorities of the kingdom.

III. Christ Predicts the Power of God in Individual Lives (vv. 4-5, 8)

As soon as Jesus ascended, his ministry would be given to his disciples. Whatever Jesus had done, they would do; Jesus promised his followers that they would not do his ministry in human strength. They would receive the power of the Holy Spirit.

We are called to serve God, and we have the power. We are called to holy living, and we have the power.

IV. Christ Attests to His Completed Ministry (v. 9)

Jesus would have never left earth if his mission had not been completed. The fact that he ascended back to the Father testified that everything necessary for the human race's reconciliation was completed.

Believers do not have to work to complete their salvation. They yield to Christ's completed and continuing work.

V. Christ Promises His Future Return (vv. 10-11)

Soon after Jesus ascended, some messengers came to some watching, stunned, lonely disciples. They told them that Jesus would come again. Who told the messengers? Jesus, of course. He promises his future return.

Christians live in hope for the Lord's return. No promise of Christ has ever been futile. This promise is not futile. It is certain he will come again.

Jesus' thirty-three years on earth were crucial. His three-year public ministry needs pondering. Also, don't forget to study his last-minute instruction before and after his ascension. *(Harold T. Bryson)*

LIVING BETWEEN D DAY AND V DAY

EPHESIANS 1:15-23

The Second World War gave to everyone who went through that era some indelible images. One of those was a word picture that has become a model of the Christian life. It is the distinction in the European conflict between D Day and V Day. When the Allies landed on the beaches of Normandy on D Day the war was not over but its outcome had been basically determined. The ultimate victory and the conclusion of the war in Europe was on the horizon. V Day would soon come.

As one thinks of the coming of Jesus in the flesh (incarnation) and his return in victory (parousia), a similar pattern can be visualized. When we as Christians celebrate Ascension Sunday, we stand between two important events and can look both backward and forward.

On the one hand, we are reminded that the Lord Jesus came to earth and, on the cross, won the "decisive" battle for our salvation. On the other hand, we know that our struggle against sin and evil is not yet complete. The ultimate victory celebration awaits our joining the Lord in his glorious victory procession at the end of time. The text from Ephesians under consideration here reminds us that while we live in this world between D Day and V Day, we can join with the apostle in his great prayer and sense our calling to live with both genuine understanding and vivid expectation.

I. We Live with Understanding

Because the world is not an ideal place, it takes a life of faith and commitment to succeed as a Christian. In this text the apostle clearly recognized the commitment of the early Asian believers (v. 15). But he prayed that in addition to their faith, the God who displayed his power in the resurrection and ascension of the Lord Jesus Christ would give these Christians a divinely inspired (spiritual) sense of wisdom and of a God-manifested (revelation) knowledge as they lived in the world for Christ (v. 17). A knowledge of who Christ is and what he has done for us is absolutely essential for living the Christian life.

II. We Live with Hope

Beyond such understanding, however, the Christian also needs to live with a sense of destiny! The world is not just an endless cycle of ages as the Greeks thought. For those who know Christ there is both purpose and expectation in the world. Faithful believers (saints) can glimpse with expectant eyes the future hope in their Christian calling. Moreover, they can gain a vision of the wonderful inheritance that will be theirs in Christ (v. 18).

Yet even now they can experience a foretaste of the power of God in their lives—that same power that was evident in the resurrection and ascension of Christ (vv. 19-21). The supreme God has made Christ the Lord of the church so that the Body of Christ (the church) might experience the powerful presence (fullness) of God in their midst.

What Christian therefore, can not fail to sing, "To God be the glory, great things he has done!" *(Gerald L. Borchert)*

LISTENING WITH AN OPEN MIND

LUKE 24:44-53

An open mind can be like a garbage can with the lid off—anything in the world may be tossed in! The Scriptures are replete with numerous warnings and admonitions regarding the mind. We are encouraged to "gird up the loins" to avoid "vain philosophy" and to be "continually transformed by the renewing of" our minds. Yet when it comes to appropriation of biblical truth, we must have an *open mind.*

I. It Is Not Enough to Simply Hear the Word of God

Paul reminds us that "faith comes by hearing, and hearing by the word of God" (Rom. 10:17 NKJV). But not everyone who hears the sound of a gospel word listens to the voice of the Spirit. In many ways our culture has become gospel-hardened. We have been inoculated with a sufficient dose of the good news to make us immune to authentic Christianity. John 3:16 printed on end-zone placards and bumper stickers is the modern equivalent of carelessly casting away the pearl of gospel truth.

II. The Resurrection Was Not Enough to Open the Disciples' Minds

The disciples had been with Jesus from the beginning of his public ministry. They had witnessed the many miracles. Now the resurrected Lord had appeared to them, but that alone could not generate faith. We cannot be argued into faith. We cannot be cajoled into listening to the Spirit.

III. Only the Lord Can Enable Us to Listen with an Open Mind

Luke tells us that the resurrected Lord opened the minds of the disciples as he reminded them of the Hebrew Scriptures that testified about him. How did he do this? We want a method, an approach, a program, or a formula to follow. We are not told. Surely the disciples had heard Jesus expound the Hebrew Scriptures before.

Perhaps the difference was in themselves—for once, they appear ready to listen. What Jesus shared with them was not new; they had heard about the Messiah before. It is in the mystery of their encounter with the risen Christ that their minds were opened.

IV. We Have Been Entrusted with a Treasure to Be Both Lived and Shared

Søren Kierkegaard reminds us that a "witness for the truth" is one who is willing to be a martyr for Christ. It is not a title to be claimed glibly. There is more to being a witness than simply mouthing truths. Jesus did not rewind a mental tape player with a canned sales pitch every time he encountered someone seeking the kingdom. He

171

modeled and shared a witness to truth that was personal and appropriate for a variety of situations. No two people are treated in exactly the same way. We must incarnate the truth and share an appropriate word of witness as we are empowered by the Spirit.

Barclay says that this passage stresses the reality of the Resurrection, the urgency of the task, and the secret to their power. Indeed, it does this and more. An open mind to the truth of the gospel is a gift that comes only through an encounter with the risen Christ. *(L. Joseph Rosas)*

MAY 18, 1997

❧

Pentecost

Worship Theme: The Holy Spirit brings power to the life of the church and the believer.

Readings: Ezekiel 37:1-14; Acts 2:1-38; John 15:26-27; 16:4*b*-15

Call to Worship (Psalm 104:31-34, 35*b*):

Leader: May the glory of the LORD endure forever;

People: **may the LORD rejoice in his works—**

Leader: who looks on the earth and it trembles,

People: **who touches the mountains and they smoke.**

Leader: I will sing to the LORD as long as I live;

People: **I will sing praise to my God while I have being.**

Leader: May my meditation be pleasing to him, for I rejoice in the LORD.

All: **Bless the LORD, O my soul. Praise the LORD!**

Pastoral Prayer:

O God of wind and fire, who has given your Holy Spirit to indwell the lives of men and women of faith, as that band of believers gathered in an upper room that first day of Pentecost to await your presence, so we gather in hope and anticipation to seek your face. Even as your Spirit was poured out upon that company of disciples, so we pray that your Spirit might be poured out upon us. Let your Spirit sweep through our midst, lifting us above the mundane and familiar, and carry us into bold and adventurous realms of faith. Anoint us with your power, that we might go forth possessed of a new purpose and perspective, and that we might be transformed into mighty witnesses to your love and majesty. Let the spirit of Christ,

173

who gave himself for us, empower us to give ourselves for others, even as we pray in his blessed name. Amen.

SERMON BRIEFS

WHAT MAKES THE DIFFERENCE?

EZEKIEL 37:1-14

When we eat a meal, the ingredients make all the difference in taste and enjoyment. A tossed salad needs a dressing. Some people think certain foods need to be flavored with ketchup. Cooks sometimes omit an ingredient from a recipe, and tasters notice the difference.

God spoke to Ezekiel when he and the Israelites were in bondage in Babylon. God wanted to teach Ezekiel what made the difference with God's people. It was not a place. It was not a government. It was God.

God used a valley full of bones for Ezekiel's lesson. God told Ezekiel to speak to the bones, and he did. They began to organize into human skeletons and to take on muscles and skin. They had form but no life. Only when God breathed life into the bodies was there vitality. God makes all the difference in the life of a nation and the life of a person.

I. Observe a Pathetic Situation (vv. 1-2)

God took Ezekiel on a journey to see a large valley of dry bones. Probably a big battle had taken place in the valley with numerous deaths. Casualties had not been buried. The bodies had decayed, and nothing was left but the bones. Ezekiel saw a pathetic sight.

God wanted Ezekiel to see another sight. He wanted Ezekiel to see the pathetic condition of Israel. They had rebelled against God, and they were reaping the consequences in Babylonian bondage.

Any person outside of Christ is in a pathetic situation. Paul says such persons are "dead through the trespasses and sins" (Eph. 2:1).

II. Ponder a Wonderful Possibility (vv. 3-8a)

God asked Ezekiel an intriguing question: "Son of man, can these bones live?" Ezekiel was stunned by the question. He did not know if or how the bones could live. So he answered, "O LORD God, thou knowest." God told Ezekiel to prophesy unto the bones, and God would cause them to live.

God wanted Ezekiel to know about the possibility of Israel's restoration. They could return to their land and would become a "light to the nations" again.

No situation is too hard for God. He can take lives ruined by sin and make them beautiful. The possibility for restoration awaits every person who desires God.

III. Notice the Absolute Necessity (vv. 8b-14)

Ezekiel saw the bones organize into skeletons. He saw these skeletons take on muscles and skin; "but there was no breath in them." God's breath is an absolute necessity.

Israel would not restore herself. Human wisdom and strength availed nothing. Only God creates vitality in a person's life. No one can come to life outside the breath of God. He makes all the difference.

God wants to indwell each person with his Holy Spirit. Allowing him to come into life creates changes and gives life. *(Harold T. Bryson)*

PENTECOST AND THE REVERSAL OF BABEL

ACTS 2:1-38

The story of Babel (Gen. 11:1-9) is a clear portrayal of the divisiveness and confusion that reign in a world that seeks to exalt itself and discredit God. The day of Pentecost marked that moment in Christian history when the reversal of Babel began. In Acts, Luke says that the believers were all gathered together when the unexpected happened (2:1).

I. Experiencing the Unexpected

Luke's Gospel closes with the disciples waiting for power and direction (Luke 24:49). What came in Acts 2 surprised everyone (v. 12). The phenomena that occurred in this event were stranger than fiction. A sound like a violent "wind" *(pnoe)* introduced the presence of "Spirit" *(pneuma)*. Tongues of fire on people (v. 3) became tongues of understanding that, for a time, completely banished the language barriers of the Hellenistic world (vv. 4-11).

Rational attempts at explaining these phenomena that took place at Pentecost by calling the disciples drunkards just would not work (v. 13). Pentecost was not some mere repeatable, human-induced experience or event. It was a special act of God that marked the start of breaking down barriers—a theme that drives the book of Acts.

From the very beginning of the book, therefore, the message is consistent: nothing can limit or restrict the scope of the gospel (Acts 28:31), not even the old Babel language barriers! The Holy Spirit can and will break open chains and prisons and barriers. The power of the Resurrection had come to the church through the Holy Spirit, and God was announcing in this special event that the confusion of Babel could be brought to an end through people who wait upon the Lord and receive, or are "filled with," the Spirit.

II. Proclaiming the Unexpected

The task of God's people was and now is to proclaim the meaning and significance of the way in which God acts in the world. The sermon of Peter (vv. 14-36) is a marvelous contextualized message in three parts, introduced by three vocative uses of *andres* (men), which address Peter's listeners at verses 14, 22, and 29. As such, the sermon provides a model of three aspects of the Christian proclamation.

The message begins where the people are and with what they have experienced. Then it reminds them that the event they have witnessed is fully in keeping with God's intention in the Old Testament that his "sons and daughters" would someday experience the power of the Spirit (v. 17; cf. Joel 2:28). The second part of the sermon reminds us that the experience of the Spirit is directly linked to the ministry of Jesus and that his death and resurrection was part of God's great plan for saving the world (v. 23).

The final part of the sermon points to the resurrection of Jesus as the foundation of the Christian witness (v. 32) and the basis for proclaiming him as Lord and Christ to the world. The only adequate response to such a message is self-examination and repentance (vv. 37-38). (*Gerald L. Borchert*)

THE PROMISE OF THE COUNSELOR

JOHN 15:26-27; 16:4*b*-15

Many Christians are afraid of the Holy Spirit. The "Ghost" of the KJV sounds like a spook. The excesses of some have caused many of us to focus more on what we don't believe about the Spirit than what we do believe. Pentecost reminds us that the reality of the Spirit's coming is the birthday of the church.

The Old Testament said little about the Spirit in personal terms. The breath of God at the dawn of creation, the Spirit of God, is an occasional empowerment in the lives of selected heroes and heroines of Israel. Jesus' words were "new" teaching in that they spoke of a whole new relationship with the Counselor—his word for the Holy Spirit. The Counselor who had been with them would be in them. There are basic truths about the Holy Spirit contained in these verses from Jesus' last words to his disciples before his departure via the cross.

I. The Holy Spirit Is "Counselor" (15:25)

He is not to be feared. He is sent by Jesus and comes from God. He "goes along beside" the believer. We should joyously embrace the Spirit's ministry in our lives. Paul refers to the Spirit as the "earnest" of our salvation. He is God's down payment and promise that he who has begun this good work in you will perform it.

II. The Holy Spirit's Ministry Is to Testify About Jesus (15:26)

The Spirit does not draw attention to himself. The gifts of the Spirit or other manifestations are intended to focus our attention on Christ. Any focus on the Holy Spirit that says more about the third member of the Godhead than about Jesus has missed the point of the Spirit's ministry. Likewise, we are genuinely spiritual not when we draw attention to ourselves, but as our lives point others to Christ.

III. The Holy Spirit Will Convict the World of Sin, Righteousness, and Judgment (16:8)

We have the obligation to preach and testify about that which we have seen and heard. But we cannot argue anyone into faith. In reality, the Holy Spirit of God must draw men and women to Christ. He is the one who lifts up Christ—the objective standard of God's righteousness that reveals human sin and portends of divine judgment. We don't find Christ. Rather, as Saint Thomas observed, Christ is like the hound of heaven who finds us.

IV. The Holy Spirit Guides Us into All Truth (16:13)

The focus here is on spiritual truth. Yet as Arthur Holmes's philosophy title suggests, "all truth is God's truth." The Holy Spirit is God's mediated presence in the world. He communicates the mind of God to the believer. The test for all spiritual truth claims is: "Does this glorify Jesus Christ?"

V. The Holy Spirit Makes the Resources of God Available to the Believer (16:15)

In the New Testament we are urged to "walk in," "be filled with," and "live by" the Spirit. Stuart Briscoe has said: "All that Christ is, He is in us and all that He is in us He wants to be through us. The invitation of the New Testament is simply, 'Let Him.'"

We have an unlimited resource in the power of God available to us through the ministry of the Holy Spirit. (*L. Joseph Rosas*)

MAY 25, 1997

৶

Trinity Sunday

Worship Theme: God has revealed himself to us in three persons: Father, Son, and Holy Spirit.

Readings: Isaiah 6:1-8; Romans 8:12-17; John 3:1-17

Call to Worship (Psalm 29:1-4, 10-11):

Leader: Ascribe to the LORD, O heavenly beings, ascribe to the LORD glory and strength.

People: **Ascribe to the LORD the glory of his name; worship the LORD in holy splendor.**

Leader: The voice of the LORD is over the waters;

People: **the God of glory thunders, the LORD, over mighty waters.**

Leader: The voice of the LORD is powerful;

People: **the voice of the LORD is full of majesty.**

Leader: The LORD sits enthroned over the flood;

People: **the LORD sits enthroned as king forever.**

Leader: May the LORD give strength to his people!

All: **May the LORD bless his people with peace!**

Pastoral Prayer:

Almighty and eternal God—creator, redeemer, and sustainer. We sing praise to you, our Lord and our God, for you have revealed yourself to us as one in three. We worship you as Father, who fashioned us from the dust and whose love is from everlasting to everlasting. We worship you as Son, our Lord Jesus Christ, who became one with us that we might be restored to fellowship with

179

God, and who gave his life for us that we might live for you. We worship you as Spirit, who convicts us of sin, who draws us to Christ, who dwells within us to strengthen and direct us in your will. We give thanks unto you and bless you, unto whom be glory and praise forever and forever. Amen.

SERMON BRIEFS

GUESS WHAT HAPPENED IN WORSHIP

ISAIAH 6:1-8

If someone commissioned me to write a book entitled *Interesting Things That Happened in Worship,* I would have abundant material. It might have to be multivolumes. Some of the volumes would be *Tragedies, Funny Experiences,* and *Strange Occurrences.*

Isaiah wrote in his prophecy what happened when he went to worship at the temple. He had a significant encounter with God. What happened to Isaiah needs to happen to us every time we come to worship.

I. We Need a Profound Awareness of God (vv. 1-4)

The most significant occurrence in worship happens when we focus our attention on God. The first thing that happened to Isaiah was he saw the Lord.

Isaiah's awareness of God produced some great assurances. He was assured of the sovereignty of God. Uzziah, the king, had died, but God is and will forever be on God's throne. Isaiah became overwhelmed with the majesty of God. Mysterious descriptions came to Isaiah in verse 2. The prophet acknowledged the holiness of God.

Genuine worship starts with God. Worshipers become aware of his presence, and as they become aware of his presence they know his traits.

II. We Need a Realistic Consciousness of Ourselves (v. 5)

As soon as Isaiah became aware of the holy God, he began to get a realistic view of himself. For creatures to be in the presence of the Creator makes creatures aware of their sins.

Isaiah had a realistic consciousness of his personal sinfulness: "Woe is me!" He elaborates on his condition with two expressions: "lost" and "unclean lips." He acknowledged that his heart condition and verbal expression did not measure up to God's expectations.

Isaiah also had a universal consciousness of sin. The sin problem prevailed in everyone else: "I live among a people of unclean lips" (v. 5b).

A realistic consciousness of ourselves always comes when we come into the presence of the King, the Lord of hosts. God does not just want us to face our sins. He wants to do something about them.

III. We Need a Generous Bestowal of Forgiveness (vv. 6-7)

As soon as Isaiah became painfully aware of his sin, God began the bestowal of forgiveness. God wants to take care of the sin problem in human lives.

Isaiah described it with two words: iniquity and sin. The world *iniquity* means "to twist." The word *sin* means to fall short of God's intention.

Isaiah experienced the remedy with God taking away his iniquity and purging his sin. God gave a complete pardon. We need God's gracious bestowal of forgiveness.

IV. We Need a Willing Spirit to Serve God (v. 8)

Isaiah did not just have an encounter with God in the temple. His experience with God led to service in the world. All kinds of needs existed in Judah. People needed the Lord. God's greatest desire is to help people with these needs.

To meet human needs, God uses human instruments. "Whom shall I send, and who will go for us?" (v. 8b). God searched for volunteers. Then Isaiah responded: "Here am I; send me!" (v. 8c). Isaiah's worship led to service for God.

The reason churches advertise "Worship with us" is because they know profitable experiences can happen in worship. When you miss worship, you never know what kind of remarkable encounter with God you may be missing! *(Harold T. Bryson)*

LIVING FEARLESSLY WITH GOD

ROMANS 8:12-17

For many people, the Trinity is a concept that does not compute. The main reason is that people often try to make three equal one. Theological battles have been vigorously fought over this idea, and Christians have declared each other heretics over their formulations of the Triune God. Rather than trying to pour the ocean of God's truth on this matter into the teacup formulations of our minds, it is far better to take a lesson from Paul and discover the power for living that is resident in the experiencing of God in three personages.

Today's focal text from Romans makes no attempt at constructing a mathematical equation. It merely sets out for us how the caring God can touch our lives in three different ways. Moreover, as in other passages of the New Testament (cf. 1 Pet. 1:2 and Rev. 1:4-5), Paul is not bound to confine himself to the later creedal order of Father, Son, and Holy Spirit. Theological formulations can often be very proper, but leave one with the feeling of being dry and dead. In contrast, Paul's words ring with vitality and power. His God is not dead! His message about living with God is dynamic.

I. Living with the Spirit

Having detailed in the previous passages of Romans the radical differences between a life that is oriented to the created world (flesh) and one that is oriented to the Creator (Spirit), Paul challenges his readers to abandon any commitments that make the world (flesh) and its desires the goal of life. Such commitments can only lead to death (v. 13), because the pattern of world orientation is insecurity and fear (v. 15).

Those who are committed to God are entirely different because they are obedient to (led by) and have a deep sense of companionship through the Spirit. Insecurity is therefore banished in their sense of relationship (sonship and daughterhood) to God (vv. 14-16).

II. Relating to the Father

Paul and the New Testament writers are theocentric. The one God is the center of their theologies. For Jews like Paul who had even ceased to use the name of God (YHWH) because of fear of taking that name in vain, the designation of God as "Father" was revolutionary. Certainly Jesus had called God "Father," but as a result he was labeled a blasphemer.

Even more significant was the fact that Jesus taught his disciples to call God "Father" (cf. Matt. 6:9). So important was this idea to Paul that he used not only the Greek word for Father but also included the Semitic word *Abba* (v. 15; cf. Gal. 4:5), which probably goes back to Jesus himself. Praying to God as "Father," therefore, probably encapsulated for Paul his dearest relationship. God cares for us and allows us to pray to him in the intimacy of a child-to-parent relationship.

III. Following the Model of Jesus

When Jesus called his disciples, he summoned them to "follow" him. The pattern of copying Jesus' model is well established in the New Testament (cf. Phil. 2:1-11). But what is sometimes difficult to accept is that the model of Jesus is one of self-giving and suffering.

Paul understood the cost of discipleship, and he wanted all Christians to realize that following the Master would likely be painful (v. 17; cf. 1 Pet. 2:21). Yet the hope of glory makes fearless living in the midst of pain possible because our future is in the hands of the living God (Rom. 8:18; cf. 1 Pet. 1:6-9). *(Gerald L. Borchert)*

BORN AGAIN!

JOHN 3:1-17

What image comes to mind when you hear the words "born again"? The 1976 election of a "born again" Southern Baptist, Jimmy Carter, introduced the national media to the term. Perhaps you think of an Elmer Gantry-type preacher thundering hellfire and damnation. Maybe you see a man with a sign reading, "Ye must be born again." Although Jesus only used the term once, it is frequently a caricature of authentic evangelical Christian faith. And that's a pity—the truth is much too important to be lost.

I. Religion Is Not Enough

Søren Kierkegaard asked rhetorically, "How does one become a Christian in Christendom?" In other words, what distinguishes authentic Christian faith from the watered-down cultural Christianity of organized religion. How do you preach to the baptized?

Nicodemus was a wealthy Jewish leader of the Pharisee sect. He was sworn to observe the law of God. Intrigued by Jesus, he came by night—perhaps to avoid public exposure, perhaps because of the urgency of his quest. But Jesus would have nothing to do with the niceties of theological dialogue. He confronts Nicodemus with the challenge, "only those born from above can enter the kingdom of God."

II. The New Birth Is a Mystery

Commentators spend a great deal of time and exegetical energy on what it means to be born of "water and spirit." Certainly physical birth precedes spiritual birth. Water baptism is important, though Christ had not yet given that command to the church, so John's baptism for repentance was all that Nicodemus would know. Certainly the washing of the word is tied to the working of the Spirit in the New Testament.

Yet Nicodemus must have missed the point entirely, or maybe we have. He was amazed by the notion of the new birth. Jesus compared the Spirit's work to the wind. You may hear its sound and feel the effect, but you never know where the wind will blow next. We spend too much time in search of a formula or spiritual laws that, when followed, guarantee new birth.

III. The New Birth Transforms Lives

We are children of God not because we remember the day and hour we prayed a prayer or on what verse of "Just As I Am" we walked the aisle. Jesus says you only know the wind has blown by the effect. The fruit of Christ's presence is the surest sign one is born again. John never forgot this lesson. In his first epistle he gave three evidences of those who are "sons of God." If we love the brethren, acknowledge Jesus is Lord, and obey his commands we are disciples. I remember an old Presbyterian missionary who taught us theology in Bible college. One day he said that he could not remember a time when Christ was not real and precious in his life. A fellow student, troubled that Brother Davidson could not remember the day and the hour he was converted, challenged him: "How do you know you are a Christian?" Brother D. pounded on his chest and replied: "Because Jesus lives in my heart." The evidence of Christ's presence was real in Brother Davidson's life.

God does love us and have a wonderful plan for our lives. We are born from above. The evidence is in the effect this blowing of the Spirit will have on our lives. *(L. Joseph Rosas)*

JUNE

❧

Mending the Net, Sharpening the Hoe

Symbol: Rock

The rock is seen as the symbol of protection as well as God's church. God is the fortress and shelter of Israel (Deut. 32:4), and Jesus spoke of building his church on a rock (Matt. 16:18).

Text:

"He is the Rock, his works are perfect, and all his ways are just. A faithful God who does no wrong, upright and just is he" (Deut. 32:4 NIV).

Invocation:

"Lord Jesus Christ, you have promised never to forsake or leave me. Accept my life and ministry as a living sacrifice to you and grant me strength to keep my promises to you. In the name of Christ. Amen." (Reuben P. Job and Norman Shawchuck, *A Guide to Prayer*)

Scripture Focus:
- Matthew 16:18
- Deuteronomy 32:13
- 2 Samuel 22:2ff.
- Psalm 18:2, 31, 46

Prayer Focus:
- Think of God's church and how your entire life has been blessed by it.
- See times when God's church has made a difference in individual lives: the poor, hungry, sick, incarcerated, lonely, troubled, and grieving.
- Thank God for opportunities to serve through his church.
- See ways of additional service for your church, community, and the world.
- See texts for the month coming alive to empower your people to service and devotion.

Prayer:

"Pour into our hearts the spirit of unselfishness, so that when our cup overflows we may seek to share our happiness with our brethren. O Thou God of love who maketh Thy sun to rise on the evil and on the good, and sendeth rain on the just and the unjust, grant that we may become more and more Thy true children, by receiving into our souls more of Thine own Spirit of ungrudging and unwavering kindness; which we ask in the name of Jesus. Amen." (John Hunter, as quoted in Harry Emerson Fosdick, *The Meaning of Service*) *(Bill Self)*

JUNE 1, 1997

੩&

Second Sunday After Pentecost

Worship Theme: God is with us even in the midst of life's struggles.

Readings: 1 Samuel 3:1-10 (11-20); 2 Corinthians 4:5-12; Mark 2:23–3:6

Call to Worship (Psalm 139:1-6, 13-14):

Leader: O LORD, you have searched me and known me.

People: You know when I sit down and when I rise up; you discern my thoughts from far away.

Leader: You search out my path and my lying down, and are acquainted with all my ways.

People: Even before a word is on my tongue, O LORD, you know it completely.

Leader: You hem me in, behind and before, and lay your hand upon me.

People: Such knowledge is too wonderful for me; it is so high that I cannot attain it.

Leader: For it was you who formed my inward parts; you knit me together in my mother's womb.

All: I praise you, for I am fearfully and wonderfully made. Wonderful are your works; that I know very well.

Pastoral Prayer:

Most holy and merciful God, we give thanks for your wondrous works. You created the universe and sustain it with the power of your word; and yet you are concerned with the life of each of your tiny creatures. As the psalmist said, even before we were born you were shaping us, making us, breathing into us the breath of life. O Lord, help us to rest secure in your love. Though life is filled with challenges and struggles, even when crisis and tragedy finds us, help us to find peace in your presence. Forgive us for the evil we have done and the good we have failed to do, and keep us close to you. We ask it in the name of Jesus Christ our Lord. Amen.

SERMON BRIEFS

COUNSELING THE CALLED

1 SAMUEL 3:1-10 (11-20)

I recently talked with a pastor who characterized a young associate who had quit the ministry as one who may have been "mama-called and daddy-led" into the ministry. Thus, he dropped out. The certainty of God's call upon our lives into the gospel ministry is usually the bedrock support that enables us to stay in when disappointments, disillusionment, and difficulty persist.

Samuel, a pivotal prophet/priest for the transition of Israel from a confederacy to a monarchy, experienced a real call from the Lord as described in our text today. He received helpful counsel from Eli as he worked through the experience of his call from God.

Perhaps you will have opportunity to give guidance to people who express to you a struggle in discerning the call of God upon their lives. Samuel's call experience provides several helpful insights that will equip you to give good advice to such folk. These insights will help them decide whether or not their experience constitutes an authentic call into Christian ministry.

I. A Real Call Involves the Experience of a Personal Word from God

In a time when a personal word from God was rare, and, consequently, proclaimers of a message from God to his people were scarce also, the Lord spoke to Samuel in such an authentic, personal way that the boy thought it was the voice of Eli, his mentor. He had no way of perceiving on his own that God might speak to him in such a way. He was inexperienced in such matters. Once he knew that the Lord spoke to individuals in a personal way, he had no problem realizing that the experience he was having was an encounter with the living God.

Whatever the particulars of the life of a person who is being called into ministry might be, the universal fact is that such an individual will perceive a profoundly personal directive from the Lord upon his or her life.

A college student who had been aimlessly wandering through life for a couple of years became sensitive to his need to have direction from the Lord. Soon after, God spoke to him a call to ministry so deep and so personal that the student responded audibly just as Samuel did. The certainty of his call into ministry has never wavered. An audible response isn't necessary for everyone, but an experience of call so real as to make an audible response seem appropriate is critical.

The circumstances of life into which God's call comes are infinitely variable. How the word is heard is multifarious. But without exception the word will be discerned as a call from God when the call is real.

II. A Real Call Experience May Involve Interpretive Assistance from a Human Advisor

Upon Samuel's third trip to him, Eli realized that Samuel probably wasn't mistaken about hearing his name called, so he advised him to respond the next time to God. He taught Samuel with that advice that God speaks to people in a personal way.

Clovis Chappell was assisted in understanding God's call upon his life by the Sunday school director in his local church. The director observed Chappell's gift of public speaking and enlisted him to give the devotionals for Sunday school assembly. Out of that experience, Chappell felt called into the preaching ministry.

God uses other people to steer us in an awareness of his call into ministry. Such people are usually those within our own local church who love us and possess spiritual discernment about what the Lord is doing in the lives of others.

III. A Real Call into Ministry Prompts a Ready Response of Commitment to God's Will

Samuel's response to the call of God was a willing, ready, "Speak, for your servant is listening." He proved his commitment to that call by delivering a difficult message to Eli, his beloved mentor. The willingness to preach a challenging message to people we love is one of the weightiest evidences of a real call to ministry.

I am skeptical of the genuineness of calls to ministry that are resentfully received. Samuel wasn't dragged kicking and screaming into ministry. Once he understood the call, he received it readily. Jeremiah was reluctant, but not resentful and utterly rebellious. Most preachers I know, once they understood clearly that God was calling them, felt honored they were chosen and gladly yielded. (*Jerry E. Oswalt*)

STRUCK DOWN, BUT NOT DESTROYED

2 CORINTHIANS 4:5-12

A popular needlepoint plaque proclaims: "Ain't nothin' going to happen today that me and the Lord can't handle!" Such must have been the sentiment of Paul. Obviously aware of his human inadequacies and vulnerabilities when standing alone, he was, however, equally convinced of the strength and stamina that come from standing with God.

Appealing to creation language, he assured the Corinthians that the same God who created light (and life) out of darkness can "shine in our hearts," however dark the world might seem.

I. Life Is Not Easy

Paul, himself no stranger to hard times and suffering, acknowledged that life is often a tough and trying journey. Many times, he said, we feel "afflicted," "perplexed," "persecuted," and "struck down."

The life of a friend seems to parallel the apostle's words. Her marriage ended with great sadness. A neurological disease forced early retirement. The same illness now limits her vision and mobility. She cares for an aging and disabled parent. Only faith and humor have navigated her through perilous waters. Recently she confessed: "I know God doesn't put any more on us than we can stand, but sometimes I wish God didn't think so highly of me." Her statement, though tongue-in-cheek, is not an unfamiliar thought to many of us much of the time. Life can be a tough and trying journey.

191

II. Even in Tough Times, God Is with Us

Paul offered no assurance that God will deliver the faithful from trials or tribulations. He did promise, however, that we do not suffer alone. Likewise, Paul told the Corinthians that God has "transcendent power" greater than whatever life could throw their way. God is with us in our moments of struggle or suffering. Thus, wrote Paul, "we are afflicted in every way, *but not crushed*; perplexed, *but not driven to despair*; persecuted, *but not forsaken*; struck down, *but not destroyed*" (v. 9, italics added).

The journey may be difficult, but made in step with God it is also meaningful. A popular gospel song by the Goodman Family Singers entitled, "I Wouldn't Take Nothing for My Journey Now," was inspired by the testimony of a poor, physically challenged man in a remote Kentucky church. "It's been hard," he said, "and there were times I didn't think I'd survive. But God was always at my elbow, guiding me through. And I learned more through the tough times with God than I would ever have known in good times alone. So, I wouldn't take nothing for my journey now."

III. In Christ, Even Death Is Not Final

The question arises: "What, though, of the ultimate tragedy of death?" More than affliction or persecution, death seems the final exclamation point that the world was really too much for us after all. Not so, argued Paul. Even facing death or grief, he wrote, "the life of Jesus may be made visible" in us. That is God's final exclamation point. Christ arose, and so shall we because of him. Even as death is at work in the world, eternal life through Christ is given to all who believe. Thus does the mortal journey lead to life that eclipses mortality.

The Creed of The Uniting Church of Canada expresses this Pauline doctrine well: "In life, in death, in life beyond death, God is with us. We are not alone." Thanks be to God! *(Michael Brown)*

CLOWNS AND JOKERS

MARK 2:23–3:6

"Clowns to the left . . . jokers to the right . . . here I am, stuck in the middle with you." Those are lyrics from a pop song, but we can apply them to worship. Some people feel stuck in the middle between the clowns on the left, who are so committed to law and ritual that they have a way of making worship legalistic and little, and the jokers on the right, who are so cynical and sophisticated that nothing is very important to them. Every day is the same as every other day. Nothing is important enough to matter.

Clowns make the Sabbath a burden with all of their requirements, and jokers make it into nothing. Whenever an act gets separated from its reason for being it becomes legalism or oblivion. When a rule or a celebration loses its motivation it becomes a burden or it becomes a joke.

I. The Sabbath Is More Than an Obligation

For the clowns on the left, the Sabbath gathering is a requirement that must be kept by all. It is blue laws and ritual. It was the clowns who said no dancing on the Sabbath, no playing cards on the Sabbath, no playing games, no working on your car, no cutting the grass on the Sabbath. The ritual has been cut off from the motive of gratitude and joy, and so the ritual itself has become important.

II. The Sabbath Is More Than Just Another Day

But the jokers on the right are trying to tell us that all time is the same. They want to be able to do whatever they want whenever they want. The Sabbath was made for humans, not humans for keeping the Sabbath. The Sabbath was given to humanity to use to get ahead—to use for enjoyment. The jokers grab the day and work so hard to find the gusto that they exhaust themselves.

III. The Sabbath Is a Gift of God

Indeed, the story in Mark does raise the question of why we gather for worship on the Sabbath. The Sabbath was given to us for our benefit. It was made for us to use for our welfare, but we are not always very informed as to what makes for our welfare. As human beings we have deep and abiding needs to mark time. Not every day is the same. We celebrate births, we remember anniversaries, and we gather to honor the passing of traditions and events in maturity, such as high school graduations.

God gave us the Sabbath so that we might use it to set aside some time each week to glorify God and enjoy his fellowship. It is a day when we might rest from our work and let God keep us safe for a time. The Sabbath is set aside so that we might acknowledge all of the good things God has given us, and give thanks. It is a day to remember all of the past victories of God's grace and so be strengthened and reminded of his gracious care in the future.

There are things we need and ask God to do for us. But there is also the Sabbath day, a day given to us by God, so that we might do the things we need to do for God and with God—to sing songs for him, to create beautiful things for him, to write words of love to him, to speak to him the deep hopes and desires of our human hearts. We come to worship to rejoice as lovers of God.

So we are stuck here in the middle—between those who want to make worship and the Sabbath a legalistic ritual, and those who think the Sabbath is just another day for indulging their favorite excesses. And we are here in the middle giving thanks to God, glorifying him forever, and enjoying his grace. There is no place else on earth we would rather be. (*Rick Brand*)

JUNE 8, 1997

❧

Third Sunday After Pentecost

Worship Theme: True fulfillment is found only in following God's will.

Readings: 1 Samuel 8:4-11 (12-15), 16-20 (11:14-15); 2 Corinthians 4:13–5:1; Mark 3:20-35

Call to Worship (Psalm 138:1-2, 4-5):

Leader: I give you thanks, O LORD, with my whole heart; before the gods I sing your praise;

People: **I bow down toward your holy temple and give thanks to your name for your steadfast love and your faithfulness;**

Leader: All the kings of the earth shall praise you, O LORD, for they have heard the words of your mouth.

All: **They shall sing of the ways of the LORD, for great is the glory of the LORD.**

Pastoral Prayer:

As we enter your heavenly courts in prayer, O Lord, direct our thoughts to you. We worship your majesty, we honor your holiness, we give thanks for your love. In a world that distracts us too often—which would focus our attention and priorities on that which is temporary and insignificant—help us to rise above petty concerns, that we might find in you alone our purpose and our security. Grant us, O Lord, the wisdom to seek your will and the strength to obey—for we know that only as we find our place in the center of your will do we truly find life's best. In every area of our lives, Lord—in our families, in our work, in our recreation, and in our community of faith—make us ever mindful to seek your will and not our own. For we pray in the name of the One who was obedient even to the cross. Amen.

SERMON BRIEFS

THE PERILOUS PATH

1 SAMUEL 8:4-11 (12-15), 16-20 (11:14-15)

Both Elvis and Sinatra released renditions of the song "My Way." This song, which sold very well for both artists, glamorizes self-deification, which is the essence of sin. It advocates the perilous path of worldly wisdom.

Samuel's Israel reflected their commitment to this perilous path in their demand for a king to rule over them. During the time of the judges, Israel had been a theocracy (ruled by God). Dissatisfied with that, they clamored for an earthly king. Even in the face of God's warning to them about the burdens a human king would place upon them, they insisted on having a monarch. Intent on having their way, they utterly rejected God's way.

When people choose the "my way" approach to life, they set out on a perilous path. Notice from the text the reasons the "my way" philosophy is a perilous path.

I. "My Way" Has a Weak Rationale

Israel's only reason for demanding a king was that they might be like other nations. A copycat mentality, shaped by covetousness and lust, has been the downfall of many people. Think of the teens you have known who were enticed into drugs, alcohol, or illicit sex because it seemed to them that everyone else was doing it. Imagine the young adults who build up insurmountable debts in an effort to keep pace with their friends in regard to material possessions.

We all should beware of the weakness of a rationale for behavior that causes us to feel that we have to pattern our lives after the world. The world is at enmity with God.

II. "My Way" Ultimately Leads to Destruction

Israel had the mistaken notion that a monarch would enable them to gain constant military victory over their enemies. Initially Saul had some military success, but when he impatiently and presumptuously usurped the place of Samuel as priest and offered an unlawful sacrifice, he lost his kingdom. From that point on, Saul's reign was doomed. He became a pathetic, emotionally distraught, spiritually empty, and largely ineffective king. Filled with jealousy and paranoia about David, he was destined to die in defeat.

Sometimes when people choose the way of the world, they seem to have everything human beings could want out of life. Eventually, however, they will experience the destruction of the perilous way.

I can't help but think of the singers mentioned at the beginning of this message—both reflected their own lifestyles in the song "My Way." Both knew great popularity, wealth, and power but also experienced great loss. One died in personal humiliation—an end that eventually befalls those who choose to live "my way" instead of God's way. (*Jerry E. Oswalt*)

A HOUSE NOT MADE WITH HANDS

2 CORINTHIANS 4:13–5:1

Frederick Buechner, in his timeless work *Wishful Thinking*, distinguishes between "immortality" and "resurrection." "Immortal means death-proof," he writes. "Those who believe in the immortality of the soul believe that life after death is as natural as digestion after a meal." Resurrection, he argues, is different from that. "It is entirely unnatural. We do not go on living after death because that's how we are made. Rather, we go to the grave as dead as a doornail and are given life back again . . . because that is the way God is made." As so frequently is the case, Buechner hits "the doornail" on the head.

I. Eternal Life Is a Gift

When Paul wrote of life beyond life, he wrote from a theology of grace: "For by grace you have been saved through faith, and this is not your own doing; it is the gift of God" (Eph. 2:8). To the Corinthians he wrote, "We have a building from God, a house not made with hands, eternal in the heavens." Life beyond life was viewed as a gift, a demonstration of God's grace.

The Corinthians wrote to Paul voicing questions about what lies on the other side of dying. They, too, had said painful good-byes they did not wish to say. They had stood with broken hearts beside graves of loved ones, asking the same questions we ask when standing beside similar graves. It was in response to those questions that Paul, the pastor, wrote.

II. Death Is Not the End of Things

"We have . . . a house not made with hands, *eternal* in the heavens." Following the tragedy at the federal building in Oklahoma City in 1995, a good deal of discussion was centered around what to do with the property. Should they build another government facility, or should they designate the property as a memorial site to those who were murdered? A writer noted that the site should be marked as a reminder of the transient nature of earthly things. "Earthly buildings explode or decay," he wrote. "The only safe and permanent dwelling is the house not made with hands." He made a point.

God has prepared for the faithful a life beyond this life that cannot be extinguished, a place where there are no bombs, no diseases, no acts of ill will, and no good-byes.

> When we've been there ten thousand years,
> bright, shining as the sun,
> we've no less days to sing God's praise
> than when we'd first begun.
> ("Amazing Grace," John Newton)

III. Heaven Is a Home

We have "a *house* not made with hands," Paul wrote. Jesus said much the same thing: "In my Father's house are many rooms" (John 14:2 NIV). In each case the image has to do with homecoming, with returning to a place of unconditional welcome where we are part of the family. A Parent is waiting there, standing with open arms beside an open door.

As Scottish evangelist Jim Small said: "It is like coming home after dark. There is a brief passage through dark woods, but then you step into the opening. There you see a house. A light burns in the window. The front door is open. The table is set. The covers on your bed are pulled back. Your mother greets you with a smile and says, 'I'm glad you're home,' and you answer, 'So am I.' "

The New Testament says dying is like a homecoming. A reunion with a loving Parent. A light in the window. A welcome at the journey's end. *(Michael Brown)*

THE HANDYMAN

MARK 3:20-35

"Hey, girls, gather round . . . I fix broken hearts, I know I really can." In this popular song, he called himself the Handyman. There is a great temptation and power in being able to fix things, but most of the time life has more problems than we can fix.

In August Wilson's play *Fences*, a mother says to her child: "When your daddy walked through the house, he was so big, so strong, such a powerful personality, that he filled up this house. That was my first mistake. Not to make him leave some room for me. And I didn't know that to keep up his strength I had to give up little pieces of mine." How do you help a woman who has been used up?

In chapter 3 of his Gospel, Mark shows us a picture of Jesus healing people—fixing them. He casts out demons. Jesus comes and things happen. The religious leaders say he is fixing things by black magic—the devil. Something is happening, but why? God's power is at work in our world, but it keeps being called by different names.

In his book *Brother to a Dragonfly*, Will Campbell tells the powerful conversation between himself and a black preacher. The black preacher reminded Campbell of how we let God's power get called by different names. "I don't believe in civil rights," the preacher said, "because I believe in God."

God wants to work in our lives. Jesus says that the only way to know the truth is to experience the power of God in our own lives, and the only way that can happen is if we don't shut out the power of God's loving Spirit. We have to let God in before we can know his power.

When we concentrate on the power and love of God, we have a way of opening our problems up to God's mercy and the problems don't seem so large. If God becomes larger in our lives, then the room we have for our problems becomes less and our problems become smaller.

If I don't invest so much of my pride in my children, or so much of my time in their affairs, then they have more room to grow and develop. If we focus more on God and less on our jobs, our jobs becomes smaller, more manageable, and we do better at them. Rather than fretting over "so much to do, so little time," we can focus on the eternity of God and discover that we have forever to accomplish God's purpose for us.

God's power is sufficient to lift our burdens and make a way for us in the wilderness. When we trust ourselves to God, we find he is able to lead us into a life more abundant. *(Rick Brand)*

JUNE 15, 1997

❧

Fourth Sunday After Pentecost

Worship Theme: God often uses the unexpected to demonstrate his glory.

Readings: 1 Samuel 15:34–16:13; 2 Corinthians 5:6-17; Mark 4:26-34

Call to Worship (Psalm 20:6-7):

Leader: Now I know that the LORD will help his anointed;

People: **he will answer him from his holy heaven with mighty victories by his right hand.**

Leader: Some take pride in chariots, and some in horses,

All: **but our pride is in the name of the LORD our God.**

Pastoral Prayer:

Almighty God, we stand before you recognizing our own sin and rebellion; we confess our foolish vanity, our selfish spirits, and our thoughtless actions. We have fallen so short of your glory, O Lord, yet in your steadfast love you have offered us restoration; in your gracious love, you have provided a means whereby we might experience new life through our Lord Jesus Christ. Thank you for the gifts you give, and grant us strength to honor your grace with lives of faith and obedience. As you have used so many others who seemed unlikely tools—the trickster Jacob, the shepherd-king David, the fisherman Peter—so we pray that you might use us as instruments of your will. Use us for your honor, as we pray in Jesus' name. Amen.

201

SERMON BRIEFS

SEEING PEOPLE AS GOD DOES

1 SAMUEL 15:34–16:13

We see the outside of people; God sees the inside. We see the body; God sees the heart.

It wasn't difficult for Samuel to anoint Saul as Israel's first king. Saul was an impressive physical specimen. He looked like a king. On the other hand, Samuel may have found it more difficult to anoint David as king after Saul, because David was a mere lad. The shepherd boy looked like anything but a king. Saul turned out to be a failure as a king. David ruled with great success.

Someone may ask: "Why did God select Saul as king? Didn't God know his heart?" Yes, of course God knew his heart. Likely, God gave Israel what they wanted, a king like the kings of other nations. They looked on the outside of Saul. He looked like a king. They would have refused the shepherd boy at that juncture. They needed to learn to see people like God sees people. So the Lord let them learn.

God frequently chooses the weak, common, unimpressive folk from human perspective to be his servants. The Messiah himself was described by Isaiah (53:2) as one whose outward appearance would not attract people to him.

How frequently we see only the outside and not the inside of people and thus make an incorrect judgment of the kind of persons they are. Think of the pastor selection committees of local churches who have given priority to external qualities rather than the character of prospective pastors. Vance Havner once quipped that he was glad he wasn't handsome, because he had noticed that people expect the preaching of preachers to live up to their looks!

Why does the Lord frequently use those who are unimpressive in the sight of man to do his greatest work? There are at least two reasons.

I. God's Power Made Obvious

People soon were astonished at David's exploits in battle. It was obvious that he didn't possess the physical prowess to accomplish those exploits; thus, God was given more credit than if David had been a powerful warrior.

Some of the apostle Paul's critics in the church at Corinth were critical of his preaching skills. Tradition teaches us that he wasn't a handsome man. Also, he had a chronic illness that hindered him physically. Yet, second only to Jesus, Paul became the dominant figure in the New Testament because he accomplished so much church-planting within the Gentile world. Paul is responsible for as many as thirteen of the New Testament writings, and is a central figure in the book of Acts. Paul gave the glory to God for all his accomplishments. Concerning his preaching, he wrote that his speech was not with "plausible words of wisdom, but with a demonstration of the Spirit and of power, so that your faith might rest not on human wisdom but on the power of God" (1 Cor. 2:4-5).

II. God Looks Beneath the Surface

The Lord wasn't surprised by David's feats. He knew the young man's heart. He saw the qualities that could be divinely enhanced within him to make him a great king.

Similarly, God perceived in Saul of Tarsus the capacity to become a great Christian missionary, even when he was a vicious persecutor of Christians. God saved him and made of him an effective apostle to the Gentiles. He was used as the most influential instrument in the hands of God to break down the barrier between Jewish and Gentile believers. *(Jerry E. Oswalt)*

NEW LIFE IN CHRIST

2 CORINTHIANS 5:6-17

In previous passages Paul has dealt with faith in life eternal and how mortal existence is just a prelude to that which is yet to come. In this lesson he draws a parallel to discipleship. Unredeemed life, he suggests, is mere prelude to converted life.

I. Eternal Life Is a Promise

Paul states, "We would rather be away from the body and at home with the Lord" (v. 8). He trusts that death is simply a bridge linking worlds, a pathway leading Home. Maurice Boyd writes of a bridge in Europe engraved with these words: "Bridges are meant to cross over. No one builds his house there." So it is with life. The journey is exciting. We love it and wish to linger. But ultimately this life is a bridge between worlds, and Home waits on the other side of crossing.

II. Abundant Life Is Also a Promise

Just as death means birth to life eternal, so does conversion mean re-birth to the abundant. "So, if anyone is in Christ, there is a new creation; everything old has passed away; see, everything has become new!" (v. 17).

Many people are familiar with Chuck Colson's story and how he underwent a personal metamorphosis. Formerly a convicted Watergate criminal, he now is instrumental in ministry to the incarcerated. Colson's previous experiences were a prelude to his new existence. The cocoon produced a butterfly.

A personal friend whose life crumbled has painstakingly rebuilt a new and devotedly Christian identity. He often concludes statements with the phrase, "That was in my former life." For him, the new birth that Christ described to Nicodemus and Paul and affirmed in this passage was a moment of starting over. My friend became a new person. "So, if anyone is in Christ, there is a new creation; everything old has passed away; see, everything has become new!"

III. Judgment Is Not Our Prerogative

"From now on, therefore, we regard no one from a human point of view. . . . if anyone is in Christ, there is a new creation" (vv. 16-17). When a person has experienced rebirth, it is not our role to judge his or her sincerity or to remind others of his or her former lifestyle.

I recall once commending a certain church member for his commitment to missions. He displayed in word and deed a genuine love for the underprivileged and dispossessed, and gave of himself graciously to assist them. A listener replied: "It's true. He has become a great fellow. I remember when he was a drunken philanderer. What a wonderful change has occurred for him." In one brief statement a person's reputation was smeared and his authentic conversion was devalued.

"I remember when he was a drunken philanderer." That statement served no purpose but to discredit and embarrass. It lacked compassion. Jesus would never have said something like that, and

204

such is the standard for judging what we, too, should and should not say about others. *(Michael Brown)*

THE KINGDOM IS LIKE . . .

MARK 4:26-34

There are so many things around us that make us wonder whether it is worth the effort to try to do mercy, love justice, and to live a life that is becoming to followers of Jesus Christ. Two thousand years of Christian faithfulness have gone by, and to judge by the mass media assaults on our consciousness, the world is worse instead of better.

What's the use of trying to do good? Where are the signs of the coming of the kingdom of God?

There have been times in history when Christians were sure that the kingdom of God was just around the corner. During the periods of 1880 and 1920 in this country, we thought the kingdom was near. John D. Rockefeller, Jr., wrote in the *Saturday Evening Post* of February 1918: "I see the church molding the thought of the world as it has never done before, leading in all great movements of history as it should. I see it literally establishing the kingdom of God on earth."

But now, as Bob Dylan once said, "We don't talk so proud." Now we are not so sure of the victory of goodness over evil.

The disciples of Jesus early in his ministry asked a lot of the same questions we ask today. "How come there aren't more people at the service, Lord? If by their fruits ye shall know them, how come goodness seems to be having so few fruits?"

In response to their questions, Jesus told a series of parables—parables about sowing seed; about the different kinds of results; about the hidden growth and the harvest; about the mustard seed. These stories help us look at this coming kingdom of God and our participation in it.

I. The Coming Kingdom Is Assured

The good news is the assurance of a harvest. The kingdom will come. As surely as you and I can predict that death will come to each of us, Jesus says you can trust the forces of God's mercy and grace and love to bring in the kingdom of God. Do not be discouraged by

205

the size of the beginning; do not be concerned about the visible signs of the fruitiness of your efforts. The kingdom of God will come.

II. It Will Not Be a Kingdom of Our Making

The kingdom is one of grace and mercy that will come because God brings it. The church and the kingdom of God are the creation of God. The farmer does not know how the seed germinates and grows. Likewise, the kingdom of God grows in hidden, mysterious ways, independently of our human efforts.

The parable suggests that we are to be faithful farmers, sowers of the seed, and we are not to worry about the crop because God will produce the harvest. We are often tempted to become so caught up with worrying about the harvest that we neglect the sowing of the seed. Or we may forget that God keeps us in this world to act as ministers of reconciliation, to be salt to prevent the rotting from getting worse. Or we may be so depressed by the apparently unconquered power of evil that we lose all faith and thus contribute to the darkness.

Also, we may become so concerned with building the kingdom here on earth that we may forget that there is so much more to come. We may focus all of our attention on the possibilities of this world and forget that this world and all it offers are under judgment by the holiness of God. We may begin to equate our efforts and achievements with God's kingdom and thus lose touch with the only true standard by which the events and accomplishments of this world can be measured.

III. God Calls Us to Faithfulness in Light of the Kingdom

When Elijah fled from Jezebel into the cave and complained to God that he was the only one left, God said, "Oh, hush, I have seven thousand who have not bowed a knee to Baal." Jesus told the parables to help us hear the good news. The kingdom of God comes because it is God's gift of mercy and grace. It comes as a wonderful surprise, as a gift of hope and as a miracle of love. Do not be discouraged; the kingdom will come. Do not neglect your part of faithfully scattering the seeds, but remember you are called simply to scatter the seeds and enjoy the new life that God has given you as his people. Do not neglect your calling; however, do not believe that your great society, your new deals, are God's kingdom. The good news is that the harvest will come. (*Rick Brand*)

JUNE 22, 1997

❧

Fifth Sunday After Pentecost

Worship Theme: Christ calls us to faithful discipleship.

Readings: 1 Samuel 17:(1a, 4-11, 19-23) 32-49; 2 Corinthians 6:1-13; Mark 4:35-41

Call to Worship (Psalm 9:9-11):

Leader: The LORD is a stronghold for the oppressed,

People: **a stronghold in times of trouble.**

Leader: And those who know your name put their trust in you,

People: **for you, O LORD, have not forsaken those who seek you.**

Leader: Sing praises to the LORD, who dwells in Zion.

All: **Declare his deeds among the peoples.**

Pastoral Prayer:

O God of unsearchable glory, we lift up our hearts in praise and adoration. You do not forsake those who seek you, and our hearts do most earnestly seek you now. Pour out upon us the riches of your mercy, that we may be strong in faith, bold in witness, and committed in our discipleship. As Christ has redeemed us through the power of his cross and resurrection, so we pray that you may use us to be ambassadors of that redemption to a lost and dying world. Help us to be useful disciples of Christ, as we offer these petitions in his name. Amen.

207

SERMON BRIEFS

THE RIGHT STUFF

1 SAMUEL 17:(1a, 4-11, 9-23) 32-49

A movie that came out several years ago about America's early Mercury and Apollo astronauts was entitled *The Right Stuff*. The title pointed to the fact that those bright, courageous men had what it took to get the job done. It could be said of the shepherd boy David that he had the "right stuff" to defend the honor of the Lord God of Israel before the challenge of the awesome Philistine warrior, Goliath.

It takes the right stuff for Christians to defeat the powerful forces of Satan with which we daily do battle. Victorious Christians possess the same qualities that enabled David to defeat Goliath.

I. The Right Stuff Includes Reverence for God

David was sent to the front lines to carry some good home cooking to his three older brothers. While visiting with them, he witnessed the taunting challenge of Goliath for Israel to send a man into hand-to-hand combat against him. He had issued this challenge daily for a period of time. No soldier in Israel's army had accepted the challenge. They cringed in fear before Goliath for good reason. He stood ten feet tall and wore armor that weighed 150 pounds. The head of his spear weighed nearly twenty pounds. Israel had no one who could begin to match up to him physically.

David was offended greatly by this event because he saw it as the dishonoring of God. He volunteered to bring Goliath and his defiance of God down. David's intense reverence for God demanded that Goliath be stopped.

Christians should have the same strong reverence for the Lord as did David. Such reverence will motivate us to live lives that consistently reflect holiness, love, and integrity to a world so ready to taunt, challenge, and even intimidate God's people.

II. The Right Stuff Includes Reliance upon God

When Saul expressed reluctance to permit David to fight Goliath, David replied that the Lord God had delivered him from the bear and the lion in the past and that he would depend upon the hand of God to do the same as he battled Goliath.

Christians must rely on the power of the Holy Spirit to gain victory over satanic temptations and trials. This is why the writer of Ephesians admonished us to put on the "whole armor of God." In God's strength we can prevail.

III. The Right Stuff Includes Being True to Yourself

David refused the offer of Saul's armor because he had not used such before. It wasn't who he was. He felt comfortable going up against Goliath with the familiar weapons of the shepherd, a stick and a sling.

Christians can win more battles against the forces of darkness when we become familiar with the spiritual weaponry God has given us, so that we are comfortable in the use of it.

Jesus used the sword of the Spirit, the Word of God to do battle with Satan in the wilderness at the outset of his ministry. The Word was a vital part of who he was, so he used it effectively.

Our challenge is to become so familiar with the Word of God that it becomes a natural weapon for us in our warfare with Satan. (*Jerry E. Oswalt*)

DEVOTED TO DISCIPLESHIP

2 CORINTHIANS 6:1-13

A couple of issues are touched in this lesson that remain as timely as they were the day Paul wrote about them.

I. Discipleship Is an Urgent Matter

"Behold, now is the accepted time; behold, now is the day of salvation." "Someday" is not soon enough when discipleship is the topic. "Now is the accepted time" to enter partnership with Christ. And, obviously, "Now is the accepted time" to dispose of any obstacles that stand between Christ and us.

Some time ago, having finished an afternoon of yard work, I was pained by a splinter in a finger. Too sore to bother with initially, I decided to wait till bedtime to remove it. By then the soreness had increased, prompting a decision to wait till morning. By morning, the soreness was accompanied by swelling and redness. I made the tactical error of mentioning that to my wife who (a) immediately grabbed my hand, (b) put me in an armlock known only to her and a handful of professional wrestlers, (c) muttered something about "not putting these things off," and (d) did unspeakable things to the end of my left index finger with a sewing needle. I appreciated her concern but was somewhat disturbed by her enthusiasm. Nonetheless, by afternoon the swelling and redness had subsided. By bedtime the finger was no longer sore. Fortunately she is willing to take action when it is time to act.

Paul concurred with that modus operandi: "Behold, now is the accepted time." When we suffer physically, there is no time like the present to take corrective measures, eliminating whatever stands between us and health. When we hurt spiritually, there is no time like the present to take corrective measures, eliminating whatever stands between us and God (be it guilt, anger, avarice, selfishness, prejudice—the list goes on an on). "Behold, now is the accepted time; behold, now is the day of salvation" (2 Cor. 6:2, KJV).

II. Discipleship Is a Matter of Commitment

Paul moves on from urgency to discipline. Devotion to a life of discipleship requires faith, commitment, and courage. It is not an easy journey. In this lesson he lists the hardships and tribulations he has suffered as a minister of the gospel. He has remained faithful only through great endurance.

There is a lesson here for every Christian. Those who seek to faithfully follow where Christ leads find obstacles along the way, many of them frightening and painful. Stand tall for truth and you often will stand alone. Take a position for morality and you may be ostracized by the crowd. Speak out for evangelism and sometimes even fellow church people will brand you a narrow-minded fundamentalist. Speak out for justice and the current climate may call you archaic, a rose-colored idealist out of touch with a commonsense world.

Follow Christ and wherever he leads the journey will be difficult. But the journey will at least ultimately take us where we need to go. In fact, only following Christ will do that. However easy (and wide) the way of the world may be, the path of Christ is still the narrow path that leads to life. Neither Jesus nor Paul promised that discipleship would be easy. Instead, the promise is that only discipleship is meaningful.

In the final tally, only life lived in the service of Jesus Christ is life worth living at all. Thus did Paul describe himself as "having nothing, and yet possessing everything." *(Michael Brown)*

WHY ARE YE AFRAID?

MARK 4:35-41

Of all the stories in the New Testament, perhaps this story is most symbolic of the Christian church. Throughout the history of Christianity, disciples have read this story and seen in it their own situations.

For you see, we are now the disciples in the boat. This very day you sit in what is called the nave of the church, and *nave* is the Latin word for ship. The Christian community has always used as the symbol of its life the ship on storm-tossed waves with the cross on top of the ship. You are now in the boat with Jesus Christ, and the storms are raging outside.

There is no need to prove that the storms are raging! You know what the storms are around you. You know what the storms in your own life are. We are in the boat with Christ, and the storms rage and they are frightening.

In the scripture story, Jesus' disciples are doing what Jesus instructed them to do. They have Jesus with them on the boat and yet the storm comes up. This story has always been important to the Christian faith because it is evidence that having Jesus with us in the boat is never a guarantee that there will not be storms in our lives. And even though Jesus is with us, many of us, like the disciples, lose hold of our faith. "Don't you care if we perish?" the disciples ask Jesus. They were not concerned about whether or not Jesus the Messiah and the mission of the Messiah might perish. In their fear they expected Jesus to care about them and to save them from danger.

Likewise, when we become afraid of the storms around us the temptation is to believe that God does not care what happens to us. With the fear there returns that old expectation that God's obligation is to protect us. Walter Bruggemann suggests that one of the marks of atheism is when we return to that "insistence on self-definition.

211

. . . for it is based on the surmise and fear that there is no one but us. And only our voice can prevent the terror of cosmic silence." Don't you care if *we* perish?

Jesus spoke the words, "Peace! Be still!" The words had an effect on both the disciples and the storm. The words of Jesus are directed to all the different forms of evil, mistrust, and fear that are working in the world. Jesus' actions to speak to the winds and the sea (those hostile storms outside) exerted control over the disciples' fear and mistrust.

Jesus demonstrates the power to protect and care for his church—his disciples. There are no storms that by the power of Jesus Christ his people cannot endure. Jesus does care and is able to keep his people from sinking and falling into the full power and control of evil. Why are ye afraid? *(Rick Brand)*

JUNE 29, 1997

❧

Sixth Sunday After Pentecost

Worship Theme: Persons in difficulty need our encouragement and forgiveness.

Readings: 2 Samuel 1:1, 17-27; 2 Corinthians 8:7-15; Mark 5:24-34

Call to Worship (Psalm 130):

Leader: Out of the depths I cry to you, O LORD.

***People:* LORD, hear my voice!**

Leader: Let your ears be attentive to the voice of my supplications! If you, O LORD, should mark iniquities, Lord, who could stand?

***People:* But there is forgiveness with you, so that you may be revered.**

Leader: I wait for the LORD, my soul waits, and in his word I hope; my soul waits for the Lord more than those who watch for the morning,

***People:* more than those who watch for the morning.**

Leader: O Israel, hope in the LORD! For with the LORD there is steadfast love, and with him is great power to redeem.

***All:* It is he who will redeem Israel from all its iniquities.**

Pastoral Prayer:

Eternal and loving God, from whom all love comes: hear our prayers, we who call upon your name, and give us a spirit of trust and receptivity, that we might sense your presence and hear your voice within us. Cleanse us from hearts of sin and unbelief, from spirits that are focused only on our own desires and lack compassion for others. Make us sensitive to those who are hurting all around us.

213

Use us to bring encouragement and support to those who are in need. Give us a desire to serve and a joy in the service, even as we remember the One who so loved and so served us that he went to a cross on our behalf. For we ask all these things in his precious name. Amen.

SERMON BRIEFS

LAMENT FOR FALLEN WARRIORS

2 SAMUEL 1:1, 17-27

Christians should lament the fall of Christian warriors (those falling into sin) as surely as David lamented the death of Saul and Jonathan. His lament for Jonathan wasn't surprising. They were best friends. His lament of Saul, on the other hand, was extraordinary, because Saul had relentlessly hated and hounded him. David was deeply grieved over Saul's death because Saul was God's anointed, the king of Israel.

Christians should grieve the fall into sin of any other Christian because we are God's elect; chosen for his glory. Our lament for fallen Christians will convey the same attitudes as David's lament for Saul.

I. The Attitude of Forgiveness of the Fallen

The whole tone of David's funeral elegy for Saul reflects his forgiveness of Saul. The greatest need of a fallen Christian is God's forgiveness. The second great need is forgiveness by fellow believers.

The prodigal son's father forgave him freely and threw a party to celebrate his homecoming. But the older brother withheld his forgiveness and refused to attend the party. That must have deprived the younger brother of a critical ingredient for him to ever enjoy and benefit fully from the restoration of relationship with his father. When we withhold forgiveness from fallen brothers and sisters in Christ, we deprive them of an essential ingredient for continued growth in Christ: the joy of Christian fellowship.

II. The Attitude of Positive Talk About the Fallen

David's lament forbade negative discussions about Saul's and Jonathan's defeat and death. Instead, David wrote of the victories and strengths of the regal father and son. He encouraged others to do the same.

In a critical football game, a running back fumbled away his team's last-minute opportunity to tie or win the game. His teammates who patted him on the back and encouraged him did the Christian thing. A member of the other team who cursed and ridiculed him did the ungodly thing.

All around us are brothers and sisters who are struggling with life's challenges. They may be struggling with marriage; or having difficulties with children; or facing vocational insecurity or even loss of a job. There could be any number of reasons for their struggle, but there is only one Christian response: to love, encourage, and be Christ's presence in the life of that brother or sister.

When Christians fall, the last word they need to hear from a brother or sister is a harsh word of judgment and criticism. They desperately need a word of forgiveness and encouragement. *(Jerry E. Oswalt)*

ATTENTION:
THIS IS NOT A SERMON ABOUT SEX!

2 CORINTHIANS 8:7-15

Several years ago a minister pondered how to maintain decent crowds for Stewardship Sunday. The topic has an uncanny way of emptying pews, and he labored at how to avoid that. So he announced in the church newsletter that next week's sermon would be entitled: "Everything You Need to Know About Sex." Predictably, come Sunday morning the pews were jammed. Even the C-and-E (Christmas and Easter) Christians had added a third worship service to their annual repertoire.

After the hymn of preparation, the pastor noted how quiet the sanctuary became. The listeners sat on the edge of their seats, anxious to hear the latest word on the world's hottest topic. The pastor mounted the steps into the pulpit, looked at the congregation, and said: "Sex was created by God as an expression of love between husbands and wives and a way of propagating life on planet Earth. Now that we've settled that, let's talk about stewardship."

No games and no gimmicks today. Instead we need to be honest and up front about this topic. Stewardship is a biblical priority. What we do with what we have been given is a subject regularly addressed in both the Old and New Testaments. In today's lesson Paul challenges the Corinthians to put their money where their mouths are, to back up their professions of charity with the practice of giving.

I. Authentic Stewardship Requires Faithfulness

Paul was collecting an offering for the church in Jerusalem. Various Christian communities (including some of rather meager means) had contributed. Corinth, of course, was a city of considerable financial ability. The believers there were capable of supporting the mission significantly. They obviously had expressed their support verbally. Now Paul was asking them to follow through. He spoke of their "readiness in desiring it" being matched by their willingness to "complete it out of what you have" (2 Cor. 8:11, RSV).

How easy it is to talk a good game about faith without being faithful. How easy it is to preach love without loving, to teach forgiveness without forgiving, to testify about missions without helping and healing, to verbally champion youth ministries without contributing or programming, to talk evangelism without inviting. Perhaps the Corinthian church was at that point, talking a good game about stewardship without being faithful stewards. Meanwhile the needs of the poor in Jerusalem were not effectively met by mere talk.

II. Authentic Stewardship Requires Giving Ourselves First

Paul said that Jesus is the model for Christian stewards: "[f]or your sakes he became poor, so that by his poverty you might become rich" (v. 9). It is an image of self-giving love that always places a priority on others.

General William Booth, founder of the Salvation Army, used to send handwritten Christmas cards to all his workers. Booth signed the cards with a single word. It was a word designed to keep them focused. It was a word designed to remind them of their calling and their duty. It was a word designed to drive them past verbalizing faith

216

to authentic fidelity. Every card he signed with the single word: *Others.*

We, too, are called by God to think of others, to share with others, to love and serve and help and heal others. And few Christian disciplines accomplish all that half as effectively as the stewardship of our finances, by which the church wraps its arms of compassion around the world, healing hurts and lifting high the cross. *(Michael Brown)*

DESPERATE

MARK 5:24-34

The woman was sick. Mark tells us she had been suffering from hemorrhages for twelve years. She went to many doctors, but none had been able to help her. Instead, her condition had grown worse.

She received reports of this man called Jesus and how he was having a remarkable effect on people. She knew what she had to do: she would go to Jesus. He would heal her.

When she gets there it is a mob scene. The crowds were pressing against Jesus. The woman believed that if she could just touch him—just the hem of his garment—she would get well. She reaches out and touches his cloak—and she is cured.

Most of us have not had this kind of experience. We are captured by the faith of the woman. She did not just believe that Jesus had the power to heal her—she was convinced that if she just touched his robe, the hem of his garment, she would be cured. She forces us to reexamine our faith in the mystery around us—that which can't be explained and is beyond reason. Whether you call it mystery, magic, or grace, Christianity has always been filled with elements that involve a trust in something supernatural.

In many quarters of the church we have tried to ignore this mystery. We have attempted to make the Christian faith rational. Meanwhile, all around us and deep within us is a hunger that reaches out for expression. We see it in the rise of witchcraft, tarot cards, and astrology.

But there is more to human life than just reason. There is a mind, and a heart, and mystery and wonder, and powers and principalities we can't explain. Jesus invites us to love the Lord our God with all of our minds—which means that we are to use and respect and appreciate the power of reason and our minds—and we are to love the Lord with all our heart and emotions and instincts, and we are to offer our souls, which is to commit ourselves to the grace of God that surrounds us. If we can just touch the grace of God, then our sin-sick world can be healed. *(Rick Brand)*

JULY

❧

Mending the Net, Sharpening the Hoe

Symbol: Rainbow

The rainbow is the symbol of union. Because it appeared after the flood it is also the symbol of pardon and reconciliation given to the human race by God. It also represents the last judgment and the final victory of God.

Text:

"I have set my rainbow in the clouds, and it will be the sign of the covenant between me and the earth" (Gen. 9:13 NIV).

Invocation:

"Almighty God, from whom every good prayer cometh, and who pourest out on all who desire it the spirit of grace and supplication: Deliver us, when we draw nigh to thee, from coldness of heart and wanderings of mind, that, with steadfast thoughts and kindled affections, we may worship thee in spirit and in truth; through Jesus Christ our Lord. Amen." (Reuben P. Job and Norman Shawchuck, *A Guide to Prayer*)

Scripture Focus:
- Genesis 9:12-17
- Revelation 4:2-8
- Revelation 10:1-7
- Ezekiel 1:28

Prayer Focus:
- Focus on the faithfulness of God in your storms.
- Focus on the deliverance of God in your floods.
- Focus on the order God has made out of human chaos, your chaos, your order.
- List areas in which you still need a victory.
- Recall times that you would not have made it had God not come through for you.

- Recall the times God has rescued you from meaninglessness and your feelings.
- Recall the times God has given to you feelings of glory and joy.
- List the people who need the same victory and ask that you may be God's vehicle to make this happen.

Prayer:

O Thou who rulest by thy providence over land and sea defend and guide and bless the messengers of Christ; in danger be their shield, in darkness be their hope, enrich their word and work with wisdom, joy, and power, let them gather souls for thee in far fields white unto harvest. O Thou who by thy Holy Spirit worketh the wonders in secret, open the eyes that dimly look for light to see the daystar in Christ; open the minds that seek the unknown God to know their heavenly Father in Christ; open the hearts that hunger for righteousness to find eternal peace in Christ. Deliver the poor prisoners of ignorance and captives of idolatry. Break down the bars of error, and despair the shadows of the ancient night; lift up the gates and let the King of glory and the Prince of peace come in. Thy kingdom, O Christ, is an everlasting kingdom! Strengthen thy servants to pray and labor in wait for its appearing; forgive our little faith in the weaknesses of our endeavors; hasten the day when all nations shall be at peace in thee, in every land and every heart throughout the world shall bless the name of the Lord Jesus, to the glory of God the Father. Amen. (Henry Van Dyke) *(Bill Self)*

JULY 6, 1997

૨ત

Seventh Sunday After Pentecost

Worship Theme: God often reveals his strength precisely at our point of weakness.

Readings: 2 Samuel 5:1-5, 12*b*-19; 2 Corinthians 12:2-10; Mark 6:1-13

Call to Worship (Psalm 48:1-3, 8-14):

Leader: Great is the LORD and greatly to be praised in the city of our God.

People: **His holy mountain, beautiful in elevation, is the joy of all the earth, Mount Zion, in the far north, the city of the great King.**

Leader: Within its citadels God has shown himself a sure defense.

People: **As we have heard, so have we seen in the city of the LORD of hosts, in the city of our God, which God establishes forever.**

Leader: We ponder your steadfast love, O God, in the midst of your temple.

People: **Your name, O God, like your praise, reaches to the ends of the earth.**

Leader: Your right hand is filled with victory. Let Mount Zion be glad, let the towns of Judah rejoice because of your judgments.

People: **Walk about Zion, go all around it, count its towers,**

Leader: consider well its ramparts; go through its citadels, that you may tell the next generation

All: **that this is God, our God forever and ever. He will be our guide forever.**

221

Pastoral Prayer:

Almighty God, we come before you this day recognizing our weakness and rejoicing in your strength. We are your creation, the work of your hands. All we are and all we possess, all of creation is a gift of your love and grace. Yet we often act as if we are the creators, as if we are worthy of the worship that belongs to you alone. Forgive our presumptuous and rebellious spirits, O Lord, and help us to see more clearly your awesome power and glory. Help us, as we submit our lives to you, to understand that you can take even our weakness and demonstrate through it your strength. Make us instruments of your love this day, O Lord, for we ask it in the name of your Son and our Savior. Amen.

SERMON BRIEFS

WORLD CHANGERS

2 SAMUEL 5:1-5, 12*b*-19

The world watched with anticipation as the Berlin Wall was dismantled, signifying the unification of a German people divided by political differences. It was an event that had global implications—a moment that would be remembered by its promises and challenges. Two governments, economies, and educational systems had to be integrated into one functioning society. If the merger was to be successful, it was essential to find an effective and widely accepted leader: a world changer.

Through a series of events, David—who had been king of Judah for seven years—was anointed king of Israel. For thirty-three years David led a united people who had once been divided. King David's rise to leadership was inevitable but not because of his political prowess. Rather, he had a variety of interests and accomplishments: celebrated athlete (1 Sam. 17:34), accomplished musician (1 Sam. 16:14), prolific writer, composer, and poet.

God is calling men and women today to change our world by unifying the loyalties and purposes of humanity for a sacred commitment. Three essential qualities of David's life emerge from this text as criteria for those who would be world changers.

I. David's Sacred Devotion Was Affirmed by a Secular Declaration

David was recognized by the leaders of the tribes of Israel as qualified for the task of uniting the kingdom. They shared a "kinship." The leaders declared "we are your bone and flesh." That statement seems to state a quality preferred even to the more generally authoritative covenantal relationship formula for the selection of leadership. World changers are local, home folk committed to Yahweh's mission.

David's leadership credentials were another important factor. Even when Saul was king, David was the driving force, the respected leader, a hidden messiah.

David's churchmanship proved to be important. The Lord had summoned David to feed the people. This idea of David becoming the "ruler over Israel," or the crown prince is an interesting development. Here, the secular designation of a king took on theological application.

Contemporary Christianity sometimes seeks to place Christians in the political arena. God chose a committed and proven secular leader to become theologian. Indeed, our religious grammar should be corrected theologically. Effective churchmen are not so much Christian physicians or Christian attorneys but physician Christians and attorney Christians.

II. David Maintained a Spiritual Conviction Which Prevailed Over Social Conscience

Verses 6-12 describe an attempt to persuade David to gain cultural approval through actions that contradicted the will of God. David, however, had a non-negotiable spiritual conviction. David faced the roar of the insensitive with the conviction that he was not alone with his spiritual convictions.

III. David's Meaningful Spirituality Resulted in a Memorable Personality

Like David, those who desire to make a lasting impact with their lives will notice the order of his two leadership priorities. David maintained an inward reflection. As he centralized the government in Jerusalem David "built the city all around from the Millo inward" (v. 9). He moved toward the temple first.

Next, David experienced an outward expansion: "and David became greater and greater" (v. 10). The scene in verses 12-19 illustrates those priorities. When confronted by opposition David sought God's will. He turned inward to the voice of God, which turned him outward to victory over the Philistines.

A lasting impression can be made on the world by those who will develop an appropriate personal spirituality consistent with God's summons. David understood God's unique plan for his life and he walked closely with God. God has called you to be a world changer, too. Will you also walk with God? *(Barry J. Beames)*

POWER IN OUR WEAKNESS

2 CORINTHIANS 12:1-10

Our society doesn't have a lot of interest in weakness. We pay to see strength, not weakness. We like to be with winners, not losers. Sometimes, however, what appears to be strength isn't all it seems. And what looks like weakness at first glance may actually be something altogether different.

The Corinthian people were not asking anything that had not been asked before. They simply wanted proof that God was really with them—to see signs and hear about miracles and revelations, things to prove that God was really strong and powerful, really present with them.

Paul had tried to dissuade them from this inclination earlier in his letter (see 10:18). But by this point in the letter, Paul seems resigned to the necessity of revealing his own "credentials" as a person who has experienced revelations from God. Reluctant as he is to do so, he goes ahead anyway. What follows is a third-person account of his own ecstatic experience of being called by God.

I. Thorns Are Present in Every Life

But then a curious thing happens. In the middle of his litany outlining his own personal strengths and credentials, Paul stops suddenly and changes his course entirely: "to keep me from being too elated, a thorn was given me in the flesh . . ." (v. 7). We don't know what that thorn was, but whatever it was, it tormented Paul without end. Repeated prayers give us a sense of his desperation in trying to contend with it (v. 8).

I have vivid memories of picking blackberries as a child near my grandparents' ranch. There is no way to remember the feelings of delight that came with filling a bucket with those wonderfully plump, juicy, purplish-black berries without also remembering the constant aggravation of thorns grabbing and snagging and scraping and pricking as we picked those luscious berries. We developed a formula for determining the ratio of berries to thorns in a blackberry patch: lots of berries, lots of thorns; a few berries, lots of thorns; no berries at all, lots of thorns!

II. God Touches Us at the Point of Our Weakness

One doesn't need the experience of picking blackberries to know about the persistent presence of thorns in life, whether physical, emotional, or spiritual—jabbing at our lives, punctuating our happiness, abbreviating our joy.

Yet we are not alone in the suffering. The word of God to Paul during his struggle was, "My grace is sufficient for you, for power is made perfect in weakness." By the end of this text, Paul's letter has taken a strange turn, and he has begun to boast of his weaknesses rather than his strengths, "for whenever I am weak, then I am strong."

Fred Craddock once observed that it is the nature of grace that it can only enter empty spaces. That is to say, God's power comes to us not when we're full and happy and everything's going our way, but when we're bereft, when the dipstick has come up dry, when we have nothing else to go on. When we are weak then, by grace, we are strong. *(Paul R. Escamilla)*

THE SACRAMENT OF FAILURE

MARK 6:1-13

Jesus was a failure. At least in this instance that is the conclusion we draw if we take this passage from Mark seriously.

Jesus went to his hometown, the town where people knew him, and they said of him, "Is not this the carpenter, the son of Mary and

225

brother of James and Joses and Judas and Simon . . . ?" They were not impressed. Thomas Wolfe said we can't go home again. Well, we can, but there is always someone there who knew us when we were growing up—and who is not impressed, or worse.

Jesus went home and taught in the synagogue, and those who heard him were offended. So Jesus gave us the line that has ever since been applied to those who go back home and find the hometown folks unimpressed: "Prophets are not without honor, except in their hometown."

It is a curious text. It follows a series of mighty acts: calming the storm, healing the Gerasene demoniac, healing a woman with a hemorrhage, restoring a little girl to life. Then Jesus went home, and no one was impressed.

How did Jesus respond to this failure, this rejection by those who knew him so well? He sent his disciples to teach and heal, and he told them what to do if they ever went to a place that would not receive them: "as you leave, shake off the dust that is on your feet." In other words, do not let the failure continue to cling to your heels. Go on with life, with the next challenge. Leave Nazareth and go to Capernaum.

It has been called the Sacrament of Failure, this shaking of the dust from one's feet. It is an appropriate text for much of our life, but it is an especially appropriate text for celebrating the sacrament of the Lord's Supper—truly a Sacrament of Failure. After all, it was on the night of his betrayal that Jesus instituted this meal—the night before the failure of crucifixion.

This world of ours does not honor failure. It does not praise weakness nor reward defeat. Yet in the sacrament of the Lord's Supper we proclaim our faith, that it was out of the failure of betrayal, arrest, and crucifixion that God brought victory. It was out of the weakness of self-sacrifice that God brought salvation. It was out of the failure of death that God brought life.

Our world loves success stories. Yet most of us know, at some time in our lives, what it means to fail, to lose, to be weak. For that reason we can take heart in this sacrament. It is the sacrament that makes it possible for us to shake from our feet the dust of failure and move on toward life's next challenge. It is the sacrament that makes it possible for us to look to the new beginning, the new possibility, the saving promise.

Come, then, to the table. Receive the sacrament. If you know or have known any failure in your life, let this sacrament be for you the moment of a new beginning. For we are people who are nourished by the heavenly food of one who looked beyond the disappointment of failure to the hope of new beginnings. Thus we are not immobilized by failure but energized by possibility. We are people for whom the promises of beginnings are stronger than the fears of endings.

So whatever the failure—of morality, of relationships, of purpose, of commitment, of hope, of vision, of intent—shake off the dust from your feet and go out into a new future. You will find beside you the Lord who gave the advice in the first place! (*J. Lawrence McCleskey*)

JULY 13, 1997

Eighth Sunday After Pentecost

Worship Theme: God's blessing is a gift of divine grace.

Readings: 2 Samuel 6:1-5, 12*b*-19; Ephesians 1:3-14; Mark 6:14-29

Call to Worship (Psalm 24):

Leader: The earth is the LORD's and all that is in it, the world, and those who live in it;

People: for he has founded it on the seas, and established it on the rivers.

Leader: Who shall ascend the hill of the LORD? And who shall stand in his holy place?

People: Those who have clean hands and pure hearts, who do not lift up their souls to what is false, and do not swear deceitfully.

Leader: They will receive blessing from the LORD, and vindication from the God of their salvation.

People: Such is the company of those who seek him, who seek the face of the God of Jacob.

Leader: Lift up your hearts, O gates! and be lifted up, O ancient doors! that the King of glory may come in.

People: Who is the King of glory? The LORD, strong and mighty, the LORD, mighty in battle.

Leader: Lift up your heads, O gates! and be lifted up, O ancient doors! that the King of glory may come in.

All: Who is this King of glory? The LORD of hosts, he is the King of glory.

Pastoral Prayer:

God of grace and glory, we unite our hearts in praise and adoration. We thank you for the gift of life and all the goodness we enjoy. We thank you for the gift of families, who love, nurture, and protect us. We thank you for the gift of friends, who help and encourage us. We thank you for the gift of your church, which teaches and supports and heals. Most of all, we thank you for the gift of your Son, whose sacrifice on the cross makes it possible for us to enjoy all of your other gifts, because it makes it possible for us to enjoy fellowship with you. Help us, Lord, to live lives worthy of your amazing gifts. And help us to be messengers of your love and grace in a world that so desperately needs to experience the transforming power of the cross. For we ask these things in the name of the One whose life, death, and resurrection are the greatest gift of all, even our Lord Jesus Christ. Amen.

SERMON BRIEFS

AN ESSENTIAL PROPOSAL

2 SAMUEL 6:1-5, 12b-19

David's attempt to restore worship, which had been in decline since Eli's death, sought to involve the whole nation in spiritual renewal. The ark narrative described the process of renewal as a national movement from disaster to blessing by eliminating inappropriate attitudes and adopting appropriate attitudes toward God. The proposal was essential if a sacred focus was to be revived.

I. Spiritual Renewal Is Interrupted by Inappropriate Attitudes

I have been challenged numerous times by the statement, "You know, we are all trying to go to the same place." While heaven and eternal life may be a common desire, not every route or lifestyle will guide you to that destiny. More precisely, Christians who live with inappropriate attitudes experience a frustrated and fractured journey. God proposed that spiritual renewal could be Israel's experience if the ark, the symbolic presence of God, was returned. But a series of inappropriate attitudes retarded the awakening.

First, the men of Israel set the ark on a new cart (v. 3). With the conviction that Yahweh deserved the very best, or in an attempt to devise a more efficient mode of transportation, the cart served to impede their renewal. Why? God's instructions in Numbers 7:9 required that the ark be carried. Carrying the ark implied specific obligations necessary for a right relationship with God, such as purification. Any time we circumvent God's directions, God's purposes are abandoned.

Verse 5 suggests another important and inappropriate attitude. Although this act of worship appears to be a correct response, close examination reveals something is missing. In the list of instruments there is no mention of the wind instruments. While it is only my conjecture, "wind" is a common symbol for the Spirit of God throughout scripture. Spiritual renewal requires one's recognition of and submission to the Spirit of God.

Another inappropriate attitude is found in verse 10, when David left the ark at the house of Obededom out of fear. David became afraid of God following Uzzah's death when he touched the ark. Granted, Uzzah spontaneously tried to protect the ark from destruction. But the action was a breach of God's instruction. Now David was confused and afraid, and left the ark in the care of a Gentile rather than taking it to his city.

All is not lost because we have had inappropriate attitudes about God. Regardless of those developments renewal was possible. Verses 12-19 guide us to understand that.

II. Spiritual Renewal Is Engraved by an Inverted Attitude

During the ensuing three months, observers noticed that the house of Obededom was blessed. Remember this principle: the presence of God is the blessing of God. What took place to secure God's blessing for Israel?

David personally retrieved the ark (v. 12). This change of attitude is evidenced by the gladness that replaced his fear. Spiritual growth is contagious. Others accompanied David in bringing the ark home.

The people became obedient. This time they carried the ark (v. 13). They would not make the same mistake again.

David led another worship service (vv. 15-19). Now their worship reflected a sacred privilege rather than the celebration of a military conquest.

Not everyone was impressed with the renewal experience. Saul's daughter, Michal, "despised [David] in her heart" (v. 16). She had an inappropriate attitude. But for those who, with David, personally identified their lives with the presence of Yahweh, obeyed the word of God, and worshiped God in sacred abandon, there was a new blessing "in the name of the LORD of hosts" (v. 18). *(Barry J. Beames)*

THE LONGEST BLESSING

EPHESIANS 1:3-14

Reading through the first chapter of Ephesians is much like looking through an old family scrapbook that has been sitting on the shelf for years. As we turn each musty page, we are reminded of people, places, events that we had long since forgotten.

Verses 3-14 are like a scrapbook for the church, tracing the history of our relationship with God to its beginnings, and even before its beginnings, to the foundation of the world. This scrapbook then goes on to show us the future of God's relationship with us.

I. The Grand Basics

In these verses we find the basics of our faith expressed, except that they turn out to be very grand basics. On a time line, the description stretches from before time to the fullness of time. On a graph, it encompasses everything—things in heaven and things on earth. On a scale, the lavishness of the plan would break the springs. The writer gives us a sense of the size and scope of these ingredients of our faith with a fascinating literary device: in the original Greek text, verses 3-14 are one continuous sentence—a rather expansive blessing!

We often speak casually about blessings. Ephesians would have us understand that we don't know the half of it. We are blessed in ways that are literally of cosmic dimensions.

II. The Greatness of God's Blessing

God's blessing toward us is expressed in three ways. First, God chooses us: ". . . just as he chose us in Christ. . . . He destined us for adoption" (vv. 4, 5). We are blessed because we have been chosen, adopted, and incorporated into both God's earthly and cosmic families.

Second, God redeems us: "In him we have redemption . . . forgiveness" (v. 7). We are, by the riches of God's grace, fashioned into new creatures, our past sin and brokenness left behind. Whatever we may have been before—however we may have sinned, however we may have failed God and others—is put behind us, covered by his redemptive grace.

Finally, God unites us. Indeed, God brings unity to all things in his creation: God "has made known to us the mystery of his will, . . . to gather up all things in him, things in heaven and things on earth" (vv. 9, 10).

From this elaborate, extravagant blessing streams a single consequence: the blessing of God (v. 3). We are destined, as recipients of all the spiritual riches elaborated in the "long sentence" before us, to "live for the praise of his glory" (v. 12). In a beautiful literary symmetry, this long, flowing "hymn" concludes the same way it opens, with the benediction of God (v. 14).

God is glorified in our blessedness. In God's glorification is our human odyssey—the long, long story of our blessedness in God—made complete. *(Paul R. Escamilla)*

BE CAREFUL WHAT YOU PROMISE!

MARK 6:14-29

To be perfectly honest, I would not have chosen this text. We lectionary preachers find that most of the time the lectionary texts are good starting places for a sermon. I have found over the years that lectionary-based preaching has provided a more well-rounded fare for my congregations than would have been the case if I simply chose my own text and topic week after week. But occasionally, I come to a lectionary reading and wonder why, under heaven, it is there. This is one of those texts.

It's a story about a paranoid ruler, about a prophet who condemned the ruler for his lust, about a resentful and vengeful woman, about a daughter-in-law's seductive dance before her father-in-law, about a foolish promise, about a spiteful request, and about an unjust and gruesome murder. It's hardly a story that invites quiet reflection on this midsummer Sunday morning! And although I would not have chosen this text, it is in the lectionary, so I have thought about it at a deeper level—beyond the unattractive nature of the story itself.

My wife and I are season ticket holders to Opera Carolina, and last year one of the operas was Richard Strauss's *Salome*. It is Strauss's dramatic and memorable telling of this tale of John the Baptizer, Herod, Herodias, and Herodias' daughter, Salome. The music was dreadfully mournful. The presentation was haunting. The set and props were terrifying—from the wailing cries of John in the well where he was held prisoner to Salome's presentation of John's head on a platter. Did I like it? No! Have I remembered it? Absolutely!

Herod had married his brother's wife, Herodias. John had told Herod that such a marriage was not right. Herodias wanted John dead, but Herod was afraid of John because Herod knew John was a righteous man. But Herod made two grave mistakes. First, he gave himself a birthday party, and Herodias' daughter danced for Herod—an entrancing dance. Though it is not in the biblical text, the "Dance of the Seven Veils" is presented in a seductive and compelling way.

Then Herod made his second mistake. Pleased by the dance of Herodias' daughter, Herod promised her whatever she wanted. He made the promise publicly. And when the girl went to her mother and asked what she should request, the deed was done: "The head of John the baptizer," said her mother. Because Herod did not want to renege on a promise he made publicly, he had John beheaded and the head was delivered to the girl on a platter. She gave it to her mother. And that's it!

Have you ever, in the excitement or enthusiasm or sensation or enticement of a moment, made a promise that you wished later you had not made? Have you ever been lured by the seductive attraction of evil to make a commitment that you wished later you had not made? Have you ever let your lesser emotions and base nature gain power over your clearer thought and your more noble intentions and devoted yourself to a course of action that you later regretted?

We are not told what became of Herod or Herodias or Herodias' daughter. But I can tell you this much: outside Jericho archaeologists are now excavating the ruins of Herod's palace. We know that he lived opulently, but he has no lasting place of nobility or goodness in history. On the other hand, the Jordan River, which flows by Jericho, is remembered as the water in which John baptized Jesus; John is remembered as the voice in the wilderness who proclaimed the coming of the Messiah; and John is remembered as a teacher of righteousness. John uttered truth as he understood it—and he paid a high price for his integrity. Herod made a promise under the influence of seduction—and he paid a high price for his foolishness. John died. Herod lived, knowing that once he made a foolish promise he had to make good on it, even though it meant he did evil he had not wished to do.

Given those choices, I hope I would choose John's integrity! (*J. Lawrence McCleskey*)

JULY 20, 1997

୬

Ninth Sunday After Pentecost

Worship Theme: Through Christ, God has come to live within us.

Readings: 2 Samuel 7:1-14*a*; Ephesians 2:11-22; Mark 6:30-34, 53-56

Call to Worship (Psalm 89:20-37):

Leader: I have found my servant David; with my holy oil I have anointed him;

People: **my hand shall always remain with him; my arm also shall strengthen him.**

Leader: The enemy shall not outwit him, the wicked shall not humble him.

People: **I will crush his foes before him and strike down those who hate him.**

Leader: My faithfulness and steadfast love shall be with him; and in my name his horn shall be exalted.

People: **I will set his hand on the sea and his right hand on the rivers.**

Leader: He shall cry to me, "You are my Father, my God, and the Rock of my salvation!"

People: **I will make him the firstborn, the highest of the kings of the earth.**

Leader: Forever I will keep my steadfast love for him, and my covenant with him will stand firm.

People: **I will establish his line forever, and his throne as long as the heavens endure.**

Leader: If his children forsake my law and do not walk according to my ordinances,

People: if they violate my statutes and do not keep my commandments,

Leader: then I will punish their transgression with the rod and their iniquity with scourges;

People: but I will not remove from him my steadfast love, or be false to my faithfulness.

Leader: I will not violate my covenant, or alter the word that went forth from my lips.

People: Once and for all I have sworn by my holiness; I will not lie to David.

Leader: His line shall continue forever, and his throne endure before me like the sun.

All: **It shall be established forever like the moon, an enduring witness in the skies.**

Pastoral Prayer:

Holy and righteous Father, who through Jesus Christ has conquered sin and death and made for us a way of salvation: You are worthy of all praise, O Lord. We praise you for your creating work, by which all things have come into being. We praise you for Christ; for his sinless life, his atoning death, and his life-giving resurrection. We thank you for your Holy Spirit, through which you have come to abide in our lives, giving us direction, purpose, and power. Forgive us, O Lord, for our rebellious attitudes and sinful actions. Help us to more fully and completely release our lives to your Spirit, that day by day we would walk more closely to your will. Transform us, O Lord, that we might be recreated into the image of Christ, in whose name we pray. Amen.

SERMON BRIEFS

STEPS TO GREATNESS

2 SAMUEL 7:1-14*a*

The best-selling book genre today is how-to books. These books are written to describe how you can successfully accomplish something: how to organize your life, become a millionaire in twelve months, start a successful home business, and on and on. Second Samuel 7 reveals how to become spiritually great in three simple steps.

This passage has been called the theological crux, the most important writing in the Samuel materials, and the summit of Deuteronomistic history. It confronts mistaken churchmanship with Yahweh's magnificent Lordship. Through reflection, King David decided to construct a house for the ark of God that would be more appropriate than a tent. Nathan, the palace prophet, initially agreed that David had a good idea. Suddenly, however, the text calls David to a greater purpose. Three spiritual principles define God's greater purpose and how you can find that purpose in your own life.

I. Accept the Call to a Greater Vision

The king desired to do something that was impossible. Yahweh's question in verse 5 implies that David could not possibly build a house to contain God. The word "you" takes the emphasis away from the person and places it on the action. The king also desired something that Yahweh never desired, never requested. Yahweh made his position clear in verse 7; he had always walked with his people and had never asked for a dwelling place.

The destruction of the temple in later years may have occurred because it had not been required by God in the first place. Notice, however, that the house of David survived! This greater vision calls the people of God to walk with him dynamically; with holy lives in daily practice.

237

II. Accept the Call to a Greater Mission

Verses 8-10 describe David's greatness in terms of what Yahweh had accomplished through him. Construction of the temple would have been a symbol of David's ability and power: temporary, decaying, limited. God's mission transcended human comprehension and ability.

Three statements in verses 9-10 detail Yahweh's greater mission. Israel would experience the establishment of God's abiding and guiding presence. David's name would also be made great by the establishment of the Davidic dynasty through a long line of descendants. Those two elements would result in Israel's being granted peace from her enemies.

A mission that transcends the physical and visible in programs, buildings, and budgets positions the church for a greater purpose. Called to become partners in God's mission, the church has a global purpose with unfathomable possibilities.

III. Accept the Call to a Greater Blessing

What David knew God deserved, God would provide for himself: "Moreover the LORD declares to you that the LORD will make you a house" (v. 11). The house of God was to be a place where the people of God would gather to celebrate the glory of God. In the meantime, David was privileged to experience the Lord in a personal, daily relationship.

Today's church gathers, regularly but periodically, to corporately celebrate God's presence. The greater blessing of the church throughout the age, however, is the indwelling presence of God. That presence is permanent, not periodic; dynamic, not symbolic. The greater blessing provides you and me with the privilege of God's personalized presence.

As a result of the greater purposes of God, the people would come to celebrate in later years Yahweh's leadership (v. 12) because of a greater vision; his adequacy (v. 13) because of a greater mission; and his mercy (v. 14) because of a greater blessing. Adopt these steps to greatness and move beyond a less than fulfilling spiritual experience. (Barry J. Beames)

NOTHING BUT GIFT

EPHESIANS 2:11-22

We live in something of an antiauthority age. Authority figures tend to be belittled, and even the very idea of authority finds little acceptance among many people in our day. Tell folks what they "should" do or "ought" to do, and you are likely to receive a questioning look, followed by a cynical, "Why?" While an earlier age could find some moral bearings in such exhortations, the loss of authority has cost many in our day their sense of moral identity. How do we know how to live?

We will not find easy material for oughts and shoulds in this corner of Ephesians. In fact, there is not an exhortation for miles around! Trying to get moral imperatives from these verses is like a dog trying to bite a basketball. Nevertheless, Paul wants us to understand that it is possible to find a moral compass. We can know how to live!

I. We Can Recognize What We Are

Paul wants us to understand that there is no need for "oughts" and "shoulds" when we truly recognize what we are and live true to our identity. Instead of telling us what we ought to be, this text announces what, by the grace of God, we are! In fact, the first three chapters of Ephesians are filled with such announcements of our identity: we are redeemed, we are adopted, we are forgiven; we are given revelation, inheritance, the Holy Spirit, aliveness, grace, kindness, peace, salvation, God's indwelling.

II. We Can Remember What We Are

No exhortation for miles around? I was wrong. There is one, if you can call it an exhortation. It is this: *Remember* (v. 11). Remember who you are—and who you used to be (v. 12). The way the word *remember* comes together in Greek tells us something about how remembering works for the Christian. *An-amnesis* literally means "against-amnesia." In other words, "avoid forgetting."

In a culture that tends to borrow resources more from the future than from the past, we often place little value on the avoidance of forgetting, on remembering who we are and who we used to be. A poster on the wall at a local recreation center says it all. A young boy decked out with sunglasses leans against a beautiful European sports car, his arms folded in self-assurance. The caption reads: "I've worked hard all my life for this."

Arms loaded down with every spiritual blessing, we are asked only one thing, seemingly a modest request: to remember from whom all of these blessings flow.

III. We Can Realize Whose We Are

God's action in Christ of reconciliation, of peacemaking, of building and growing, leads to a culmination: that your life is "a dwelling place for God" (v. 22). A mystical image, perhaps hard to picture concretely, the idea hints at the very best part of the whole range of gifts enumerated here: God's life with us.

So if we haven't read it between the lines so far, the author makes it all clear now: the bestower of all these wonderful gifts has one further purpose in mind—to live with us forever! In such a way, the Giver becomes the ultimate, consummate Gift.

Ever hear anyone say, "I'm trying to get in touch with my true feelings"? God has taken us one step beyond. He has made it possible for us to get in touch with who we really are. And as we see ourselves for who we are, we will see God for who he is—and for all he has done for us! *(Paul R. Escamilla)*

RENEWAL, BELIEVING, AND WHOLENESS

MARK 6:30-34, 53-56

Have you noticed how people want instantaneous miracles these days? Ours is an instant-gratification culture. We want not just miracles, but *instantaneous* miracles. We want illnesses cured, and we pray for them to be cured now. We want financial difficulties relieved, and we buy lottery tickets in hope that all our difficulties will be relieved instantly. We want to lose weight, so we go on another miracle diet that promises us quick and permanent weight loss. We want what we want, and we want it now! Moreover, we want what we want to be bestowed on us with little or no effort on our own part.

These reflections on our instant-gratification society may seem a long way from the text about Jesus' retreat to a lonely place and his response to people who came to him for healing. But the distance is much less than it seems. The text is divided into two sections. Together they tell us two important things about wholeness.

First, we see that Jesus understood the need for regular replenishment and renewal. When the disciples tell Jesus about their travels and teachings, they report that they were surrounded by crowds of people who wanted to be near them and to hear their words. Jesus knew the wear and tear of constantly being available to people. As important as such ministry is, even Jesus could not keep it up without time for renewal and replenishment. So he said to the disciples, "Come away to a deserted place all by yourselves and rest a while."

Throughout my ministry, I have struggled with my need to take time off. It is easy for us to reason that the ministry of the church, or the work at the office, or the volunteer program, or the community project will not get done if we take time off. Have we ever stopped to think that such a view of our indispensability is idolatrous—that we are so important that everything depends on us? And when we try to fulfill the impossible expectations we end up frustrated, or angry, or depressed, or disillusioned. Only then do we realize that we simply cannot meet all the expectations and care for all the needs.

If Jesus knew that he needed time for renewal, prayer, meditation, and refreshment, who are we to think we can continue to minister in his name without replenishment? We are, remember, the culture that has coined the term "workaholic." How desperately we need to recover the practice of retreat, replenishment, spiritual nurture, and care of our souls. That's the first thing this text tells us about wholeness: that we need to replenish the springs of our souls.

And the second thing is this: wholeness is not so much "dropped" on us out of the blue as it is a gift of God to those who believe that God can give it. The text tells us that once people recognized Jesus, they brought their sick to him to be made well. They believed that they would be made whole if they could simply touch the fringe of his cloak. And, "all who touched it were healed."

Think of "healing" in as broad a sense as possible—as physical healing to be sure, but also as a restoration to wholeness. Think of it in terms of healing body, mind, and spirit, which represents wholeness. Think of it as healing the past, which frees persons from captivity to guilt and sin. Think of it as healing the psyche, which releases one from anxiety and restores one to a life of trust and confidence. Then ponder the faith of those who anticipated and expected healing if they could simply touch the fringe of Jesus' cloak.

In the New Testament there is close correlation among the words *healing, wholeness,* and *salvation.* To be healed—physically, mentally, spiritually—is tantamount to being made whole; it is tantamount to being saved. And Christ is the giver of such healing, wholeness, and salvation to those who believe. But believing is not some kind of magical method of getting what we want from God. Rather, it is faith that Christ is the key that can open the door to allow the healing of mind, body, and spirit to come into our lives.

With such a strong connection among healing, wholeness, and salvation in the New Testament, we do well to remember that healing may not always be what we hope for. We may hope for physical healing, but the healing that comes may be strength of spirit and confidence of will to sustain us and see us through the difficulty of a physical illness.

In my first pastorate thirty-four years ago, there was a woman who suffered from severe physical injuries. She had been in a automobile accident years before, in which her husband had been killed and she had been critically injured. Many of her broken bones never knit back together again. She had to be lifted in and out of bed each day. In her last hospitalization, shortly before her death, I was praying with her, and I prayed that we would always know that God is present with us, whatever the circumstances. As I said "Amen," she said, "He is! He is!" Physically she was never restored. But in every other way she was as whole a person as I ever knew.

I believe that Jesus knew something important about the ministry of wholeness, healing, and salvation. He knew that the caregiver must from time to time be replenished. And he knew that wholeness comes to those who, in faith, both expect it and leave its shape to God. If Jesus knew both these things about renewal, believing and wholeness, shouldn't we take a cue from him? (*J. Lawrence McCleskey*)

JULY 27, 1997

❧

Tenth Sunday After Pentecost

Worship Theme: Prayer is God's gift that allows us access to his presence and power.

Readings: 2 Samuel 11:1-15; Ephesians 3:14-21; John 6:1-21

Call to Worship (Psalm 14):

Leader: Fools say in their hearts, "There is no God."

People: They are corrupt, they do abominable deeds; there is no one who does good.

Leader: The LORD looks down from heaven on humankind to see if there are any who are wise, who seek after God.

People: They have all gone astray, they are all alike perverse; there is no one who does good, no, not one.

Leader: Have they no knowledge, all the evildoers who eat up my people as they eat bread, and do not call upon the LORD?

People: There they shall be in great terror, for God is with the company of the righteous.

Leader: You would confound the plans of the poor, but the LORD is their refuge. O that deliverance for Israel would come from Zion!

All: When the LORD restores the fortunes of his people, Jacob will rejoice; Israel will be glad.

Pastoral Prayer:

Our holy and loving God, before whose righteousness we tremble, we confess our sins this day, the many ways we have brought dishonor upon your name and disruption upon our lives. We have fallen short of your great desire for us: to walk purely, to live justly, and to show compassion. Yet we thank you, merciful Lord, for even as we miss the mark, you have provided a means of redemption and reconciliation through Christ our Savior. And because he has given his life for us, O Lord, we praise you that we can now walk with boldness before your throne of grace. Even now, our Father, we stand in your presence in prayer—what an incredible privilege you have given us! Even as we lift up our hearts in praise, so enable us to lift up our lives in service and our voices in witness to the One in whose name we pray. Amen.

SERMON BRIEFS

DON'T PLAY WITH FIRE

2 SAMUEL 11:1-15

For most of her life, a seventy-year-old cleaning woman had worked for the company. Fellow employees decided to honor her and planned a surprise party to express their appreciation. When news of the party was leaked and the woman found out about the plans, she pleaded for them not to throw the party. "That's sweet of you," said her boss, "but it's not necessary for you to be so modest."

"Modest, my foot!" she exclaimed. "I just don't want to have to clean up all that mess!"

King David learned that sin invites us to a party and leaves us to clean up the mess it leaves in our lives. The account of David's sin of adultery with Bathsheba recorded in 2 Samuel 11 reveals three common aspects of sin to motivate us not to play with fire.

I. When You Sin, You Can Expect Public Exposure

David wanted to keep his sin a private experience. In his attempt to remain anonymous David employed others to act on his behalf. He surveyed individuals in the palace to find who the woman next door was. One person told David her name was Bathsheba (v. 3). David also sent others to bring Bathsheba to the palace.

When Bathsheba became pregnant, she sent a messenger to tell David the news. Sin can be defined as an outward expression of inward resistance or rebellion to God's purpose. Even individual acts are known by God. David's choice had consequences beyond his own spirituality. Bathsheba's shame, Absalom's and Uriah's deaths, and preservation of the act in scripture all made a moment of private desire a public event.

II. Sin Results in Accelerated Panic

Verses 6-14 do not reflect a calm and composed response: David panicked. Immediately he sent for Uriah under false pretenses. When Uriah arrived, David tempted him with the privilege of going home to wash his feet, or rest. David also tempted him with royal advantage by catering a feast at Uriah's house (v. 8). The pace quickened when David realized Uriah slept on the porch. Uriah was enticed to an altered state of mind through intoxication. David's attempt was not foiled just by Uriah's patriotism. Even intoxicated, Uriah was more pious than David.

Out of desperation the king became more aggressive. Uriah carried his own death wish as part of a well-orchestrated murder plot. David's actions could never cover his sin. Panic only accelerated the consequences.

III. Personal Exemption: Obedience to God

Personal exemption is a third dimension of the sin event exposed by specific words throughout this text. Notice the supporting characters in this drama.

The word *Bathsheba* means "daughter of Sheba" or "daughter of oath." It was David who disregarded the ritual cleansing rites. Bathsheba was so respected that as "the wife of Uriah" she is mentioned in the genealogy of Jesus in Matthew 1:6.

Uriah means, "Yahweh is my light." According to verse 11, the ark accompanied the army, implying that it was a holy war. Uriah acted with honor, and from innocence. Out of loyalty he never failed to live up to his title, the servant of David (v. 21).

When you outwardly express an inner resistance to the will of God you can expect the public exposure of your sin to result in an accelerated panic that throws life out of control. Or you can experience personal exemption from the consequences of sin by conditioning your life to obey God. *(Barry J. Beames)*

A PRAYER FOR ALL SEASONS

EPHESIANS 3:14-21

Is there a special prayer that has great meaning in your life? For some it might be the Lord's Prayer. For others, the Prayer of Saint Francis has special significance. Both of these prayers are written in the first person: "*Our* Father, who art in heaven"; "Lord, make *me* an instrument of thy peace."

What if we're feeling the need to pray for another person or community, but are not sure how to pray? Paul's prayer on behalf of the Ephesians gives us a good model for such intercession, as he asks essentially three things for them: power, love, and the fullness of God.

I. We Pray for Power

Paul prays for the church to be strong (v. 16). Immediately we think of physical strength, or financial strength, or mental strength. But this prayer is for strengthening "in your inner being with power through his Spirit." In other words, this intercession asks that the Ephesian church be strong where it really counts: deep within. As easily as we might tend to ask for other kinds of strength for another person or for a congregation, this prayer bypasses those strengths for an inner power that steadies and strengthens every other aspect of one's life. This power—spiritual power—is the very best means of support.

II. We Pray for Love

The next phrase of Paul's prayer asks for Christ to dwell in their hearts as they become "rooted and grounded in love" 6. 17). Notice that love is not a free-form emotion that waxes and wanes, comes and goes, ebbs and flows. Neither is it a feeling that we conjure up and tailor to our own disposition.

Love is a "groundedness," a "rootedness," deriving from the occupancy of Christ within the very heart. In other words, there is an objectivity about this love, having to do with the standard of self-giving set by Christ. It is Christ who is to order the heart toward love by living there; such a love should grow deeper, stronger and sturdier with time.

I remember a small Inter-Varsity booklet entitled *My Heart, Christ's Home* The title speaks for itself, and in the course of the booklet various "rooms" in the person's heart are opened up to the question of whether Christ is really welcome there. It is one thing to visit with a friend over lemonade on the front porch, and quite another to invite someone into our medicine cabinet, the family room, or the refrigerator! "May Christ dwell in your hearts," the prayer goes, probably knowing full well how subversive and life-changing such an intercession could turn out to be.

III. We Pray for Fullness

Lastly, Paul prays for something rather peculiar. Put in other words, I would say he's praying for the Ephesian church to be slightly over-whelmed. Here he wants them to comprehend the incomprehensible: breadth, length, height, depth, love that surpasses knowledge . . . so that "you may be filled with all the fullness of God" (v. 19). It is with such a fullness that we can pray with the psalmist, "You, LORD, are all I have, and you give me all I need; my future is in your hands" (Ps. 16:5, GNB).

Power for faithful Christian living; hearts of love; a sense of the fullness of God in our lives. These are not things we should pray only for others; let's ask God to make each of these things living realities in our own lives. *(Paul R. Escamilla)*

A MIRACLE OF MULTIPLIED WITNESS

JOHN 6:1-21

On the northwestern shore of the Sea of Galilee, in an area where much of the ministry of Jesus occurred, there is a small church at a place called Tabgha. Built by Benedictine Fathers in 1982, this church is on the site of two earlier churches, the first built about A.D. 350 and the second about a hundred years later. The second church was destroyed in the early seventh century, and over 1,300 years passed before archaeologists excavated the site and found the re-mains of the two churches.

In their excavations the archaeologists found a beautiful mosaic that had formed part of the altar of the second church building. The mosaic shows a basket of loaves, with a fish on either side of the basket. Very early in the Christian community's life, this site was apparently regarded as the place where Jesus' feeding of the multitude occurred.

It is not surprising that the early Christians would have marked this particular event from the life of Jesus. This miracle story, or "sign" as

John would have designated it, was very important in the early church. It is the only miracle of Jesus that is reported in all four Gospels.

After a particularly intense period of ministry, Jesus had gone off by himself. But the crowds followed him, and at the end of the day they were hungry. So Jesus had the people sit down; he took five loaves and two fish from a boy in the crowd, gave thanks to God, and distributed the food. After everyone had eaten, the disciples gathered up twelve baskets of fragments. And the crowd wanted to make Jesus king, but he went off by himself.

What do you make of this experience reported by all the Gospel writers? All kinds of attempts have been made to rationalize the story: everyone who had food must have shared it; the feeding really referred to spiritual food; it was a symbolic prefiguring of Holy Communion; it was a literal miracle of multiplying food. But all these approaches seem to miss the point.

The text leaves an element of mystery in the account. It says only that the people ate what they wanted and were satisfied. It preserves the element of mystery. Halford Luccock wrote: "The story is a wonderful picture of a tremendous truth of Christian history, that Jesus does multiply above measure for human use whatever of worth is put into his hands. Whatever we give him he will enlarge for the service of human need" (*The Interpreter's Bible,* Vol. 7, p. 743). And George Buttrick once said: "The main truth is that of alliance between man's little and God's abundance. Let reminder be given for our cheer that, if we do what we can in trust and consecration, God will give the increase" (*The Interpreter's Bible,* Vol. 7, p. 432).

Is it not sufficient to say that our task as disciples is simply to do what we can in trust and consecration and leave the increase to Christ? Is it not sufficient to say that our task as disciples is to offer what we can to the causes of Christ—our efforts, energies, money, prayers, concerns, time, love—and allow Christ to take what we offer individually and make of it corporately far more that we are able?

I believe I know at least part of the reason the early Christians regarded this experience of Jesus so seriously. They had seen the attractive and expansive power of the gospel to nourish spiritual hunger and to minister to physical need. And this experience from the life of Jesus reminded them of both dimensions of the gracious and loving ministry of Christ and the church. They believed in the miracle of multiplied witness because they had both received and shared its power. (*J. Lawrence McCleskey*)

AUGUST

୪

Mending the Net, Sharpening the Hoe

Symbol: Stag

The stag has come to typify piety and religious aspirations (Ps. 42:1). It is also the symbol of purity of life and solitude because it seeks refuge in the high mountains.

Text:
"As the deer pants for streams of water,
so my soul pants for you, O God" (Ps. 42:1 NIV).

Invocation:
Almighty God, in Whom I find life, health, and strength, and through Whose mercy I am clothed and fed, grant me a thankful and faithful heart. In the name and spirit of Christ. Amen.

Scripture Focus:
- Psalm 42
- Habakkuk 3:17-19
- Amos 9:13-15
- Exodus 3:1-5

Prayer Focus:
- Pray that you may be refreshed in body and spirit.
- Focus on ways you may accomplish this.
- Recall times in the past of high spiritual energy and refreshment.
- Visualize a time for privacy, reflection, and solitude.
- Seek the discipline of Jesus. Pray early in the morning, and longer than you usually pray.
- Seek the discipline of Jesus to break away from all duties for refreshment and prayer.
- Seek not the gifts of God but the presence of God.

Prayer:
"Come, O Lord, in much mercy down into my soul, and take possession and dwell there. A homely mansion, I confess, for so glorious a majesty, for such as thou art fitting up for the reception of thee, by holy and fervent desires of thine own inspiring. Enter then, and adorn, and make it just as thou can inhabit, since it is the work of thy hands. Give me thine ownself, without which, though thou should give me all that ever thou hadst made, yet could not my desires be satisfied. Let my soul ever seek thee, let me persist in seeking, until I have found, and am in full possession of thee. Amen." (Saint Augustine) *(Bill Self)*

AUGUST 3, 1997

ࣝ

Eleventh Sunday After Pentecost

Worship Theme: We are to live lives that are worthy of God's call.

Readings: 2 Samuel 11:26–12:13*a*; Ephesians 4:1-16; John 6:24-35

Call to Worship (Psalm 51:1-12):

Leader: Have mercy on me, O God, according to your steadfast love; according to your abundant mercy blot out my transgressions.

***People:* Wash me thoroughly from my iniquity, and cleanse me from my sin.**

Leader: For I know my transgressions, and my sin is ever before me.

***People:* Against you, you alone, have I sinned, and done what is evil in your sight, so that you are justified in your sentence and blameless when you pass judgment.**

Leader: Indeed, I was born guilty, a sinner when my mother conceived me.

***People:* You desire truth in the inward being; therefore teach me wisdom in my secret heart.**

Leader: Purge me with hyssop, and I shall be clean; wash me, and I shall be whiter than snow.

***People:* Let me hear joy and gladness; let the bones that you have crushed rejoice.**

Leader: Hide your face from my sins, and blot out all my iniquities.

***People:* Create in me a clean heart, O God, and put a new and right spirit within me.**

Leader: Do not cast me away from your presence, and do not take your holy spirit from me.

All: Restore to me the joy of your salvation, and sustain in me a willing spirit.

Pastoral Prayer:

Almighty God, we lift up our prayers in thanksgiving for your daily care and for the provisions of life; for the joys of family and friends; for the help and encouragement of brothers and sisters in Christ; for the saving love of our Lord and Savior, Jesus Christ. We pray that you will free us from the power of sin in our lives, that we might experience the power and freedom of Christian discipleship. Help us to live day by day in such a way that Jesus will be honored in our words and actions, and that his greatness will be proclaimed through our lives. We ask these things in his wonderful name. Amen.

SERMON BRIEFS

HEALING THE HEART

2 SAMUEL 11:26–12:13a

In Sholem Asch's novel *The Nazarene*, the miracles of Jesus are mocked by a blind man. The blind man could have been healed if he had asked. Jesus responded to his remarks by questioning what shall it avail one to be made seeing with the eyes and have the heart remain blind. God initiated spiritual healing of David's blind heart through an encounter with Nathan.

Known as a judicial parable, this text disguises a real-life violation of the law as a parable told to the guilty person in order to lead him to pass judgment on himself. Spiritual failure obscures God's dynamic purpose for your life. That purpose can be restored, as it was for a broken King David, by healing your heart through a threefold spiritual/therapeutic process.

I. Sin Must Be Raised to a Personal Consciousness

In verses 1-4 of chapter 12, David was brought face to face with his sin. Nathan gave David a parabolic illustration of reality. David had confused fact with fiction by rehearsing his own self-justification. But the significance of the offense is implied by Nathan's use of contrasting opposites: rich man, poor man; many flocks, one lamb. David's personal consciousness was also raised by a private illumination of his resistance to God. The important issue was not the specific act but the nature of the offender. David ignored the sacred value of marriage, revealing the true nature of his heart.

His consciousness was raised further by the prophetic incrimination of his own reticence. In 11:25, David told Joab to not be displeased by Uriah's death, implying that the Lord was pleased with this holy war. The Lord, however, was not pleased with the king.

II. Healing of the Heart Also Requires Prescribed Consequences

Verses 5-6 of chapter 12 confront us with the inconsistency of human judgment. David said the offender "deserves to die." Literally, the word means "son of death" and describes the person's character, not David's sentence. His anger motivated an irrational demand. Verse 6 records the correct legal sentence, according to Exodus 22:1, a fourfold restitution. We do not judge the seriousness of sin the way God does.

An inverted holy justice is another prescribed consequence in verses 7-12. David was told that the sword would never depart from his house, that his wives would be taken from him, and that his secret would be made public. When holy justice replaces human inconsistent judgment, we understand the devastating effects of sin.

The prescribed consequences also reveal an impatient heavenly jealousy. According to verse 14, David's actions had provided God's enemies the opportunity of blasphemy that would bring shame and ridicule on the name of God. The consequences of David's sin were transferred to the child. That severe judgment would immediately restore reverence to Yahweh's name.

III. A Penitent Confession

This is the final phase of the heart's healing. The confession in verse 13 minimizes the person. David accepted full responsibility through an honest confession: "I have sinned."

The confession also maximized David's failure. The word "sinned" is unqualified. Confession of sin must be made without explanation or excuse. The confession of sin must also magnify the Lord. David stated, "I have sinned against the LORD." Yahweh was the object of the confessional act. Although our sin impacts others, it is a rebellious action defying the authority of God.

Your heart can be healed through spiritual therapy that includes a personal consciousness of sin, prescribed consequences for sin, and a penitent confession of sin. *(Barry J. Beames)*

BY WAY OF THANKS

EPHESIANS 4:1-16

Everything thus far in the letter to the Ephesians has been a gift. Beginning from the very first words of the letter ("Grace to you and peace"), every line seems to place more bread in an already overflowing basket. Chapters 1 and 2 give us the announcement and extensive elaboration of the many aspects of God's grace as it has been poured out upon us. Chapter 3 opens with Paul's own self-description as one whose very imprisonment is a sacrifice of love toward those to whom he writes. That chapter closes with an assurance that Paul is giving something else to the church—prayer. Indeed, the very text is almost a gift of praying.

No other passage in the entire New Testament is so fully saturated with a sense of the blessedness of God's people in the church. Reading chapters 1-3 truly gives us a feeling of having been richly gifted. But receiving even the most beautiful and sought-after gift can make us feel awkward if we are not allowed to express due thanks for it. Chapter 4 gives us an opportunity to respond with thanksgiving.

I. The Great "Therefore"

In verse 1, the writer states, "I therefore . . . beg you to lead a life worthy of the calling to which you have been called." In this case, the word "therefore" is the fulcrum balancing all that came before with all that follows. It is the center point between gift and task, call and response, blessing and gratitude.

In Luke 19, Jesus shows love to Zacchaeus; therefore, Zacchaeus redistributes his wealth. In 1 John we are told that God first loves us; therefore, we are able to love. In Acts, the Holy Spirit is given to the church; therefore, the church goes out in mission. And in Ephesians we are reminded that God has showered us with grace and blessings (chapters 1–3); therefore, we can respond with gratitude (chapters 4–5).

II. Worthy Means Shared

The way the writer talks about responding to God's overwhelming initiative is by asking for a "worthy" life in response. By "worthy," the writer means living cooperatively with others. All the virtues enumerated here address what Bonhoeffer referred to as "life together." Verse 3 sums up this emphasis nicely ("making every effort to maintain the unity of the Spirit in the bond of peace"), and the verses immediately following have become the hallmark of the modern ecumenical movement: " . . . one body . . . one Spirit . . . one hope . . . one Lord, one faith, one baptism, one God and Father of us all."

Asking for unity, however, does not require uniformity. On the contrary, the tribute to unity is followed closely by a marvelous litany of the diversity of gifts and graces given to the Body of Christ (v. 11). Many voices make up the gospel song. The goal of unity is not monotone Christians, but harmonizing Christians, whose variety of gifts "promotes the body's growth in building itself up in love" (v. 16). Our best means of showing gratitude to God for all that has been expressed in three chapters of this letter turns out to be more horizontal than vertical. To appreciate God's bounty to us is to live graciously with one another. *(Paul R. Escamilla)*

WHAT IS IT?

JOHN 6:24-35

In this conversation between Jesus and some people who had followed him across the Sea of Galilee, there is a reference to an important event in the history of the Jewish people. After Jesus fed a crowd of 5,000 people, he crossed the Sea of Galilee only to be followed the next morning by some of the crowd. In this conversation about food that perishes and food that endures, the people reminded

Jesus of an event from their history: "Our ancestors ate the manna in the wilderness" (v. 31).

It's a story worth recalling.

The Israelite people had been led out of slavery in Egypt and had wandered for about two months in the wilderness east of Egypt, the area we know as the Sinai peninsula at the northern end of the Red Sea. They believed that it was God, through Moses, who had led them out of Egypt, and this freedom became the defining event in their history. They owed their freedom to God. But two months after they left Egypt, they ran out of food. They began to complain that in Egypt, even though they were slaves, at least they had food to eat.

So Moses talked with God about the situation, and God told Moses that he would "rain bread from heaven" for the people (Exod. 16:4). The next morning dew covered the ground, and when the dew evaporated a flaky substance was left behind. It tasted, we are told, like wafers made with honey, and it could be ground and made into cakes. The story says that when the wandering Israelites first saw the flaky substance on the ground, "they said to one another 'What is it?' For they did not know what it was" (Exod. 16:15).

They called it "manna," and there is an interesting play on words here. The Hebrew phrase for "What is it?" is pronounced something like *man hu*. Man hu; what is it? Manna—"the bread that the Lord has given you." And they ate it for forty years.

When he was reminded of the story, Jesus carried the meaning a step further: "I tell you, it was not Moses who gave you the bread from heaven, but it is my Father who gives you the true bread from heaven. For the bread of God is that which comes down from heaven and gives life to the world." And the people made a request: "Sir, give us this bread always." Jesus said to them, "I am the bread of life. Whoever comes to me will never be hungry." (vv. 32-35).

Remember this the next time you come to the Lord's table for the sacrament of Communion. When we partake of the sacrament we eat bread that resembles the manna provided in the wilderness. And we claim that it represents Jesus, the very Bread of Life.

What is it? It is freedom from the distress of life. It is sustenance in the wilderness of life. It is grace in the pain of life. It is God's presence in the loneliness of life.

What is it? It is rest in the demands of life. It is peace in the disruptions of life. It is community in the isolation of life. It is security in the uncertainty of life.

What is it? It is manna rained from heaven. It is bread that nourishes the soul. It is Christ, the Bread of heaven, which will "feed me till I want no more." (*J. Lawrence McCleskey*)

AUGUST 10, 1997

❧

Twelfth Sunday After Pentecost

Worship Theme: We can encourage others through both words and actions.

Readings: 2 Samuel 18:5-9, 15, 31-33; Ephesians 4:25–5:2; John 6:35, 41-51

Call to Worship (Psalm 130):

Leader: Out of the depths I cry to you, O LORD. Lord, hear my voice!

People: **Let your ears be attentive to the voice of my supplications!**

Leader: If you, O LORD, should mark iniquities, Lord, who could stand?

People: **But there is forgiveness with you, so that you may be revered.**

Leader: I wait for the LORD, my soul waits, and in his word I hope; my soul waits for the Lord more than those who watch for the morning,

People: **more than those who watch for the morning.**

Leader: O Israel, hope in the LORD! For with the LORD there is steadfast love, and with him is great power to redeem.

All: **It is he who will redeem Israel from all its iniquities.**

Pastoral Prayer:

God of wonder and glory, we gather before you in worship; we lift our hearts to you in praise. You are the creator of all, and by your grace you have redeemed us from sin and death. Though we are unworthy of your love, yet you have graciously showered your compassion upon us. You have forgiven us and placed your Spirit within us; surely we can do no less than praise your name. Even as you have touched our lives, O Lord, we know that you wish to enfold many more within your loving embrace. Use us, Lord, to be messengers of divine grace; allow us, Lord, to be instruments of your kingdom work. And even as you support our spirits day by day, so help us to be encouragers of others, making your presence seen and felt through our words and actions. We ask all these things in the name of the One who gave himself for us. Amen.

SERMON BRIEFS

THE HUMPTY-DUMPTY SYNDROME

2 SAMUEL 18:5-9, 15, 31-33

Absalom lay peacefully in his mother's arms as his father, David, looked on. But what a paradox. The child whose name meant "peaceful" would burst upon the pages of history with a vengeance. Murder, seduction, hatred, rebellion, and war would become his trademarks. Even his death would be anything but peaceful.

Absalom suffered from what we could call the "Humpty-Dumpty syndrome." Like the character in the children's rhyme, Absalom thought he couldn't fall, but life came crashing in on him and he did fall! And all the king's horses and all the king's men couldn't put Absalom together again.

What caused Absalom's downfall? How can we avoid his mistakes?

I. Absalom's Life Demonstrated Revenge

The Bible describes the trickery of Absalom's half brother, Amnon, who raped Absalom's beautiful sister, Tamar (2 Sam. 13). Like a cancerous cell, revenge spread quickly in Absalom's heart until it dominated his every waking moment. Revenge asks how to take the law into one's own hands to carry out the punishment of the guilty. David never punished Amnon for his despicable act, but Absalom planned in his heart the steps necessary for revenge, and carried them out (2 Sam. 13:32).

The character flaw of revenge appears as:

- a relentless pursuer never satisfied until hatred is fulfilled.
- desire, not for justice but for selfish victory over another.
- restlessness—until a twisted action is taken.
- fanaticism that leaves logic in the dust.

What about your life? Has someone hurt you so deeply that you have lost sight of equitable punishment and allowed revenge to rob you of life's peace? Get a grip on revenge now. Ask God for forgiveness. Deal with the matter with human help. Get on with life.

II. Absalom's Life Demonstrated a Lack of Moral Responsibility

Absalom carried out his plan by murdering his brother Amnon. He then flees from his act of violence to Talmai, his maternal grandfather (2 Sam. 13:38). At his home he found asylum.

The question of morality is on the mind of the nation. Who is right and who is wrong? Where do we get our morality?

Christians look to the Bible as the foundation for our morality, for which the Ten Commandments forms the basis. The Beatitudes are the principles of sacred attitude (Matt. 5:1-12). Truth, righteousness, and holiness become our watchword and song in life—all of which point to moral responsibility.

III. Absalom's Life Demonstrated a Divorce in Relationships

There is a sad verse in 2 Samuel 16, which reads, "then all the Israelites will hear that your father is your enemy" (v. 21b, New Century Version). Divorce culminates in separation from any type of relationship. Somewhere in Absalom's heart he divorced his dad. It may have started when David refused to punish Amnon for Tamar's rape, but probably it developed years before in quite subtle ways. David's busy schedule of running a nation, going off to war, and ruling a palace all interfered with his relationship with Absalom. What legitimate activities have separated you from someone you love?

IV. Absalom's Life Ends Without Remorse

Remorse never entered Absalom's mind when he became entangled in the large oak tree (2 Sam. 18:9). He probably died cursing his father as he had done all of his life, even as Joab threw the first javelin into his heart (2 Sam. 18:14).

Many people die without any remorse for the things they did or the way they acted. Revenge, immorality, separation, and hatred all contribute to a great fall in life. How can we avoid this kind of scenario? Only by asking God for help, repenting for wrong motives and actions, and daily consecrating ourselves to God. *(Derl G. Keefer)*

LEARNING HOW TO ENCOURAGE OTHERS

EPHESIANS 4:25–5:2

Remember the old children's verse, "Sticks and stones may break my bones, but words will never hurt me"? The older we become the more we realize that words do hurt. Hurtful words coupled with hurtful actions are much more painful than "sticks and stones." The sting of hurtful words and actions can remain with us for years.

Christians ought to encourage others with their words and actions. We often are not sure how to do this. In Ephesians 4:1–5:2, the apostle Paul instructs believers in how to encourage others through words and actions. In these verses we learn six ways to encourage others.

I. We Encourage Others by Speaking the Truth in Love

The first way we can encourage one another is by removing falsehood and speaking the truth in love. This is one coin with two sides. One side states that we must stop lying to each other, while the other side of the coin says we must speak the truth in a loving manner. Many times we try to avoid conflicts by fudging on the truth. We do not want to hurt the other person's feelings, or so we tell ourselves. Actually, we probably don't want to get involved to the point that we put ourselves at risk. Loving relationships, though, mean that we do put ourselves in the place where we can be hurt for another's welfare.

At the same time we must not be blunt to the extent that we needlessly offend. Love must be our guide. We must ask ourselves what is the most loving way to express the truth.

II. We Encourage Others by Not Allowing
Our Anger to Become Sin

A second direction for encouraging others is found in verse 26. While anger is an emotion that arises in any relationship, we must not allow our anger to become sin. Biblical anger always involves a righteous reaction to sinfulness. But biblical anger is always seasoned by love and redemption. Sinful anger wants to hurt and get revenge. Don't allow your anger to damage a relationship. "Do not let the sun go down on your anger."

III. We Encourage Others by Working Hard

Paul expresses a third manner in which we can encourage other people, and that is through sharing the goods we have gained through hard work. In verse 28 we are admonished not to steal but to work hard in order to have something to share with those who are in need. Sometimes the best thing we can do for someone is to supply a material need. Providing food or clothes or paying a medical bill can build others up in ways we could never imagine. The only way we can meet such a need is to be in a position financially to do so. Consequently, our income through gainful employment becomes a means for encouraging others.

IV. We Encourage Others by Speaking Positive Words

Verse 29 is a verse that seems to tower over the rest of the passage. Words are not neutral. The words we say are either positive, which means they build up other people, or they are negative, which means they tear down other people. Evaluating our words as to whether they are positive or negative is one of the most difficult things for us to do.

We need to be concerned with more than what we say and why we say it. We must be mindful of the way the other person hears and receives what we say. Perhaps the most encouraging thing we can do for others is to use our words to build them up.

V. We Encourage Others by Forgiving Them

The fifth way our passage teaches us to build up others is by forgiving them. Forgiveness means not taking into account wrongs we suffer. Forgiveness also involves treating the one who has sinned against us as though he or she has not done anything to us. We can forgive others even if they do not ask for our forgiveness, but full reconciliation takes place only when they admit their wrongs and ask our forgiveness.

Think of the times in your life when you have had to ask for forgiveness. Can you remember how encouraging it was when you received forgiveness? So we need to be "tenderhearted, forgiving one another, as God in Christ has forgiven you."

VI. We Encourage Others by Walking in Love

Paul's final exhortation on how we can encourage others is to walk in love. Our whole attitude and demeanor should be characterized by love. Such a character trait includes putting others before ourselves, wanting and working for the best for and in others, being patient and kind, and hoping and believing in others. Love is an action and not soupy sentimentality. We can encourage others best when we love them most.

The apostle Paul has given us practical instruction into exactly how we can encourage other people. The hard part for us is to apply what we know is right. Our relationships with each other deserve the greatest effort we can exert. When we put into practice what the Scriptures teach us we enjoy healthy and happy relationships. (*Douglas Walker*)

SATISFACTION GUARANTEED

JOHN 6:35, 41-51

Hunger hurts! When you haven't had enough to eat it is painful. I vividly remember a meal shared with fellow theological students. After we had said grace one student said to me, "I just don't understand why we pray over our food. None of us have ever been without food. Most of us have eaten too much of it today, and we are struggling with a weight problem. We should not be grateful for food, but grateful when we can resist its allure."

This person's problem was that he had never been without food before, never been weakened because of the lack of food. The average person in the world will eat one small meal today, and 10,000 will die due to the lack of food. Hunger hurts!

Hunger for food was assumed in biblical times, and with the context of this universal experience Jesus spoke the controversial words, "I am the bread of life." It was a statement that was sure to get everyone's attention. What was Jesus saying about himself?

I. I Am a Staple

Verse 41 says that "the Jews began to complain about him because he said, 'I am the bread that came down from heaven.' " It didn't take them long, did it? Wouldn't you complain about me if I said, "I am the bread of life." You would consider that outrageous! They thought it was ridiculous that Jesus should make such an audacious claim. "Is not this Jesus, the son of Joseph, whose father and mother we know?" (v. 42).

Bread is a universal staple. It was in biblical times, and it is now. According to *Webster's*, a *staple* is a "chief item of trade, regularly stocked and in constant demand"; "a most important, leading principal." Jesus is claiming that life is made up of many pressures, many opinions, many struggles, many decisions, but there is one thing that is basic to all of life—himself.

The Jews had every right to complain about someone who would make such a broad claim. Either Jesus was someone they had never encountered before, or he was in need of the services of the mental health clinic.

II. I Satisfy

It is no secret that God has created us with a "God-space" in our lives, and until we fill it with God we will be hungry and thirsty. Job expressed this when he cried, "Oh, that I knew where I might find [God], that I might come even to his dwelling!" (23:3).

Jesus guarantees that he will fill the hunger that we all have for spiritual fulfillment.

Job's cry is the cry of everyone. Nothing satisfies our longing for the Deity but the Divine. Junk food may relieve our hunger for a time, but a steady diet of junk food will produce indigestion. Likewise, if we try to fill our spiritual hunger with things of the world, we will never be satisfied. Jesus is the staple that permanently satisfies our desire to have fellowship with our Creator. When we accept Jesus we are satisfied. Satisfaction guaranteed . . . by God. (*C. Thomas Hilton*)

AUGUST 17, 1997

❧

Thirteenth Sunday After Pentecost

Worship Theme: Prayer is a means of bringing our lives into submission to God's will.

Readings: 1 Kings 2:10-12; 3:3-14; Ephesians 5:15-20; John 6:51-58

Call to Worship (Psalm 111):

Leader: Praise the LORD! I will give thanks to the LORD with my whole heart, in the company of the upright, in the congregation.

People: **Great are the works of the LORD, studied by all who delight in them.**

Leader: Full of honor and majesty is his work, and his righteousness endures forever.

People: **He has gained renown by his wonderful deeds; the LORD is gracious and merciful.**

Leader: He provides food for those who fear him; he is ever mindful of his covenant.

People: **He has shown his people the power of his works, in giving them the heritage of the nations.**

Leader: The works of his hands are faithful and just; all his precepts are trustworthy.

People: **They are established forever and ever, to be performed with faithfulness and uprightness.**

Leader: He sent redemption to his people; he has commanded his covenant forever. Holy and awesome is his name.

All: **The fear of the LORD is the beginning of wisdom; all those who practice it have a good understanding. His praise endures forever.**

Pastoral Prayer:

Our Father and our God, we come to rest in the shadow of your throne, weary from our daily struggle and seeking the comfort of your presence. Thank you, Lord, that you allow us to come into your very presence, despite our unworthiness. Though we are a sinful people, rebellious and prone to follow our own foolish will, yet you have redeemed us, forgiven us, and given us access to your presence through our Savior and your Son, Jesus Christ. Even as we lay before you our intercessions—the anxieties, the concerns, the needs of our lives—we are comforted in the knowledge that you know our needs before we know them, and that you will provide for us in the way that is for our good. Help us to know your will more clearly and to obey you more faithfully. In Christ's name, Amen.

SERMON BRIEFS

A PRAYER FOR WISDOM

1 KINGS 2:10-12; 3:3-14

The message of the text reveals Solomon's desire to be a man communicating with God. At this point in his life he was unencumbered with selfishness, distractions, and the allure of unlimited power. The prayer he uttered shows a preoccupation with faithfulness, obedience, and fellowship with God.

At this innocent time in Solomon's life he was inviting the Almighty to rule over him. Later in his life this king would lose sight of God and begin to prostitute himself with foreign gods. Here, at the beginning of his rulership, he was accountable to the true God.

Let's examine Solomon's prayer for true wisdom.

I. It Is a Prayer of Praise

Solomon remembers the graciousness and kindness of a loving God. Walter Bruggemann wrote: "Solomon sets himself in the history of Yahweh with his people. The context for prayer is a recital of the long history of graciousness which reshapes and redefines this moment of prayer. Such prayer is never in a vacuum, but always in a context of faithful remembering and a grateful resolve to continue this family in faith."[1]

Life is lived to the fullest when we remember God is in charge. Our praise reaches God's heart as we reach out in availability to him. True praise goes to him for who he is, not because of what he gives us materially. He must be the object of our adoration, reverence, and awe. Praise glorifies God.

Richard Lee has said, "Oh, for a heart that is fixed on God no matter what happens. Oh for a devotion to Him that is steadfast, for lips that will praise His unchanging love and faithfulness, though all the world crumbles around our feet. This is the praise that pleases the Father and brings glory to His name."[2]

II. It Is a Prayer of Submission (3:7)

Honest submission understands where life and power originate. This prayer waits on God. Solomon solicits God's power and submits to it.

Stephen Beck observed that while driving down a country road one day he came to a very narrow bridge. In front of the bridge was a sign stating, "Yield." Since no other cars were coming he continued across the bridge to his destination.

On the return trip he came to the same one-lane bridge, but from the other direction. To his surprise there was another yield sign posted. The two signs were placed on each end to help prevent drivers from having head-on collisions.

When we submit to God for all of life, it is to avoid a head-on collision with God's will for our lives. A quick outline to help us remember that submission is God's plan follows:

Submission is the secret of power.

Submission is the source of praise.

Submission is the steam of purpose.

Submission is the satisfaction of planning.

E. Stanley Jones wrote: "Life holds nothing within it which Christ has not conquered." Solomon would have understood that perfectly.

III. It Is a Prayer of Concern (3:9)

Notice that Solomon wanted a listening heart to hear God speak. He does not ask for personal wealth, health, or power; but rather for *wisdom* to lead. It demonstrates a compassion and concern for the people he rules. That was his passion.

Janet Curtis O'Leary said, "Pity weeps and runs away; Compassion comes to help and stay." Wisdom knows the difference between the two.

IV. It Is a Prayer that God Answers (3:10-13)

The miracle of this prayer rests on God. He answered the king in a way that far exceeded Solomon's hopes or dreams. God surpasses the minimal heart requests and gives him that for which he does not ask—riches and honor.

When we submit ourselves in faith and obedience, God will provide blessings for us beyond anything we anticipate. *(Derl G. Keefer)*

---

[1] Walter Brueggemann, Knox Preaching Guide (John Knox Press, 1982), p. 11.
[2] Richard Lee, Windows of Hope (Multnomah Press, 1992), p. 84.

FOLLOWING THE INSTRUCTIONS

EPHESIANS 5:15-20

Recently I was reminded that it is important to carefully read the directions when putting together children's toys. My son had been wanting a basketball goal, so my wife and I gladly obliged. In order to save a little money we went to Sam's Wholesale and purchased a goal that we had to assemble. I was tired (can you tell I am already making excuses?) and hurried through the complicated assembly instructions (another excuse?).

The first step stated to put one pole inside another and beat on the ground four to six times to ensure a proper mesh. My error was that I put the wrong ends together and beat furiously until I couldn't separate the two poles. We ended up having to order another pair of poles from the manufacturer. Needless to say, I have heard from my family about the importance of carefully reading instructions.

In one sense the New Testament is an instruction manual for life. When you and I carefully read the instructions and follow them, our lives run much smoother.

In this text, the apostle Paul gives us some instructions for living the Christian life. Our task is to read carefully and to follow completely the directions we read. Notice the three clear directives in this section of Scripture.

I. Walk Wisely

The first instruction says to be careful to walk wisely. Verse 16 clarifies that Paul most likely has in mind what we would call time management. We need to be wise in how we spend our time. In this last decade of the twentieth century, schedules are fuller and demands on time are greater than at any other period in history. Christians have the opportunity to demonstrate their commitment to Christ simply by the way we choose to spend our time.

With the proliferation of calendars and other scheduling helps, time management has become an industry unto itself. Christians should think in terms of priorities when planning schedules. Part of our daily calendars ought to include quality time alone with God and with our family, ministry opportunities, as well as our regular work routine.

II. Understand the Will of the Lord

Paul's second suggestion is to not be foolish but to understand the will of the Lord (v. 17). The context seems to indicate that this verse is linked to the preceding two verses. This verse would then relate to knowing God's will for our lives on a daily basis.

Often we are concerned about knowing God's will for the big things in our lives, such as job, school, or mate. God is not only interested in the big decisions of life but also in the daily development of character and our own practice of the Christian life. Knowing God's will for how we schedule our routine every day seems to be the direction of Paul's thought.

The big question becomes, "How do we know God's will?" At this point Paul gives no definitive answer; however, the last three chapters of Ephesians comprise a textbook of sorts of how we ought to conduct our lives. Learning more of how we are to live the Christian life answers the question of what God's will is on a daily basis. Here, being wise means that we organize our lives around the things we ought to be doing, which is the will of God for our lives.

III. Be Filled with the Spirit

The final instruction for living the Christian life that Paul writes in this passage is to be filled with the Holy Spirit. We are to be controlled by the Spirit of God in the same way a drunk is controlled by alcohol. The analogy should show us the importance of the work of the Holy Spirit in our everyday life.

What does it mean to be filled with the Spirit? According to verses 19-20, three things occur when we are filled with the Spirit: we speak with joy to one another, we are joyful in our hearts, and we give thanks to God. If one is filled with the Spirit, he or she speaks to others in psalms, hymns, and spiritual songs. The one who is filled with the Spirit also makes melody and sings in his or her own heart. Joyfulness of the inner person is the evidence of the Holy Spirit's control. Finally, the one who is filled with the Spirit gives thanks to God for all things.

Just as following the instructions will lead to success in assembling a child's toy, following the instructions for the Christian life will lead to successful living. *(Douglas Walker)*

A DARING DISCOURSE

JOHN 6:51-58

What in the world was Jesus doing that stirred up so many people? First, Jesus' hearers complained (6:41), and now they "disputed among themselves" (v. 52). He didn't seem to bring much peace of mind; instead he caused controversy wherever he went. He seemed to be a troublemaker who was out to make waves as big as he could.

I. A Literally Repulsive Idea

Cannibalism is repulsive, and so Jesus was daring to talk about eating his flesh and drinking his blood. The Jews especially would find such talk repulsive because of their dietary law (see Lev. 17:10, 11). They did not drink the blood of animals and certainly would not drink the blood of humans. Jesus was intentionally risking offending his hearers with that kind of talk. But he took the risk, knowing full well the consequences.

He took the risk because he wanted to reveal as clearly as possible the biblical God. He took the risk, knowing full well that some would intentionally misconstrue what he said in order to ridicule him. He knew that would happen. All public speakers have their opponents. All preachers have challengers who feel they don't know anything about anything, and if an opportunity comes along to give a double meaning to something these people jump on it. This was such a double-meaning statement, and Jesus' listeners jumped on it.

For Christians today, the body and blood of Christ are symbolized by the bread and cup in the sacrament of Holy Communion. The meaning behind the symbolism is what brings us to the Lord's table, and that meaning is what many of Jesus' listeners failed to grasp.

II. We Become One with Christ

In this text, Jesus is encouraging his disciples to be so closely aligned with him that their flesh becomes one. Our daily lives are to become so closely identified with his that we become one with Christ. This is a reminder that as Jesus lived and died in the flesh so we too live and die in the flesh; that as Jesus suffered, so will his disciples suffer; that as Jesus died and rose again from the dead, so will we who have put our faith in Jesus Christ as our Lord and Savior one day die and rise again to new life.

Loretto McMahon died on August 28, a few years ago. Her obituary in the Ft. Lauderdale paper said she was eighty-eight years old and "was born and raised in Chicago, Illinois, where she spent most of her life in the food services industry as waitress, secretary, and owner of a tea room in Aurora, Illinois. She retired to Ft. Lauderdale, and although she never married, she created an extended family of wonderful friends. She was courageous and caring. She is best remembered as a woman who recognized that making a meal for friends is a way of sharing time, talent, and treasure. In lieu of any form of memorial, why not share a meal with friends and tell them you love them."

When you do this the "living bread" (v. 51) will continue to live in you. (*C. Thomas Hilton*)

AUGUST 24, 1997

Fourteenth Sunday After Pentecost

Worship Theme: God has provided the tools we need to win spiritual victory.

Readings: 1 Kings 8:(1, 6, 10-11) 22-30, 41-43; Ephesians 6:10-20; John 6:56-69

Call to Worship (Psalm 84):

Leader: How lovely is your dwelling place, O LORD of hosts! My soul longs, indeed it faints for the courts of the LORD;

People: my heart and my flesh sing for joy to the living God.

Leader: Even the sparrow finds a home, and the swallow a nest for herself, where she may lay her young, at your altars, O LORD of hosts, my King and my God.

People: Happy are those who live in your house, ever singing your praise.

Leader: Happy are those whose strength is in you, in whose heart are the highways to Zion. As they go through the valley of Baca they make it a place of springs; the early rain also covers it with pools.

People: They go from strength to strength; the God of gods will be seen in Zion.

Leader: O LORD God of hosts, hear my prayer; give ear, O God of Jacob!

People: Behold our shield, O God; look on the face of your anointed.

Leader: For a day in your courts is better than a thousand elsewhere. I would rather be a doorkeeper in the house of my God than live in the tents of wickedness.

People: **For the LORD God is a sun and shield; he bestows favor and honor.**

Leader: No good thing does the LORD withhold from those who walk uprightly.

All: **O LORD of hosts, happy is everyone who trusts in you.**

Pastoral Prayer:

O holy and righteous Lord, we offer to you the praise that is your due, and we worship you with glad and joyful hearts. We praise you, O Lord, for providing us a fellowship of believers, where we can come to worship and where we find fellowship and family. In the midst of a challenging world, where paganism seems to flourish and your love is so often ignored, help us to have a renewed faithfulness to the service of your kingdom. Give us strength for the battle; equip us for the struggle. And yet, Lord, help us to remember always that the battle ultimately is yours; unless we rely on your power, we will not find true victory. Give us grace and power for the living of these days, even as we ask it in the name of the Living Christ who has already won the victory. Amen.

SERMON BRIEFS

GOD IS THE PROMISE

1 KINGS 8:(1, 6, 10-11) 22-30, 41-43

Inside the human spirit there rises a desire to seek, know, experience, and please God. Sometimes there is a question as to whether God will meet us. Yet on other occasions we boldly claim God's presence and feel God's special touch on our individual lives or in our public services.

Like a printer's trademark of several years ago, God draws a circle and writes, "I never disappoint." God makes promises to his people.

I. God Promises His Presence (vv. 1, 6, 10-11)

Solomon is the faithful king with much promise, but he keenly realizes the desperate dependency of his rulership on God's presence. In preparation for the temple dedication he brings out the symbol of God's promises—the Ark of the Covenant. Inside the ark were the two tablets of stone with the law written on them and—according to the writer of Hebrews—a pot of manna and Aaron's rod. These were constant reminders that God would not leave nor forsake his people.

Today there are symbols to remind us of God's presence. Symbols for the New Testament church abound, such as the cross, bread and fruit of the vine, the empty tomb, and a crown. They help us along our spiritual journey to visualize God's leadership and presence by giving us proper understanding of God's glory.

II. God Promises His Covenant Love (vv. 22-26)

Solomon's prayer of temple dedication begins with a statement of promise that God would give his love. However, for Israel to maintain its favored nation status, it must meet the condition that God laid down—wholehearted devotion to him. This accomplishment would occur if the people walked with him in obedience and trust. The question was not if God would love them, rather would they love God?

That remains the question today. God loves us, as John 3:16 states emphatically. The "whosoever will believe" gives us the condition. Acceptance of the promise gives us the special "favored person" status.

III. God Promises His Concern (vv. 27-30)

These verses indicate that God can be visited in his sanctuary made by hands; however, God is not limited to just the temple. The Almighty God dwells in heaven and is on the earth, literally everywhere. We cannot box him in or domesticate him. He is distant, yet closely attentive to the needs of his people. He quite literally is the awesome God with a personal touch. Only a God free from us can really help us.

God's love is concerned with our circumstances. He abides with us and works with us. He graciously makes a difference in our lives. God inclines his heart, ears, and eyes toward us. We can have genuine confidence in this great God that Solomon speaks of in this text.

IV. God Promises His Answer (vv. 41-43)

The Lord is the answer to life's needs, questions, and sins. This God of promise comes to all who genuinely seek to know his forgiveness, love, and presence. Step by step God will lead us if, in faith, we follow. Our lives can be built on him. Our need is to worship God in spirit and in truth! Will you? *(Derl G. Keefer)*

SPIRITUAL WARFARE

EPHESIANS 6:10-20

Everyone who has ever tried to live the Christian life would admit that it is a struggle. Our vision is so limited that we only see the physical things with which we wrestle. We focus on ourselves, our circumstances, and others. In the later portions of Ephesians, chapter 6, the apostle Paul attempts to redirect our sights. He tells us our struggle is not really with flesh and blood, those things upon which we most often focus. Our real conflict is spiritual and with spiritual forces!

This is one of those passages we must read with the eyes of faith. We cannot see with our physical eyes the things about which Paul speaks. More important, Paul discusses how we may have victory in this conflict, which we accept we are in by faith.

We know Paul's exhortation as spiritual armor. Paul gives spiritual meaning to the armor of a Roman soldier. By putting on the armor of God we, too, will be equipped to fight and win in the spiritual struggle in which we find ourselves. Paul describes six pieces of our spiritual armor.

I. We Wear the Belt of Truth

The first part of our spiritual armor is truth. Two ideas are significant about truth. First, Christians should know and believe the truth about who God is and what God has done. This relates to cognitive facts about what the Bible says about God and his mighty acts. Human notions of God will not do. Second, we must be truthful people. Telling the truth to ourselves and others, in love, is essential in the spiritual battle in which we are engaged.

275

II. We Wear the Breastplate of Righteousness

Another aspect of our spiritual armor is right living. Many a believer has been sidelined due to corrupt behavior. The visual image is the piece of armor that protects the chest and heart. In order to protect this large area of the body a large sheet of metal was fashioned to guard it. The protection for our spiritual lives is personal holiness.

III. Our Feet Are Shod with the Gospel of Peace

This third item of equipment calls us to evangelism and missions. Every believer is to be actively involved in sharing the good news of salvation in Jesus Christ alone. When we fail to spread the word about Christ we are unprepared for spiritual conflict. Along with personal evangelism we can be part of mission efforts away from our homes. Church planting, church construction, and short-term mission volunteers are specific ways we take the gospel of peace to those around us and the world.

IV. We Wear the Shield of Faith

A defense device that allowed the bearer to fend off arrows and spears was the shield. Likewise, Christians can extinguish the fiery darts of the enemy by clinging to faith in the Lord Jesus Christ. Defining faith is often easier than explaining how to live by faith. A life of faith is characterized by dependence on the Lord. Paul wrote to the church at Rome that whatever was not of faith was sin (Rom. 14:23). Perhaps another way of looking at the life of faith is to think in terms of pleasing the Lord. Does what I am doing bring pleasure to the Lord? Faith is a vital part of our spiritual armor.

V. We Wear the Helmet of Salvation

Even in ancient days helmets were used to protect the head from injury. Perhaps no part of the body is as susceptible to a mortal wound as is the head. We safeguard our heads by wearing helmets when we ride bicycles and play sports.

In the spiritual realm this important body part represents salvation. Nothing can rival the necessity of our own salvation for victorious Christian living. The assurance of our salvation becomes a security from doubts and dismay. Discouragement, which is one of our very real opponents, is thwarted by confidence that the Lord has saved us. Salvation by grace through faith stands as a pillar of strength in the midst of our spiritual conflict.

VI. We Carry the Sword of the Spirit

The final piece of our spiritual armor is the sword of the Spirit. Of course the analogy refers to the Word of God. As believers we should hear, read, study, apply, memorize, and meditate on the Bible.

It's interesting that Scripture is the only part of the equipment that is for offense in this spiritual conflict. While Holy Writ is not to be a weapon for us to use in order to beat others over the head, it should serve to help us move forward in the Christian life. Apart from the Word we have no clear guidance and would be left only with our feelings. God's Word enables us to press the fight toward our spiritual enemies who are not flesh and blood.

Paul concludes this section of scripture with a clear admonition to prayer. As we take up the full armor of God and couple it with prayer we can conquer the spiritual forces that wage war against us. (*Douglas Walker*)

DIFFICULT TEACHING

JOHN 6:56-69

Jesus is preaching in the synagogue at Capernaum to people of faith. This is not a public discourse in the sense that he was standing on the street corner preaching to people with no religion. Jesus knew the Jews believed. Jesus knew the Jews practiced their faith. Jesus knew the Jewish faith and claimed to the Jews that their faith had now been fulfilled by his arrival. He did not try to destroy their faith, but to fill it more full of divine truth.

Jesus claims to be the "bread" that "came down from heaven" and that the "one who eats this bread will live forever." When his life became their own life then they would live forever, just as Jesus was going to live forever.

I. The Disciples' Difficulty

One could assume that the casual attender at the synagogue would have difficulty with such a teaching, but one would hope that his disciples would "get it." They didn't! John goes out of his way to point out that many of the close followers of Jesus found this teaching to be difficult.

Other translators have the disciples responding: "This is very hard to understand. Who can tell what he means?" (TLB). "This is more than we can stomach!" (NEB). "This is intolerable language. How could anyone accept it?" (JB). Such comments from a casual observer could be expected, but not from his faithful followers. John says that Jesus' disciples were complaining. Jesus' claim to be the living bread that would provide eternal life for all who believe in him was dividing people into camps.

Jesus' response was to say to his disciples, in so many words, "So this offends you? Wait until the Ascension. If my claim to come from God is difficult teaching, wait until I return to God after the Resurrection. You haven't seen anything yet. Stick around." Many did not. They had had enough and they went back to their Judaism, or whatever. But not Peter.

II. Nowhere Else to Go

When the outer circle of disciples began to thin, Jesus turned to his inner circle of twelve and challenged them to make a decision. Peter then made it clear that he (for a while anyway) got the gospel message and he would cast his lot with Jesus. As a matter of fact he felt that there was nowhere else to go, for Jesus had "the words of eternal life."

The challenge here is to those of us who already consider ourselves disciples. Jesus keeps stretching our faith. Jesus keeps saying, "You have come this far, come a little farther. You have committed this much, commit a little more. You love these people, now open your arms to these people. You have compassion for the one hurting person in front of you, now broaden that compassion to all hurting people in God's world."

Grow, grow, grow. Jesus is continually trying to remold us into his likeness, which means that there are few way stations along the journey at which we can rest.

Clarence Jordan visited an integrated church somewhere in the southern United States. He asked the uneducated preacher, "How did the church get this way?" The pastor explained the message he preached: "If you're one with Jesus, you've one with all kinds of folks. And if you ain't you ain't."

"What happened?" Jordan asked.

"Well," the preacher said, "the deacons took me into the back room and told me they didn't want to hear that kind of preaching no more. So I fired them deacons! Then I preached that church down to four. And not long after that it grew and grew and grew. And I found out that revival sometimes don't mean bringing people in, but gettin' the people out who don't love Jesus."

Jesus knew his teachings would be difficult in a fallen world. He never promised us an easy time. He promised us his presence. *(C. Thomas Hilton)*

AUGUST 31, 1997

꙾

Fifteenth Sunday After Pentecost

Worship Theme: Outer obedience results from an inner transformation.

Readings: Song of Songs 2:8-13; James 1:17-27; Mark 7:1-8, 14-15, 21-23

Call to Worship (Psalm 45:6-7):

Leader: Your throne, O God, endures forever and ever.

***People:* Your royal scepter is a scepter of equity;**

Leader: you love righteousness and hate wickedness.

***All:* Therefore God, your God, has anointed you with the oil of gladness beyond your companions.**

Pastoral Prayer:

Our Lord and our God—almighty, glorious, beyond human comprehension. We thank you that you have revealed yourself through Jesus Christ and shown us that you are a God of love as well as power; that you are Lord of grace as well as of judgment. You are our source of life, our sanctuary, our redeemer. Even as you have performed the miracle of creation, so we pray that you will do a miraculous work in our lives and hearts. We need to be transformed, not simply on the outside but from within. Let your Spirit flow freely in our hearts, that we might day by day be more like Jesus, in whose name we pray. Amen.

SERMON BRIEFS

THE DREAM OF LOVE

SONG OF SOLOMON 2:8-13

The theme of the book of the Song of Solomon is a "celebration of love." Bible scholars have interpreted this passage several ways.

Some scholars believe that this love is between a man and a woman. Many view the song as a love poem about King Solomon and his bride. Others view it as a triangle of love: a shepherd figure who is the real lover and who wins the girl's heart over the romantic advances of the king. Still others view this as a collection of unrelated love poems with no overarching story line at all. And some Bible interpreters comment that this lover's song is an allegory depicting either God's wholesale love of the nation of Israel or Christ's love for the church.

The text can be titled, "The Dream of Love," and seen as a dream of romantic love or spiritualized as a dream for the divine love of God. In the text, notice first:

I. The Excitement of Love (vv. 8-9)

Have you ever been away from your sweetheart for any length of time? What was missing? The touch, eyes, and voice. Most of all what was missing was the companionship! Companionship is the ability to share surface conversation and intimate thoughts as well. When I am with my love, my wife, she doesn't have to speak a word. Simply knowing that she is near comforts me. There is a calming effect that all is well. When I have been away for a conference and get close to home, my heart starts beating faster and I begin to visualize her in my mind. When we embrace, I know that all is right with the world and a peace settles over me.

The crescendo of love heightens as the girl anticipates her lover "leaping across the mountains, bounding over the hills" (v. 8, NIV) in order to be with her. It is great to have someone love us. God's love for us is like that.

II. The Invitation of Love (v. 10)

Even when sin separated us from God, God still loved us so much that he sent his one and only Son out searching for us. In our foolishness we mistreated him by ignoring his invitation to abide with him. Yet our hearts were lonely and empty and there was a longing for real life. God dealt with us through his preachers and laypeople sharing the gospel and being people of intercession—praying for us to respond to the invitation of Jesus.

When we began facing the truth and understanding the God that longed for us, we responded. A new excitement filled our hearts! He created in us a new heart with new ambitions and goals. He became our friend for eternity!

III. The New Life of Love (vv. 11-13)

In Palestine the winter dumps heavy, cold rain upon the ground and people. The gray clouds give off a feeling of despair and gloom.

The spring ushers in a new sense of optimism with its warm sun that calls forth life from the moist earth. With the arrival of spring comes the ripening of the figs on the trees and the blossoms become tender grapes. The migrating turtledove returns with the warm weather. All is new. All of this new life in nature creates the mood, the ambiance, the feeling of lovers in love. Life is fresh and exciting.

The obvious spiritual comparison unfolds for us. When we find our lover, God, the newness is everywhere. We have a new name: Christian. A new heart: transformed. A new personhood: redeemed. A new home: heaven. But new life comes only because we have the lover with us—God! (*Derl G. Keefer*)

PUTTING IT INTO PRACTICE

JAMES 1:17-27

There are moments when golf is one of the most exhilarating games on earth. Two minutes later golf can be the most frustrating game on earth. Golf is a sport where many times a player knows what to do but just can't do it. A golfer sometimes has difficulty putting into practice what he or she knows to do.

The Christian life at times is like golf. The Christian knows what to do but sometimes just doesn't do it. The book of James helps and encourages us as Christians to put into practice what we know to do. In this passage from James we find three clear exhortations to do what we know to do. James answers the question: "How can I put into practice what I know I should do?"

I. Acknowledging God's Perfection (vv. 17-18)

James lists for us some of God's perfections. Every good thing that is given and every perfect gift comes from the Father, which demonstrates his perfection. The blessings of life, such as family, food, friends, health, and material blessings, are all evidences of God's goodness and grace. As we acknowledge God for his perfection our hearts should overflow into thanksgiving to him.

Our heavenly Father exists in such perfection that there is no variation in him or shadow of turning. What a stark contrast between the creatures and the Creator! As further evidence of God's perfection, James speaks of God's will in bringing us to salvation. All of this should evoke in us an acknowledgment of who God is, which will enable us to put into practice what we know.

II. Thinking of Others First

James instructs us to place others before ourselves in order to put into practice what we know. We are to be quick to hear, slow to speak, and slow to anger. When we practice these characteristics, we genuinely put others before ourselves and show them the kindness and respect of Christ. The hard part, of course, is being consistent in our conduct; James reminds us that our anger and haste does not accomplish the righteousness of God.

Furthermore, we are to be humble and remove all filthiness and wickedness. Such acts show we are thinking of others before we are thinking of ourselves and placing their interests before our own. A lifestyle characterized by thinking of others first demonstrates that the word has been implanted in the soul of that individual.

III. Doing God's Word (vv. 22-27)

The clearest expression of our need to put into practice what we know comes in this section. James pleads with us to be doers of the Word and not mere hearers. The warning is strong for those who do not do the Word—they are deluding themselves.

These words call for personal examination. Each of us should reflect on our own lives to see if we apply what we know. A wise Christian once told me that spiritual maturity is not based on what you know, but on what you do with what you know.

Application of God's Word is the real test for our walk with God. James argues that we deceive ourselves when we do not apply the Bible. In fact, these are some of the strongest words in all of Scripture that warn of self-deception. It is not enough for us to hear and read the Bible if we do not put into practice what we know. As illustrations James cites our ability or inability to bridle the tongue and our willingness to minister to widows and orphans—those with great need.

All of us need to be reminded of the necessity of putting into practice what we know to do. All of us need encouragement and help from time to time to be strong enough to keep practicing what we know is right. May God give us the grace and strength to help and encourage one another to put into practice what we know. (*Douglas Walker*)

INSIDE JOB

MARK 7:1-8, 14-15, 21-23

The world has a crude expression—taken from computer terminology—that goes like this: "garbage in, garbage out." It is meant to warn people that they should carefully select what they read, the movies they see, the friends with whom they associate, and the television programs they watch, for the danger is that you may become that which you see, hear, and associate with. The corollary is, "you are what you eat."

Many people feel that participating in a corrupt world will ipso facto produce a corrupt person. They always assume that the dark will overcome the light and the light will never overcome the darkness. The Bible tells us it can go either way.

I. When the Inner and Outer Don't Match

Inner faith will produce outer actions—there is no doubt about that, and Jesus has no quarrel with that. If, when you feel like praying, you fold your hands, bow your head, close your eyes, and kneel, then your outer posture is rightfully expressing your inner feelings. If you love someone and you greet that person with a hug as a manifestation of your endearment, then your actions are expressing your inner feelings. If you thoroughly enjoy the company of an individual and hence spend most of your time with that person, you are expressing with your body the inner feelings of your heart and mind. Your inner feelings and your outer actions are expressing the same emotions.

Hypocrisy comes when you display the outer actions without the inner feelings: when you bow your head to pray but do not feel like praying; when you hug a person you do not like; or, like Judas Iscariot, when you kiss a person but do not use the kiss as an expression of affection but as some other kind of sign. If you spend time with others in order to use them but do not really like their company, you are being hypocritical because your actions are not an extension of your inner feelings. You must have not only the "words" but the "music" to go along with words.

Jesus wants his hearers to know that their Jewish religion supports such inner faith for he quoted the prophet Isaiah (29:13) "These people . . . honor me with their lips, while their hearts are far from me." That is hypocrisy! Pretending to be something you are not and have no intention of being.

II. It's What's Inside That Counts

If I told you I saw a local pastor one night coming out of a notoriously risqué bar with his arms around some of the drinkers singing loud songs, what would you think? You would wonder what he was up to! I neglected to mention that the pastor had on a Salvation Army uniform and they were singing "Amazing Grace." Well, that's a little different then, isn't it? The pastor's motivation was to witness to Jesus Christ and to rescue the perishing, not join them in their revelry.

The difference is inner motivation. All evil things come from within, but so do all good things. The outward act can be ambiguous and therefore we must look, as God does, upon the inner motivation.

The Christian faith is an inside job. The apostle Paul encouraged the Christians at Philippi with these words: "[W]hatever is true, whatever is honorable, whatever is just, whatever is pure, whatever is pleasing, whatever is commendable, if there is any excellence and if there is anything worthy of praise, think about these things" (Phil. 4:8).

Think and act on these things. When you do, your Christian life will have both the words and the music. *(C. Thomas Hilton)*

SEPTEMBER

❧

Mending the Net, Sharpening the Hoe

Symbol: Lamp

The burning lamp is the symbol of the living personality of God (see Psalm 132:17). Because of its light it is the symbol of wisdom and piety. The Word of God is the lamp unto the faithful.

Text:

"Here I will make a horn grow for David and set up a lamp for my anointed one" (Ps. 132:17 NIV).

Invocation:

"Almighty God, unto whom all hearts are open, all desires known, and from whom no secrets are hidden: Cleanse the thoughts of our hearts by the inspiration of thy Holy Spirit, that we may perfectly love thee, and worthily magnify thy holy name; through Christ our Lord. Amen." (From *The Book of Worship*)

Scripture Focus:
- Psalm 132:17
- Psalm 119:105
- Judges 7:9-25
- Psalm 62:5-8
- Matthew 25:1-13
- Proverbs 6:23
- Proverbs 13:9

Prayer Focus:
- Visualize your pulpit as a lamp burning.
- See your heart and mind as a flaming torch in God's hands.
- Focus on people by name who should see the light of God.
- See the paths of righteousness being lit by God's burning lamp.

Prayer:

"Grant me, even me, my dearest Lord, to know thee and to love thee, and to rejoice in thee. And, if I cannot do these perfectly in this life, let me at least advance a higher degree every day, until I can

286

come to do them in perfection. Let the knowledge of thee increase in me here, that it may be full hereafter. Let the love of thee grow every day more and more here, that it may be perfect hereafter; that my joy may be great in itself, and full of thee. I know, O God, that thou art a God of truth; make good thy gracious promises to me, that my joy may be full. Amen." (St. Augustine) *(Bill Self)*

SEPTEMBER 7, 1997

❧

Sixteenth Sunday After Pentecost

Worship Theme: Authentic faith produces Christlike actions.

Readings: Proverbs 22:1-2, 8-9, 22-23; James 2:1-10 (11-13), 14-17; Mark 7:24-37

Call to Worship (Psalm 125):

Leader: Those who trust in the LORD are like Mount Zion, which cannot be moved, but abides forever.

***People:* As the mountains surround Jerusalem, so the LORD surrounds his people, from this time on and forevermore.**

Leader: For the scepter of wickedness shall not rest on the land allotted to the righteous,

***People:* so that the righteous might not stretch out their hands to do wrong.**

Leader: Do good, O LORD, to those who are good, and to those who are upright in their hearts.

***All:* But those who turn aside to their own crooked ways the LORD will lead away with evildoers. Peace be upon Israel!**

Pastoral Prayer:

Almighty God, our souls bless thee, our lips magnify thee, and our spirits within us exult in your presence. We praise you for the glorious redemption you have made available to us through Christ—through his atoning death and his vindicating resurrection. Yet, Lord, we know that too often we fall short of your perfect will for our lives; despite our professions of faith, we still allow temptation to draw us from your path. Forgive us, Father, and help us to find that greater submission to you in which we will also find your perfect peace. Help

SEPTEMBER 7, 1997

us to live, to speak, to act in such a manner that those we encounter
will sense your power and presence within us. May Christ be honored in all we do, all we say, all we think, and all we are, for we ask
it in his precious name. Amen.

SERMON BRIEFS

WHAT'S IN A NAME?

PROVERBS 22:1-2, 8-9, 22-23

A name is only composed of letters that make a sound. It is the
person that bears those letters who is important. No matter how
many other people in the world carry your name, each is different
and you are the only you. I want my name to stand for God.

Solomon wrote in Proverbs 22 some of the characteristics that I
want people to see in me when they call my name.

I. I Want My Name to Carry Honor (vv. 1-2)

How can we gain respect and honor for our names? It comes
through high ethical and moral conduct—label it *integrity*. We
adhere to a high standard of justice and responsibility that is derived
from our connection to God.

The word *honor* for a Greek living during Christ's lifetime meant
"weighty" or "heavy." Gold, for example, was the best example of
something of honor because it was both heavy and valuable. When
we give honor to certain people, we're saying that they carry great
weight with us.

People will honor us because we are faithful to our spouse, ethical
in our conduct at work and church, and have a godly standard. We
are an asset to God.

II. I Want My Name to Be Synonymous
with Generosity (vv. 8-9)

An African boy listened carefully as his teacher explained to the
class why Christians give presents to each other on Christmas Day.

289

The teacher said, "The gift is an expression of joy over the birth of Jesus and friendship for one another."

When Christmas Day arrived, the young boy waited around after class to see his teacher. When everyone had left he handed her a sea shell of exquisite beauty. The beauty startled the teacher and she inquired where he had found such an unusual shell. He told her that there was only one spot where these particular shells were to be found—a certain bay several miles away.

"Why it's gorgeous, but you should not have walked all that way to get a gift for me," the teacher told him.

His dark eyes sparkled as he answered, "Long walk part of gift."

Generosity often means sacrificial giving that comes from deep inside the heart.

III. I Want My Name to Be Synonymous with Compassion (vv. 22-23)

The world lacks compassion. Sometimes it seems as if all we do is shove to get to the head of the line, like junior high students at lunch time. Let somebody else be the last. Who cares? The Greek word for *sympathy* signifies that we are "to feel or suffer with." We align ourselves with the hurting of the world.

Generosity is the response to people's need whereas compassion is the reason. Compassion comes because God's Son is with us. With Jesus' eyes we see the hurt, bleeding, dying world with new appreciation. We see the external and internal needs of humanity. (*Derl G. Keefer*)

LIVING FAITH

JAMES 2:1-10, 14-17

I have two plants in my office. One is alive and the other is artificial. The artificial one is a very low maintenance plant with only occasional dusting required. It never blooms and never gives any signs of life, even though it is green. The living one shows all the signs of life. It needs water and sometimes the leaves bloom. Other times some leaves turn brown and must be trimmed. A cursory glance at the plants will not reveal which one is living and which one is plastic. A closer and more thorough examination does reveal which plant is the living one.

Some people in the church resemble the two plants in my office. While some are genuine and alive, others only give the appearance of spiritual life but in reality are fake. How can I know whether I have a living faith or a false faith? The second chapter of the book of James helps to give us some answers to that question.

I. Living Faith Is Impartial (vv. 1-10)

Discrimination is evidence of partiality. James is quite clear that we should not hold our faith in the Lord Jesus Christ as a sign of personal favoritism. Nor should we be partial to anyone. As we read this passage in James chapter 2, we must be struck with how similar our day is to James's day. We tend to cater to those who are wealthy or are dressed well or look good. In so doing we are showing partiality.

How do you and I respond to the person who doesn't dress as well or smell as nice as others? A living faith is one that welcomes equally the poor and rich, the black and white and brown, the educated and uneducated, the well-dressed and the poorly dressed. While we might downplay this type of sin, James is quick to say that whoever breaks the law at one point is guilty of breaking the whole law. Discrimination is sin and we need to call it such, no more or less loudly than we speak of every sin.

Living faith, on the other hand, is not concerned with skin color or bank accounts or anything except the individual person. May God grant us a faith that shows no partiality!

II. Living Faith Produces Good Works (vv. 14-17)

While I was in high school and college one of my sisters lived in Florida. Every spring break I made a visit to see her. Driving through the orange groves I began to stop and enjoy the sights, smells, and tastes. Those trees naturally produced oranges because that is what they were—orange trees. The oranges grew from the inside of the tree out.

In the same way, Christians ought to produce good works because on the inside God has changed us. To use another biblical analogy, we have been transferred from the kingdom of darkness to the kingdom of light. We are not the same anymore, and because we have been changed from the inside out we naturally produce good works. It is as natural for a Christian to produce good works as it is for the orange tree to produce oranges.

Good works for the Christian, as do oranges, come in all shapes and sizes. Developing Christian character, ministering to the needs of others, and sharing the Word of God are all examples of good works. Time would not permit an exhaustive list of good works that the believer could perform. The key is that a living faith produces good works.

Living faith is the result of the work of God in bringing a person to salvation. Impartiality and good works are the results of a living faith. Just as the true nature of the two plants in my office will be eventually revealed, so will a living faith and a false faith be made plain. A living faith produces good things that bring praise and glory to our Lord and Savior Jesus Christ. *(Douglas Walker)*

BEYOND THE BORDERS

MARK 7:24-37

In the preceding verses Jesus declared all foods are clean (v. 19), because it is what is in the inner person that counts. In these stories, Jesus declares all persons clean, whether a Syrophoenician woman in Tyre, or a man of unknown but non-Jewish race in the region of the Decapolis. These two stories recorded by Mark are also documented in Matthew (15:21ff.).

We should not get bogged down in the details of the story, but rather see the broad sweep of the theological brush. We have here two examples of the same religious principle illustrating Jesus' repudiation of the traditional Jewish beliefs that the true faith is only for those of the house of Israel.

While as a matter of strategy Jesus started with Israel, as a matter of practicality he expanded beyond those borders. These two stories make this point clear. The Christlike God is a God for all people, who seeks all people everywhere, who calls on them for faith in him and is desirous for the commitment of all, so that all might be saved. As Paul wrote counseling Timothy: "This is right and is acceptable in the sight of God our Savior, who desires everyone to be saved and to come to the knowledge of the truth" (1 Tim. 2:3-4).

To the best of our knowledge this is the first and only journey of Jesus beyond the borders of Israel, and the fact that he traveled here is symbolically significant. His actions speak volumes of words.

Jesus often stated that it was his intention to go first to the house of Israel, to those of the Jewish faith. He never claimed to be starting a new religion. He was brought up a Jew and knew well his Jewish Bible (Old Testament), often quoting it, even on the cross (see Mark 15:34; Ps. 22:1). He claimed that he had come not to destroy Judaism, but to fulfill it. To fill it full of new meaning. To bring it to its proper climax. To fulfill the words of the Jewish prophets. This was his intention.

While he still desired this, he had what spaceflight engineers would call today a "midcourse correction." He drew his circle larger to include the Gentiles—all non-Jews—and this is nowhere more evident than this passage where a desperate Gentile mother pleads with him to come and heal her daughter, who was possessed with "an unclean spirit."

He states first his original intention to go to the Jews: "Let the children be fed first, for it is not fair to take the children's food and throw it to the dogs" (v. 27). The Jews often referred to Gentiles as "dogs." Jesus uses here the common vernacular, as he often did in order to be understood by the common people. The woman's clever repartee drew him out so that he healed a foreigner in a foreign country, an astounding theological event for one who claimed to come to fulfill Judaism.

The second episode, where a person who cannot hear or speak is healed, is recorded more for the comments attributed to the crowd than for the actual healing. The healing was not a new lesson, other than it was again done to a Gentile beyond the border of Israel.

The most astounding thing was that the people were now saying, "He has done everything well; he even makes the deaf to hear and the mute to speak" (v. 37). These were carefully crafted words that were used to echo the prophet Isaiah who, when he spoke of the coming Messiah, said, "Then the eyes of the blind shall be opened, and the ears of the deaf unstopped; then the lame shall leap like a deer, and the tongue of the speechless sing for joy" (Isa. 35:5-6a). The use of these words verified in the minds of those using them that Jesus was in fact the Christ spoken of by their prophet Isaiah.

When General Douglas MacArthur was forced to leave the Philippines because of the advancing Japanese army during the Second

World War, he told them, "I shall return." When he returned near the end of the war, he chose very carefully his words when he landed and said, "I have returned." It was a fulfillment of his earlier promise. Jesus is claiming to be the fulfillment of the prophet Isaiah by going beyond the border to non-Jews. *(C. Thomas Hilton)*

SEPTEMBER 14, 1997

❦

Seventeenth Sunday After Pentecost

Worship Theme: Christ calls us to bear his cross through obedience and commitment.

Readings: Proverbs 1:20-33; James 3:1-12; Mark 8:27-38

Call to Worship (Psalm 19:1-2, 7-14):

Leader: The heavens are telling the glory of God; and the firmament proclaims his handiwork.

People: Day to day pours forth speech, and night to night declares knowledge.

Leader: The law of the LORD is perfect, reviving the soul;

People: the decrees of the LORD are sure, making wise the simple;

Leader: the precepts of the LORD are right, rejoicing the heart;

People: the commandment of the LORD is clear, enlightening the eyes;

Leader: the fear of the LORD is pure, enduring forever;

People: the ordinances of the LORD are true and righteous altogether.

Leader: More to be desired are they than gold, even much fine gold;

People: sweeter also than honey, and drippings of the honeycomb.

Leader: Moreover by them is your servant warned; in keeping them there is great reward.

People: **But who can detect their errors? Clear me from hidden faults.**

Leader: Keep back your servant also from the insolent; do not let them have dominion over me. Then I shall be blameless, and innocent of great transgression.

All: **Let the words of my mouth and the meditation of my heart be acceptable to you, O LORD, my rock and my redeemer.**

Pastoral Prayer:

God of unsearchable glory and unmeasurable majesty, we praise you for your revelation of yourself in Jesus Christ, our Lord. In Christ, we have come to know you as a God of love and mercy, a God of grace and compassion. Through Christ we have sensed your touch and experienced your blessing. On the cross he conquered sin and death, and through his cross we have received life and light. Even as he was willing to sacrifice his very life on that cross that we might be reconciled to the Father, so give us the strength and courage to carry that cross each day—to carry it to the poor and oppressed; to carry it to the sick and imprisoned; to carry it to the lost and loveless. And as we carry that cross in our own lives and words and actions, may your Holy Spirit nurture in us a flame of righteousness and holiness that this world cannot extinguish—a flame that will burn with power and purpose until that day when we gather around your throne and sing praises to the One who hung on that cross for us, for we pray in his name. Amen.

SERMON BRIEFS

WISDOM'S CALL

PROVERBS 1:20-33

This text focuses on two characters: wisdom and simple ones. Wisdom is personified as one calling out and warning that she needs to be heeded. She is calling to "simple ones," those who reject her and fail to acknowledge her warning.

What kind of wisdom is being rejected here? Verse 29 demonstrates that simple ones, mockers, and fools hated her knowledge in their refusal to fear the Lord. "Fear of the Lord" is the theme of the book of Proverbs (cf. 1:7) and is the content of wisdom's message. This is not the fear of the abused toward the abusers, but a loving reverence submitting to the Lordship of God.

I. Wisdom's Attempt to Call (vv. 20-21)

The call of wisdom is not for some elite few who have achieved academically to master a philosophy of God. On the contrary, her call is public and for anyone willing to heed. She does not call out in the theology classroom alone but in the street and in public squares for common folk to hear her important message. She does not limit her work to quiet halls of academia but cries out in the midst of the noise of the streets and in the gates of cities.

Wisdom shouts loudly amidst all the other voices that claim truth, but she has the only answer that will remedy humanity's ailments: "Fear the Lord."

II. Simple Ones' Rejection (vv. 22-25)

Simple ones do not want to complicate their lives with truth and the harsh reality that a change or reordering of their lives might be needed to remedy their ailment. They love simple ways, burying their heads in trivial matters and avoiding the truth at any cost. If they cannot hide from reality, their "plan B" is to mock the truth and maintain an arrogant false superiority toward the truth, which is by New Testament terms "foolishness" to them. Their ultimate problem is that they hate such knowledge.

Wisdom was always ready to aid and assist them, but they refuse to hear her rebuke. Human nature never likes to hear rebuke or reproof. Human nature tends to seek out voices that confirm our own thoughts and do not challenge us to make changes in our comfort zones. Wisdom calls out even in nature so the Psalms tell us, but moving along on our own course is the most comfortable path to take.

297

III. Wisdom's Response (vv. 26-28)

Initially, one may read these verses and think, "How cruel!" However, wisdom attempted to alert simple humanity to the truth, but in rebellion they fall into disaster and calamity. Now wisdom mocks and laughs at the arrogant yet ignorant who failed to heed her call.

So many of humanity's worst problems are because we have failed to listen to a simple truth and move in obedience. To look for wisdom to lead the way after such disaster was forewarned is meaningless. More is at stake here than wisdom saying, "I told you so!" There are principles and cycles set from the foundation of time.

We have no choice but to live by the biblical principle of reaping and sowing. To fail to heed means we face the consequence of disaster. We brought such disasters upon ourselves by failing to "fear the Lord." (*Joseph Byrd*)

THE TYRANT, THE TONGUE

JAMES 3:1-12

Out of the heart come all kinds of evil (Mark 7:20-23), and the first place they go is the tongue (v. 6). How many of us have wished we had not said that careless word or made that too quick response? Of course, we all have. Whoever invented the saying, "Sticks and stones may break my bones, but words can never hurt me" never had a parent scold him, a fianceé break an engagement, or a doctor give him a cancer diagnosis.

James considers the tongue, the instrument of words, a tyrant that is managed by an even greater power, the human heart. The words we say reflect much of what we are inside.

I. The Tongue: A Teacher's Instrument

Verse 1 warns those who would be teachers of their greater responsibility and accountability in comparison to others. The New Testament held teachers in high esteem. First Corinthians and Ephesians list the teachers immediately following the apostles and prophets.

As carriers of the truth of the gospel, they are warned to be especially careful. The very clarity and purity of the gospel was theirs to explain and exemplify. The Bible does teach a double standard. The standard for the ordinary Christian is very high. Jesus said, "Be perfect." James adds that teachers will be judged by that standard even more strictly than the ordinary believer. And what instrument do teachers use more than their own tongues?

II. The Tongue: A Universal Instrument

Verse 2 broadens the importance of careful consideration of the tongue to all. A mature person, James says, is easily recognized if he/she can control his/her tongue. Because the whole body follows what the tongue says, verses 3-8 graphically illustrate the power of the tongue.

The tongue is compared to a rudder for a ship, a small fire to a forest fire, and a bit for a horse. These small things do control their larger complements. So the tongue manages one's life. In verse 8, James declares it evil. He is referring to all the misuses of the tongue, such as gossip, backbiting, slander, and rumors.

III. The Tongue: Indicator of the Heart

Echoing the teaching of Jesus, James reminds his readers that the tongue may be a tyrant, but it takes its power and direction from the heart. James refers to the fact that bitter and sweet water cannot flow from the same source. Fig trees cannot bear olives, and those who praise God cannot curse their fellow men.

James recognizes that apparently such contradictions do happen. He reminds us that we have failed and have praised God in one breath while cursing our brothers with the next. But, he shouts, "This should not be."

Even Paul struggled with this apparently universal predicament. He, too, declared a dualism in his inner self when he spoke of doing things he wished he had not done and leaving things undone he had done. If so great a saint had such difficulty, is it not to be expected that all of us need to be alert? *(Carolyn Volentine)*

299

THE BURDEN OF THE CROSS

MARK 8:27-38

During a battle a soldier was frantically digging in as shells fell all around him. Suddenly his hand felt something metal and he grabbed it. It was a silver cross. Another shell exploded and he buried his head in his arms. He felt someone jump in with him and looked over and saw an army chaplain. The soldier thrust the cross in the chaplain's face and said, "I sure am glad to see you. How do you work this thing?"

When Jesus talks about bearing our cross, we want to know, "How do you work this thing?"

I. Peter Started with the Right Idea

Poor magnificent, blundering Peter. Someone said the only time Peter took his foot out of his mouth was to switch feet. He did it again. Jesus asks the disciples, "Who do you say that I am?" In a flash of insight Peter answered, "You are the Messiah."

When Jesus explains how that will translate into everyday life, however, Peter reprimands Jesus. A suffering Messiah can't be right; it didn't fit any of Peter's preconceptions about Messiah. Jesus, in turn, reprimands Peter.

The cross is essential to Mark's understanding of Jesus' purpose and mission as Messiah.

II. What Bearing the Cross Isn't

The cross is central to our faith but, like Peter, we cringe at cross-bearing. What does Jesus mean? People say, "I guess that's a cross I have to bear," generally with a poor-pitiful-me tone of voice. Is that really cross-bearing? No!

Cross-bearing doesn't refer to meaningless or even involuntary suffering that has to be endured. Suffering terminal cancer or AIDS is a horrible misfortune, but it's not bearing a cross. To offer your cancer- or AIDS-weakened self by reaching out to others and helping them, that's taking up your cross.

III. What Bearing the Cross Is

Bearing our cross is a choice. It is a voluntary form of sacrificial obedience that identifies us completely with Christ. Bearing our cross is not making the best of a situation or circumstance. It is something we deliberately take up and bear.

We don't like that. We would rather wear a cross than bear a cross. The cross is all about discipline, hard work, obedience, and commitment. It isn't easy, but it is possible. It draws us closer to Christ and makes us more Christlike.

Some women who live near Washington D.C. wanted to show God's love to a special group of people. They heard about a group of babies who were rarely held and destined to live and die in hospitals because they had AIDS. The babies didn't get much attention, so they began to cry silently. No one had responded to their crying out loud so they stopped doing it. But they still shed tears.

Even though these children would die by their second birthdays, the women took a number of the AIDS babies home. The women would respond to the silent tears by holding and rocking the babies. Soon these unloved, cast-off AIDS babies began to cry out loud again. They had been spoken to in the only way they could understand. They had been spoken to in the language of love by women willing to deny themselves and take up their cross.

To experience life in Christ requires feeling the weight of his cross in our daily discipleship. It's not easy, but it's not impossible. When we say yes to the cross, we don't have to bear the load alone. The burden of the cross is no burden at all—not when we're yoked with Christ. Deny yourself by giving yourself for others in Christ's name. Take up your cross and follow him. *(Billy D. Strayhorn)*

SEPTEMBER 21, 1997

❧

Eighteenth Sunday After Pentecost

Worship Theme: The presence of Christ within us enables us to overcome the power of sin.

Readings: Proverbs 31:10-31; James 3:13–4:3, 7-8*a*; Mark 9:30-37

Call to Worship (Psalm 1):

Leader: Happy are those who do not follow the advice of the wicked, or take the path that sinners tread, or sit in the seat of scoffers;

People: **but their delight is in the law of the LORD, and on his law they meditate day and night.**

Leader: They are like trees planted by streams of water, which yield their fruit in its season, and their leaves do not wither. In all that they do, they prosper.

People: **The wicked are not so, but are like chaff that the wind drives away.**

Leader: Therefore the wicked will not stand in the judgment, nor sinners in the congregation of the righteous;

All: **for the LORD watches over the way of the righteous, but the way of the wicked will perish.**

Pastoral Prayer:

Most holy and merciful God, we come before you with praise and adoration. You are worthy of all honor and praise, O Lord, for you are both Creator and Redeemer, both Judge and Savior. We are the work of your hands, Lord, yet in our rebellion we have fallen short of your glory. Though we are undeserving of your compassion, still you reach out to us with healing and loving arms. How we want to know your presence and power in our lives, Lord. Teach us to walk in your paths day by day; empower us to be faithful and bold disciples of Christ. Help us to yield our lives more fully to your Holy Spirit, that we might know your glory in our own lives. For we ask it in the name of Christ. Amen.

SERMON BRIEFS

HONORING THE VIRTUE OF A WIFE

PROVERBS 31:10-31

Often we look at this passage as a standard to which women need to live up to to be of good character. Perhaps there is merit to such an approach, but one truly wonders if the writer is simply considering the blessing of his wife or mother and noting her qualities. The text could read more like poetry expressing deep love and appreciation for labors and qualities rarely found in people of our day. It could be an expression of thanks, noting all the benefits provided from such a noble and caring wife. In fact, the text tells us as much about how to treat a virtuous wife as it describes her.

I. The Virtues of Her Labor (vv. 11-19, 24)

The work of this wife is such that it cultivates complete confidence from her husband because she has consistently worked for his good and not his harm. Such are many of the wives and mothers with which God has blessed the church—often quietly laboring to make a positive effect on their family.

In this text, her work is described as selecting materials for linen and being enterprising enough to provide meals, sacrificing her sleep to maintain such a level of accommodation for the entire family. Her work is accomplished with vigor, and her labor is done to work the advantage toward the family. She does not accept shortcuts to accomplish her responsibilities. This text does not condemn the "working woman"; it takes note and honors the stay-at-home moms.

II. Her Care for Her Family (vv. 21-23, 27)

This wife has tended to her family with preparation well in advance. Verse 23 seems to indicate that she takes a role in the respect that her husband has within the community. How true it is that any spouse can edify or destroy the character of a mate. This is not an idle woman; she is a good steward of her home and all with which God has blessed her. She is a wife who has the management capabilities of a corporate executive.

III. Her Character (vv. 20, 25, 26, 28-30)

One may praise an individual for his or her actions; however, that person's character involves his or her attitude while doing the tasks that must be accomplished. This woman is praised for her character and for her activities. She is a woman whose lifestyle demonstrates generosity. She is a woman of dignity and strength. There is no sense of femininity equating to "wimpiness" here. Her character is such that those who know her best, including her flaws, call her blessed and praise her. Her nobility is beyond the norm for others; she settles for nothing less than purity in her life.

Finally and most important, all of her character is shaped by her wisdom to fear the Lord. Here is the beginning and the end of such a virtuous woman: her faith in God.

A simple message to us today from this text is to call us to look beyond the choices of career a woman may make and focus upon her character. The next century needs women of character whose values are shaped by their faith in God. (*Joseph Byrd*)

THE BATTLE WON

JAMES 3:13–4:3, 7-8*a*

"Love's redeeming work is done . . . Fought the fight, the battle won." These familiar words from the hymn, "Christ the Lord Is Risen Today" by Charles Wesley, remind us that Christians are on a winning team. James and the rest of the New Testament present a worldview that the kingdom of God is in tension with the human desire to be king, the world's desire to establish its own kingdom, and the powerful supernatural kingdom of Satan.

I. The War Situation

Although the ultimate war is won, there are daily skirmishes. Like a general, James barks out his assessment of our personal and social warfare in verses 3:3-18. The background context for flesh sins focuses on the social sins. He contrasts "evil wisdom" with "wisdom from above." This evil wisdom reveals itself in the area of destructive interpersonal relationships.

Bitterness is the first identified culprit. This includes bitterness against others, circumstances, ourselves, and God. Next comes jealousy (vv. 14-16), arrogance (v. 14), and self-deception or lying against the truth (v. 14). Encouraging the root of bitterness is always the foul fertilizer of unforgiveness. Refusal to forgive encourages many toxic weeds of interpersonal conflicts and sin. Bitter, prideful, negative emotions yield the fruits of disorder and, as James calls it, "every evil thing."

The sin energy of our self-centered wills attracts the even greater destructive forces of Satan and his demons. James is not saying that all who reveal negative wisdom are completely ruled by Satan. He is saying those with negative wisdom are allowing confusion and other negative manifestations because they are allowing themselves to be influenced by the evil one. James does not allow for rationalizations. He clearly defines sin as sin and orders his readers to be faithful and loyal.

II. Command One

Therefore, he orders clearly and forcefully: "Submit yourselves therefore to God." The opposite of rebellious pride is submission to God. Verses 4:3, 7-8a clearly give the Christian his/her orders. As we draw near to God in worship, prayer, and thanksgiving we will know God's presence as we have never known it before. The book of Revelation describes the work of heaven as that of praise. We can draw into God's presence by that same activity and focus now, in this present age.

III. Command Two. Promise One

"Resist the devil" (v. 7b). How? We resist the devil the same way Jesus did—by verbal confrontation based in the truth of God's word. The word of God in the New Testament is often referred to as a weapon. Resistance of the devil is both offensive and defensive. The promise of God is that the devil will flee from us as we resist him.

IV. Command Three. Praise Two

Verse 8*a* says, "Draw near to God." Worship him. Praise him. Glorify him. By deliberately bringing our attention to him, we are putting ourselves in the position to receive his presence. And his presence is what we are promised. "Draw near to God and he will draw near to you."

Clean-up skirmishes against flesh, the world, and the evil one continue. But the praise of God makes the Christian a conqueror so that he may sing: "Soar we now where Christ has led; / Following our exalted Head; / Made like him, like him we rise; / Ours the cross, the grave, the skies, Alleluia!" *(Carolyn Volentine)*

A DIFFERENT SORT OF GREATNESS

MARK 9:30-37

As a teenager, I always wanted to belong to an "in" crowd. But I didn't live in the right neighborhood or I didn't wear the right clothes. I always seemed to stand on the outside looking in. I also wanted to be a leader. I wanted to be in charge and have people respect me and ask me for advice. In the role of leader I saw a certain amount of power and prestige.

I. The Disciples' Attitude

That's how the disciples must have felt. The Pharisees and Sadducees were the privileged class. They got the best seats at banquets. Others paid attention to them. The disciples stood on the outside looking in and longed for what these people had. No wonder they were discussing who among them was the greatest. Maybe, at first, they were innocently discussing how the kingdom would come about and what role they would play. But the innocent talk got out of hand. Then again, maybe the power of their newfound positions went to their heads. Whatever the case, Jesus asked them what they had been arguing about. The look in his eyes told them he already knew. So he taught them about servanthood.

II. Being a Servant Leader

He didn't berate or belittle them. Instead, he took a child in his arms. A child is the classic example of the powerless. A child can't reward or repay. Jesus held that child in his lap and said, "Whoever welcomes one such child in my name welcomes me, and whoever welcomes me welcomes not me but the one who sent me" (v. 37).

His message made their arguments about greatness as meaningful as arranging the deck chairs on the Titanic. Jesus said: "Whoever wants to be first must be last of all and servant of all" (v. 35).

That's an odd way of thinking. Our whole economy and social structure is based on being number one. We constantly push and shove to see who will be in charge and who will have the most influence. We honor those folks who come in first. Contrast that to the portrait of Jesus painted by his own words: "Whoever wants to be first must be last of all and servant of all."

III. Sacrificial Service

Greatness and servanthood—both attitudes are natural in us. The first illustrates that to which most people aspire. The second illustrates that for which we were created. One indicates our quest in life, the other exhibits our best in life.

A mother celebrating her birthday was treated to a party by her family. Mom was told to sit in her favorite chair. One by one, the father and the two older children solemnly presented Mom her gifts on a tray, as if she were royalty. The youngest girl, who was really too young to have had much of a role in picking out the gifts, had been left out of the plans. But she rose to the occasion. She suddenly appeared with the empty tray. Approaching her mother she placed the tray on the floor, stepped on it, and with a childish wiggle of joy said, "Mommy, I give you ME!"

Jesus, the only Son of God, had everything and yet claimed nothing. Out of his unselfish service and obedience came our salvation. He calls us to live and pursue a different kind of greatness, the greatness that comes from giving yourself to Jesus and being a servant. *(Billy D. Strayhorn)*

SEPTEMBER 28, 1997

❧

Nineteenth Sunday After Pentecost

Worship Theme: Prayer is a precious gift that enables us to relate to God.

Readings: Esther 7:1-6, 9-10; 9:20-22; James 5:13-20; Mark 9:38-50

Call to Worship (Psalm 124):

Leader: If it had not been the LORD who was on our side—let Israel now say—if it had not been the LORD who was on our side, when our enemies attacked us,

People: **then they would have swallowed us up alive, when their anger was kindled against us;**

Leader: then the flood would have swept us away, the torrent would have gone over us; then over us would have gone the raging waters.

People: **Blessed be the LORD, who has not given us as prey to their teeth.**

Leader: We have escaped like a bird from the snare of the fowlers; the snare is broken, and we have escaped.

All: **Our help is in the name of the LORD, who made heaven and earth.**

Pastoral Prayer:

Almighty God, creator of heaven and earth, who sustains creation by the power of your word: we praise you, O Lord, for you have given us the breath of life; you have provided all that we have and are. We praise you, O Lord, for even while we were in bondage to sin you extended your love to us. We praise you, O Lord, for you have provided to us a means of reconciliation—even Jesus Christ, our Savior. And we praise you, O Lord, for you have given to us the

SEPTEMBER 28, 1997

enormous privilege of entering into your very presence through prayer. We who have proved ourselves to be such rebellious and presumptuous creatures, have nevertheless been allowed to access the power of your divine kingdom through prayer. What amazing love, O Lord! May you shape us more and more in the image of your Son, that we might honor your great love with lives of steadfast obedience like unto the life of Jesus, in whose name we pray. Amen.

SERMON BRIEFS

THE HUMBLE HEROINE

ESTHER 7:1-6, 9-10; 9:20-22

This text is surrounded by a truly captivating story: God's people are living in exile, yet God is present with them, directing the affairs that affect them and protecting them. As believers, we may not find ourselves in the greatest circumstances; we may even be threatened by our adversary. However, we can trust in our God of deliverance to be faithful and make a way out for us.

Haman had created a scheme to destroy the Jews. Our text demonstrates his humiliation and ultimately his fate for transgressing against God's people.

I. God's Placement (7:1-6)

The rise of Queen Esther to the throne is a drama of its own. Here, however, we consider that God placed her in a position to work for the good of those he loves. Haman's plot to annihilate the Jews could have been successful, but God had placed Esther (the heroine of the story) in a place to frustrate Haman's plan. Esther wisely and humbly requests of her king her life and the lives of her people.

Our society seems to think that shouting will gain the hearing needed to bring justice. This story indicates that prayer and fasting (4:1-3) working through God's placement of the circumstances accomplished more than any sort of demonstration. Faith and prayer to a sovereign God moved through the circumstances to avert an evil plan.

309

II. God's Judgment (7:9-10)

Haman's evil plan becomes his own undoing. He was blinded by his own agenda and arrogance (cf. 6:6), and the consequences were as severe as his intentions toward the Jews. Haman is hanged on the gallows he prepared for Mordecai. His brand of evil is not ancient history. The evil of a self-absorbed spirit is present in today's world.

In chapter 6 Haman is humbled, but in chapter 7 he is accountable for his decisions. Today's world does not want to hear of a God of justice. Yet without a sense of conviction there can be no relief of condemnation through redemption. This text demonstrates there are consequences for taking a stand against God's people.

III. Sorrow Turned to Joy (9:20-22)

These verses comprise one of the primary purposes of the book of Esther: to explain the institution of the annual festival of Purim. The Jews were on the verge of being annihilated, but God rescued his people and relieved them from their enemies. This was cause for generous celebration with feasting and gift-giving.

Christians' greatest enemy has truly been defeated, and we should pause to consider that the appropriate response to God is one of worshipful celebration and generous living. God is faithful to deliver his children! (*Joseph Byrd*)

PRAYER: OUR LIFELINE TO GOD

JAMES 5:13-20

Prayer is a mystery. To the Christian, prayer is a truth revealed but not fully apprehended. Like the words *trinity* and *sacrament,* prayer helps us talk about how we experience God. John Wesley boldly proclaimed, "God does nothing but in answer to prayer." But what is prayer?

Prayer is our talking to God and God talking to us. Prayer is communication and communion with God. Prayer assumes there is a God. The Christian knows that God not only is there, but he is good and his will is ever directed toward his children's good. When we pray, we recognize the sovereignty of God.

Prayer, like life itself, is a gift from God. It is only possible because he reveals himself to us that we may converse with him.

SEPTEMBER 28, 1997

I. Prayer Is Our Response to Life

Prayer comes in as many forms as there are circumstances. It ranges from the "Oh, my God" type of prayer when believers are in crisis situations, to the lovely "Now I lay me down to sleep" prayer of a child preparing for bed. James urges us to bathe all of life in prayer. He focuses on four general areas common to us all: trouble, happiness, illness, and sin.

II. Prayer Is Our Response to God

When James says to pray "in the name of the Lord," he is pressing us to remember that we are not living in a powerless, lonely state. We are living in Christ's ruling presence. We pray in response to our Savior's presence and involvement in life with us, praying not from a position of "rights" but from a position of reception of his grace. We know a God of superlatives; omniscient, omnipotent, and also omnipresent.

III. In Prayer We Hear God's Response

James declares: "The prayer of a righteous man is powerful and effective" (NIV). God responds to those who know him, who humble themselves to be his servants. Such a servant was Elijah. James summarizes the Old Testament story about Elijah and the rain. But just in case we misunderstand, James assures us that Elijah was a human being, just as we are. It was Elijah's righteousness that made him able to communicate with God.

The fifth century Talmud records a story about righteous Elijah and the power of prayer. The story says that Elijah would frequently visit a certain rabbi. One day the rabbi waited but Elijah did not come. The next day, when Elijah did arrive, the rabbi asked him, "Why didn't you come?"

Elijah replied, "I had to wake up Abraham, wash his hands, wait while he prayed, then make him lie down again. Likewise I had to wake up Isaac and Jacob, wash their hands, wait until they prayed, and make them lie down again, each in his turn."

"But why didn't you awaken them all at the same time?"

"Oh, no," Elijah replied. "I know that if they prayed together, their prayers would be so powerful that they would bring the Messiah before his time."

311

The Talmud's story and our text in James both press us to know that the prayers of a righteous man are powerful and effective. James then projects: if all of life is to be held before God in prayer, is it not logical that if someone does wander from the truth, he can be brought back? Even a multitude of sins will be covered. The sinner will escape eternal death, thus receiving the greatest benefit of healing from the prayer of faith. *(Carolyn Volentine)*

WHO IS ON OUR SIDE?

MARK 9:38-50

A man ran a newspaper ad for a system "guaranteed to cut any and all of your bills in half." The system cost only $29.95. Upon investigation, authorities discovered that for the $29.95 plus postage and handling, the man would send people a three-dollar pair of scissors. He was subsequently arrested for mail fraud.

All around we see a world out of control. It's a world where no one says no; where success, money, and self-gratification mean everything; where betrayal is easy and family and commitment finish last; where integrity is just a word. When will it end? We want to shout, "That's enough. Everybody back to square one. Let's start all over again."

I. Christ Set the Example We Need

The Son of God came as one of us, tempted in every way like us, but he did not give in. He gives us the chance to start over, to be transformed through forgiveness. He gives us the chance for reconciliation through grace. He also came to show us what faith, discipleship, love, and obedience are all about. He showed us what courage and integrity are by taking up his cross and bearing our sins. He calls us to follow him and to live by kingdom standards.

II. Christ Gave the Direction We Need

Who is on our side? That's the question the disciples bring to Jesus. During the history of the church there have been times when that has been a very important question. Are they for us or against us? Today there are so many groups who claim to be followers, how do you tell them apart? How do you tell who are the real players and who are only playing at this thing called faith? Is it the creed they espouse? Is it the amount of Scripture they can quote?

Jesus says the secret is to have salt in ourselves. We're called to live our faith in such a way that there is no doubt who we follow. Jesus speaks of not putting stumbling blocks in the way of others. He speaks of living a life that is not offensive to others or to the values of God's kingdom—a life that doesn't lead another astray.

III. Christ Provided the Vision We Need

Turning the other cheek; loving our enemy; forgiving those who sin against us; showing no partiality; being honest; living with integrity and faithfulness; bearing our cross—these are not options for the followers of Christ. Nor are they unattainable ideals. They are the order of the day—the minimum daily requirement, the standard by which we live and breathe and relate to people both inside and outside the faith.

The story is told that one day General Robert E. Lee was speaking in the highest terms of another officer, when one of the men interrupted him: "General, do you know that man is one of your biggest enemies, and misses no opportunity to ridicule you?"

"Yes," Lee replied. "But I was asked to give *my* opinion of *him*, not *his* opinion of *me*."

The Son of God calls us to act with the same integrity, no matter what is going on in the world. How we act reflects upon Christ. Christ is on our side helping us to live our faith. Bishop Woodie White said, "No matter how bad the bad news gets—the final word is always the good news of Jesus Christ." We are called to remember that and seek to glorify God with our lives. *(Billy D. Strayhorn)*

OCTOBER

৯৯

Mending the Net, Sharpening the Hoe

Symbol: Salt

Salt as a preservative is a symbol of the eternal covenant between God and his people. It was also valued as a seasoning for food. Thus, it is a seasoning for our lives.

Texts:

"Season all your grain offerings with salt. Do not leave the salt of the covenant of your God out of your grain offerings; add salt to all your offerings" (Lev. 2:13 NIV).

"You are the salt of the earth. But if the salt loses its saltiness, how can it be made salty again? It is no longer good for anything, except to be thrown out and trampled by men" (Matt. 5:13 NIV).

Invocation:

"Almighty God, grant that those who worship you this day may present their bodies as a living sacrifice, holy, and acceptable to you. By the power of your Holy Spirit make us strong to fulfill our ministry this day. In the name of Christ. Amen." (Reuben P. Job and Norman Shawchuck, *A Guide to Prayer*)

Scripture Focus:
- Habakkuk 3:17-19
- Psalm 1
- Leviticus 2:13ff.
- Matthew 5:13-16

Prayer Focus:
- Focus on your gratitude to God for being his child.
- Focus on your joy in leading God's church.
- Visualize the wide influence of your congregation.
- Focus on ways to make it wider.
- Visualize ways to give your church a salty tang in its ministry.

314

OCTOBER

Prayer:

"I have been careless, cowardly, mutinous. Punishment I have deserved, I deny it not; yet have mercy on me for the sake of the truth I long to learn, and of the good which I long to do. Take the will for the deed, good Lord. Accept the partial self-sacrifice which thou did conspire for the sake of the one perfect self-sacrifice which thy didst fulfill upon the cross. Pardon my faults, out of thine own boundless pity for human weakness. Take not my unworthy name off the roll call of the noble and victorious army, which is the blessed company of all faithful people; and let me, too, be found written in the Book of Life, which even though I stand the lowest and last upon its list." (Charles Kingsley) *(Bill Self)*

OCTOBER 5, 1997

ॐ

Twentieth Sunday After Pentecost

Worship Theme: God's work in our lives can overcome any challenge.

Readings: Job 1:1; 2:1-10; Hebrews 1:1-4; 2:5-12; Mark 10:2-16

Call to Worship (Psalm 26):

Leader: Vindicate me, O LORD, for I have walked in my integrity, and I have trusted in the LORD without wavering.

People: **Prove me, O LORD, and try me; test my heart and mind.**

Leader: For your steadfast love is before my eyes, and I walk in faithfulness to you.

People: **I do not sit with the worthless, nor do I consort with hypocrites;**

Leader: I hate the company of evildoers, and will not sit with the wicked.

People: **I wash my hands in innocence, and go around your altar, O LORD,**

Leader: singing aloud a song of thanksgiving, and telling all your wondrous deeds.

People: **O LORD, I love the house in which you dwell, and the place where your glory abides.**

Leader: Do not sweep me away with sinners, nor my life with the bloodthirsty,

People: **those in whose hands are evil devices, and whose right hands are full of bribes.**

316

Leader: But as for me, I walk in my integrity; redeem me, and be gracious to me.

All: My foot stands on level ground; in the great congregation I will bless the LORD.

Pastoral Prayer:

Divine Father, from whom flows all that is lovely, all that is good, all that is worthy of praise, we thank you for your Word, which reveals to us your truth. We thank you for your Spirit, who gives direction to our lives. We thank you for your Son, whose sacrificial death has enabled us to experience eternal life. O Lord, we live in a world characterized by sin and hopelessness, a world tainted by evil, a world in which illness and tragedy are all too frequent companions. There are those within this congregation today who are carrying terrible burdens, O Lord—burdens of loss, burdens of fear, burdens of anxiety. Enfold them in your love this day, our loving Father. Bring your comfort and encouragement to each one who is struggling this day. Help us to realize, Lord, that no matter how great the challenge, you are even greater. Give us courage for the living of these days, for we ask it in the name of the One whose resurrection gives us hope. Amen.

SERMON BRIEFS

TOUGH FAITH

JOB 1:1; 2:1-10

The story of Job is well known, although few of us really want to apply it to our lives so that we can understand painful circumstances. We have the natural human desire to avoid anything that will bring us pain or discomfort. Job clearly teaches us that bad things do happen to good people.

However, good people have something that helps them make some sense of their experience. This is not to say that we never question or feel pain or discomfort; it is simply a promise that eventually the circumstances will make sense and God will work all things together for our good.

I. A Man of Integrity (v. 1)

Job is described with particular words that are significant enough to be repeated in the text. They seem to imply more than just a brief description of him. These words identify his character—that is, his truest self.

He is first described with the terms *blameless* and *upright*. These mark his moral character. He was complete, undefiled, or uncompromised. Put simply, he was pure in his intention, single-minded, and single-hearted. He also was upright or righteous in the sense of being straight. He could have been the example of correct living.

Job is also described by the phrases, *fearing God* and *shunning evil*. The fear or reverence of God is prominent in the wisdom literature of the Old Testament. Here it takes on an even more in-depth meaning. Not only was Job righteous, but he lived such a life in piety before a Holy God. Moreover, Job was not only called to God; he was also called away from evil. The term literally means he removed or departed from evil. Such a man is one who walks before God in spiritual integrity.

II. Maintaining Integrity After Disaster (vv. 1-3)

The scene in heaven in these verses follows Satan's attack upon Job by destroying his livelihood and his children. Job did not sin in all of the disaster that was brought upon him. In all the ruin that had come upon Job, he still maintained his integrity. The idea here is that Job courageously held strong to his integrity or true character. We must come to understand that life's tests in the crucible will determine our integrity or true character. Job remained true.

III. Accepting Pain (vv. 4-10)

Satan is further allowed to attack Job directly and physically. In the pain and discomfort of physical problems coupled with the emotional agony of losing his family and livelihood, Job's integrity would face the ultimate test. In verse 9, his wife questions if he still will hold to his integrity.

It is a question still asked today. Is our integrity really worth feeling the pain? The temptation to give up and not focus upon principles and convictions is always present for the believer. Job's reply is appropriate for today. Can we accept the good from God without

318

accepting the trouble? In a society geared to convenience and minimizing discomfort, this rhetorical question is alien.

Not only should our lives be shaken to truly examine the occasional time of suffering, but we also should underline the preceding undeserved blessings that we so often take for granted. Job was willing to live with suffering; he saw it as part of the territory of being a servant of God. Even here, Job did not sin in what he said.

We may not count our words with such weight, but Jesus said that it is out of the abundance of our hearts that our mouths speak. How's your integrity? *(Joseph Byrd)*

FAMILY TIES

HEBREWS 1:1-4; 2:5-12

All large cities now have a variety of international restaurants. Whether you are in New York City, Nairobi, London, or Moscow, you will find any number of culinary tastes. The world's largest cities also offer a wide variety of catering to religious tastes. There are Moslem mosques, Baha'i temples, Buddhist temples, Shinto temples, Jewish synagogues, and Christian churches, just to name a few of the religious opportunities.

The writer of Hebrews knew what it was like to live in a smorgasbord of religious culture. Therefore, it was not only urgent and important, it was imperative he clearly focus his readers' attention toward their definitive Christian beliefs.

The one reservoir of truth from which all Christian truth springs is that the one true personal God exists as Father, Son, and Holy Spirit. The trinitarian view of God is the point at which Christianity separates from its sister religions, Judaism and Islam. Hebrews adamantly argues it is God the Son who supremely reveals God's Self to us.

I. The Glory of God in Christ Presented to Man

Hebrews 1 pronounces Jesus Christ to be the culmination of Jewish history's saga. "In the past God spoke to our forefathers through the prophets at many times in various ways" (NIV). But now we have something "better," even the "best." The word *better* appears twelve times in this letter. Jesus the Son of God and everything that is affiliated with him is better than what was previously available.

In verses 2 and 3, Jesus' superiority is demonstrated in seven declarations. 1) God has given him ownership of everything. Literally, God has made him "heir of all things." 2) As also taught in John 1:3 and Colossians 1:16, God created the universe through him. 3) He is the concentration of God's glory, who God is and what he does. 4) He is the exact representation of God. That is, he is the essence of God made understandable to us. 5) Echoing the declarations of John 1:1 and Colossians 1:17, Hebrews identifies Jesus as the word of God, which not only creates but also holds all things together. 6) Jesus' cosmic functions prove his power to relate to humanity's need for restoration from its sin. The Son of God, therefore, is better than all that has gone before because he has done what no one else or nothing else could do. He has provided purification for sins. 7) Having done so, he is exalted to more than a better position than that of all others. He is awarded equality with God as described in the phrase, "sat down at the right hand" of God. Thus he is intimately involved with God and intercedes for those who trust him.

II. The Best Brings Men to the Best Position

After the author of Hebrews thoroughly explains Jesus as the Son of God, he proceeds to proclaim the humanity of Jesus. What greater argument for Jesus' humanity can there be than Jesus' suffering— suffering even unto death. Jesus, the Son incarnate, literally taking on flesh, put himself in the same vulnerability as flesh, a position a little lower than the angels. But from that position he has been exalted now above all. He has imparted to flesh his holiness. That holiness is available to all who will receive him.

They who receive him are, therefore, truly his brothers: he sharing their flesh, they sharing his holiness. He has brought "many sons to glory." (*Carolyn Volentine*)

LET THE LITTLE CHILDREN COME

MARK 10:2-16

Why do we have children? If you ask people that question, you're likely to get one of three responses:

- *We had children to populate the earth.* Now times have changed, and having large families is not necessary or even popular anymore. Procreation alone isn't reason enough to have children.
- *We had children so we would be less lonely.* There's some bad news, I'm afraid: children make parents feel more lonely, not less. At first, it feels good to be needed twenty-four hours a day. Soon you're lonely for adult conversation. Thinking about the future makes you lonely. The future comes and the kids leave home. That makes you lonely.
- *We had children because they give meaning to life.* Viewed like this, children become another possession, like a Rolex or a BMW. Treat children as things and they'll grow up with no sense of self-worth or values.

Then, why *do* we have children? William Willimon and Stanley Hauerwas, in their book *Resident Aliens: Life in the Christian Colony,* write: "Christians have children, in great part, in order to be able to tell our children the story. . . . It is our privilege to invite our children, and other's children, to be a part of this great adventure called the Church."

That's a great reason for Christians to have children. It reminds us whose we are. By telling and living the story, we invite and enable the children to come to Jesus. It is a great privilege to tell the story. It's an even greater privilege to empower children to tell it. The child's point of view helps us maintain the awe and mystery of faith.

Sometimes we fail to notice what is in plain sight. It's not that we don't care—it's that the things we walk by every day become so commonplace that we forget they are there. Children help us see with new eyes and ears. Their experiences enhance our faith experience.

Children can be a pain. They leave fingerprints, spill soft drinks, and get crumbs all over everything. They're loud, noisy, and sometimes disrespectful. But they can also be angelic and reverent. Our job is to help the children hear the story, because sometimes they can even be God's messengers.

The day after our denomination began a campaign to raise money for our camp, nine-year-old Erica wanted to give me something for the camp. I thought she meant a dollar or two. Instead, she shocked me by giving me $100. I started not to take it, but the light in her eyes said I had to. It was a sacred offering. Her mother said Erica prayed about how much to give. Do you know where she got the money? It was the money she received for her birthday and Christmas combined with the money she earned for good grades and picking up aluminum cans.

Erica's gift gave us a fresh understanding of love and giving. I called the camp administrator and told him about Erica's gift. He told our denominational newspaper and the newspaper ran a story about it. Other preachers called, and they shared the story with their congregations. There is no telling how much more money that $100 generated. But no matter how much was given, there was no gift as great or as large as what Erica gave. Through her unselfish gift we heard our Master's voice.

Sometimes children are God's messengers, sent so that we can hear the message in fresh ways. The Good Shepherd laid down his life for the sheep. Sometimes we get so caught up in keeping the pasture clean and tidy that we can't hear the Shepherd's voice. That's when we need to let the lambs of God speak to us. Listen closely and you'll hear the Master's voice. *(Billy D. Strayhorn)*

OCTOBER 12, 1997

❧

Twenty-first Sunday After Pentecost

Worship Theme: Christ demands first place in our lives.

Readings: Job 23:1-9, 16-17; Hebrews 4:12-16; Mark 10:17-31

Call to Worship (Psalm 22:1-11):

Leader: My God, my God, why have you forsaken me? Why are you so far from helping me, from the words of my groaning?

People: O my God, I cry by day, but you do not answer; and by night, but find no rest.

Leader: Yet you are holy, enthroned on the praises of Israel.

People: In you our ancestors trusted; they trusted, and you delivered them.

Leader: To you they cried, and were saved; in you they trusted, and were not put to shame.

People: But I am a worm, and not human; scorned by others, and despised by the people.

Leader: All who see me mock at me; they make mouths at me, they shake their heads; "Commit your cause to the LORD; let him deliver—let him rescue the one in whom he delights!"

People: Yet it was you who took me from the womb; you kept me safe on my mother's breast.

Leader: On you I was cast from my birth, and since my mother bore me you have been my God.

All: Do not be far from me, for trouble is near and there is no one to help

323

Pastoral Prayer:

Almighty God, ruler of heaven and earth, we worship your majesty; we bless your steadfast mercy. You are above all; in you alone glory and honor reside. We praise your name, for your love is never-ending, your compassion is beyond understanding. When we were yet sinners, you gave your only Son to die on a bitter cross, that we might have life. How can we fathom love so divine? Let your Spirit fill our hearts, O Lord, that we might know your presence with renewed power. Help us to yield ourselves more fully to your will, that we might experience your strength in our own lives. Protect us from evil, O Lord, that we might maintain absolute fidelity to your truth and your way. Enable us to so order our lives that we place no priority higher than service to your kingdom. We ask all these things in the name of our loving Savior, Amen.

SERMON BRIEFS

LIFE'S HARD QUESTIONS

JOB 23:1-9, 16-17

It is easier for us to reflect on the story line of Job without entering into the pain of his conversations with his friends. In these conversations we see a Job who is human. He is a man of integrity, yet he is also a man of questions and a man who struggles with his agony. We are not only told of Job's incredible faith and great feats; we are also told of his weaknesses and shortcomings.

Here, Job is wrestling with his questions by giving a response to Eliphaz's rebuke in chapter 22. Eliphaz has just admonished Job to turn to God in repentance so that he may be restored—he assumes Job's calamity is based on sin in his life.

I. The Questions of Agony (vv. 1-2)

Job begins his response to Eliphaz by describing his emotional and attitudinal condition. He has a "complaint" against God. As he perceives God putting him through his ordeal, Job is asking the wrenching question, "Why?" God's hand remained heavy despite his pleas. Within the cycle of grieving all humans enter into a time of asking why. We cannot forbid this questioning nor can we give answer for God. This is a stage in which the human heart simply cries out, "I do not like what I am feeling!"

II. The Futility of Arguing One's Righteousness (vv. 3-9)

If he could speak to God face-to-face, Job believes that he could state his case. In reality he wants to rationalize his questions and find answers for his calamity. However, even Job is theologian enough to know that God would not use supernatural power to destroy him. He is convinced that he would be acquitted of the wrongdoing of which Eliphaz is accusing him.

Yet God is not a human who can be found and met face-to-face to discuss the issues. Job argues that he is practically defenseless because God cannot be found and bring to rest the accusation of sin, which supposedly has brought Job disaster. The process of rationalization of our righteousness or our circumstances is truly futile. God's ways and thoughts are beyond human capacity. In all, Job is left with frustration, which is shared by many people who are struggling in the face of helplessness.

III. Reverent Questions (vv. 16-17)

Job responds by noting the true awesomeness of God and his power to make the human heart faint. Even in his questioning, Job still has the wisdom to "fear God." Verse 17 points out, though, that it does not silence his questions. He does not understand his dilemma and still has agonizing and self-searching questions that remain unanswered. It's a little messy when you do not have black and white answers to difficult situations.

Our text seems to indicate there is a way to question and yet fear God. Perhaps that is what faith is. Maybe we must believe and reverence God without all of our questions being answered. Life is messy, but faith is holding onto God, even when it doesn't feel like God is there. Because the promise of Scripture is that God is always with his children, even when they are struggling. Trust him—he is there. (*Joseph Byrd*)

AN AUDIENCE WITH THE KING

HEBREWS 4:12-16

Most of us have never had the need or opportunity to seek an audience with a king. Nigeria is a country, however, in which kings are still very real social powers. Although the country holds elections, traditional kings are still acknowledged. Every village, town, and city have a king. Anyone who wants to promote an event has to visit the king to get permission to do so. A king may be very rich or very poor, but he is still king and must be consulted about events in his domain.

An audience with the king can be a challenging experience. Approaching the throne requires courage and humility, and frequently a previously scheduled appointment. To speak to the king, one needs an advocate, someone who can introduce you to the king and explain your cause.

In the Old and New Testaments, God is described as Israel's king despite the presence of earthly rulers. The priest was the intermediary or advocate between the people and God. The book of Hebrews announces that the most superior of intermediaries is now available, God's own Son. He is the high priest who intercedes for us and answers us.

I. Awareness of the Need for Grace

Verses 12 and 13 describe for us what the word of God does in our lives. It strips us of pretense and lays us bare before God. There is no room for denial of guilt or projection of fault. The word of God is so precise that it separates us joint from marrow—distinguishing between the soul, that which Greek thought defined as a living being, and the spirit, which is the center of thought. Only God could so separate our selves and scrutinize our very being.

It is the quality of God to so know us that we recognize we are being judged. Is it any wonder then that we become keenly aware of our need for God's grace?

II. Assurance of Grace

Grace is that wonderful word for God's favor and blessings. Verses 14 and 15 assure us that grace becomes available to us—we are not to despair. Our judge is not a distant king but one who has joined with us in the adventure so completely that he, as the Son of God, put on our flesh and thus knew every attack that we have known. He has experienced our limitations and been subjected to our weaknesses, liabilities, and infirmities. And he was triumphant. In contrast to us, he did not sin. He never allowed anything to separate him from God.

III. Abundance of Grace

Verse 16 urges us to make use of our audience with God the king to receive the abundant grace God desires to give us. We are to go to God fearlessly and confidently, with the assurance we shall receive God's favor and earthly blessings—help that is appropriate and well-timed for every need. We can endure God's intimate scrutiny because in Jesus Christ we see God's great love for us. Therefore we come as we are.

God in his grace recognizes our human weaknesses but does not allow us to stay trapped by those conditions. Jesus Christ, the high priest, provides companionship with God, which produces the holiness intended in our lives.

The author of Hebrews encourages us to bring to the audience with the king our weakness and receive his strength. We bring our infirmity and receive health. We bring our trouble and receive help. Thanks to Jesus Christ the mediator, the priest, life is no longer a trap but an adventurous assignment from the king. (*Carolyn Volentine*)

TAKING THE LAST STEP

MARK 10:17-31

Sitting in a park one day, I saw a group of children playing on a slide. In the midst of all the energy and excitement there was one boy who held back. He was reluctant to go down the slide. The others were encouraging him to try. All of a sudden you could see the look of determination on his face as he boldly marched to the slide.

Step by step he climbed the ladder. But when he reached the top and his young eyes saw how far it was to the end of the slide, his resolve crumbled. You could see the fear and disappointment on his face and in his shaky knees as he slowly made his way back down the ladder. He stood on the brink of a momentous decision and was unable to take the last step.

I. Another Young Man Faced a Decision

This passage is about decision making, commitment, and separation from God. It's wrapped around wealth and a rich man's struggle. It calls into question the things, attitudes, and practices in our lives that keep us from total commitment. It's about ending the separation and taking that last step. Like the young boy on the slide, the rich young man comes to Jesus and stands on the brink of a momentous decision.

The rich young man responded to the compelling nature of Jesus' voice and message. He was good and faithful, but he realized something was missing. So he came seeking answers. Jesus loved him immediately. Jesus saw the boundless potential in him.

The Great Physician diagnosed the problem and said, "You lack one thing; go, sell what you own, and give the money to the poor, and you will have treasure in heaven; then come, follow me" (v. 21). But the price was too high. With shaky knees, the rich man slowly backed down. He couldn't take the last step and "went away grieving."

II. God Will Not Take Second Place

Jesus wasn't condemning money or wealth. Jesus was warning the disciples, the crowds, and us about decisions concerning money. Money and things cannot have first place in our lives. When they take first place we view everything in terms of price, not value. Money and things fix our heart on the world, not God. They can separate us from God.

It's not just love of money that separates. A thousand things can separate us from God. An attitude. A prejudice. Jealousy, political positions, indifference, a hobby, an unforgiving spirit, even a theological position; all of these can separate us from God if they take first place in our lives. We're called to fix our heart on God. God will not take second place in our lives.

III. It Is a Challenge Beyond All of Us, but Not Beyond God

The disciples were amazed at Jesus' pronouncement concerning the rich. It was popular belief that riches were a sign of God's favor. They asked, "Then who can be saved?" Jesus said, "For mortals it is impossible, but not for God; for God all things are possible" (v. 27).

We can't do it on our own. But God can do it for us. That's grace. Salvation comes through faith in God through Christ. That's the step the rich young man couldn't take, giving up all and following Jesus. This passage confronts us in the one area we don't like being confronted—our commitment. It challenges us to probe deeply and honestly into our faith relationship with God. It calls us to stand on the brink with shaky knees. It challenges us to take that last step. (*Billy D. Strayhorn*)

OCTOBER 19, 1997

❧

Twenty-second Sunday After Pentecost

Worship Theme: Authentic success is found only in authentic service.

Readings: Job 38:1-7 (34-41); Hebrews 5:1-10; Mark 10:35-45

Call to Worship (Psalm 104:1-9, 24, 35c):

Leader: Bless the LORD, O my soul.

People: O LORD my God, you are very great.

Leader: You are clothed with honor and majesty, wrapped in light as with a garment.

People: You stretch out the heavens like a tent, you set the beams of your chambers on the waters,

Leader: You make the clouds your chariot, you ride on the wings of the wind,

People: you make the winds your messengers, fire and flame your ministers.

Leader: You set the earth on its foundations, so that it shall never be shaken.

People: You cover it with the deep as with a garment; the waters stood above the mountains.

Leader: At your rebuke they flee; at the sound of your thunder they take to flight.

People: They rose up to the mountains, ran down to the valleys to the place that you appointed for them.

Leader: You set a boundary that they may not pass, so that they might not again cover the earth.

People: O LORD, how manifold are your works!

Leader: In wisdom you have made them all; the earth is full of your creatures.

All: Praise the LORD!

Pastoral Prayer:

Almighty and everlasting Father, we lift our praises unto you. We bless and magnify your name; we thank you for the grace you have shown to us through our Lord Jesus Christ. Preserve in us your truth; implant in us your will; reveal in us your power. Though we do not deserve your steadfast mercy, yet we are thankful that your love has been poured out upon us. Help us, Father, to remember day by day how great a debt we owe to you. And help us, Lord, to be willing to be empowered by your Holy Spirit, that we might be bold and effective servants of your Kingdom. For we know, Lord, that it is only in your service that we will find true freedom; it is only in your service that we will discover our true purpose. Use us that Jesus might be honored in all we do and say, for we ask it in his wonderful name, Amen.

SERMON BRIEFS

FINDING THE ANSWER IN THE WHIRLWIND

JOB 38:1-7 (34-41)

When a whirlwind of adversity strikes, how do you deal with it? We often ask "Why?" or "Why me?" Some stoic may keep silent or feel guilty about questioning, but most of us seek answers.

Viktor Frankl suffered through years in World War II concentration camps; he lost everything. Frankl later wrote, "If one has a why to live, he can endure almost any how." The Old Testament account of Job reveals that sometimes the why isn't given, but an even better answer can be found. How do we find the answer in the whirlwind of illness, death, war, bankruptcy, or natural calamity?

I. The Answer Comes When We Remember Who We Are

We don't have all the answers. A couple lost their son in a tragic motorcycle accident. Friends of the mother found it easy to say, "God

331

needed a flower for his garden." The "friends" of Job had easy answers. They offered conventional wisdom—"sin brings adversity; righteousness brings prosperity." Righteous Job didn't know what was happening, but he didn't buy that line.

Job stood defiantly before God and sought an audience to plead his case. He demanded a judicial hearing (31:35), but got far more than he expected. God said, "Who is this . . . ? Gird up your loins like a man; I will question you" (38:2-3).

Because we often consider ourselves "the masters of our fate," it is easy to slip into pride and self-sufficiency when adversity strikes. We defend ourselves, justify our actions, point to past faithfulness. We demand an answer, or give out easy answers. God reminds us who we are—a person limited in knowledge and power whom he may be teaching some lessons with adversity.

God placed Job on the witness stand and displayed multiple exhibits of creation's mysteries. "Where were you . . . ? Have you commanded the morning . . . ? Is it at your command that the eagle mounts up?" Since none of us can fathom the mysteries of life, we ought to keep more silence in the midst of the whirlwind of suffering.

II. The Answer Comes When We Remember Who God Is

With the splendor of creation spread before him like an Imax theater, Job realized anew the power of God. But what he needed even more—and what we need as well—was the presence of God. The Powerful One became the Present One. "Then the LORD answered Job out of the whirlwind" (38:1). Our God is "a very present help in trouble" (Ps. 46:1). If we are willing we can find the reality expressed in the old hymn, "He walks with me and talks with me, and tells me I am his own."

Job's attention was directed to the rhinoceros and the crocodile. David Cline observed, "These too are part of God's creation though we may see no value in them or indeed may find them positively malevolent. It is the same with suffering, sometimes indeed it may have a recognizable purpose, but sometimes it may be just as enigmatic and hurtful to man as the wild animals can be. Nevertheless it is part of God's order for the world, and he knows what he is doing in allowing it to be" (*The International Bible Commentary*, F. F. Bruce, ed., p. 547).

The liberation forces in Europe found written on a prison wall, "I believe in the sun even when it is not shining. I believe in the day, even when it is dark, and I believe in God, even when he is silent." Look and listen for God in the midst of your whirlwind. He does work "in all things for the good of those who love him" (Rom. 5:28). *(Bill D. Whittaker)*

QUALIFIED TO SERVE

HEBREWS 5:1-10

Whenever there is a local election, most newspapers run articles or charts that provide information on the background, experience, and views of the candidates who are running for office. That's because when a person is elected, or chosen for a job, the list of qualifications is always important. The candidate's abilities, experience, and knowledge are all a part of his or her qualifications.

In Hebrews 5, Paul outlines the duties of a high priest. And as the responsibilities are listed, he points to Jesus Christ as the supreme example of a high priest, who ministers on behalf of sinners who need his help. He reveals that Christ alone is qualified to serve.

I. The Role of the High Priest (v. 1)

Paul writes that "every high priest is appointed to represent them (men and women) in matters related to God." The high priest becomes a mediator between God and mankind; he brings the petitions and needs of man to the throne of God's grace and in turn he reveals to mankind the will and Word of God. The high priest makes the connection, facilitates the exchange.

When I preached in some evangelistic services in Brazil, a key person in every service was the translator. Brazilians speak Portuguese and I speak "Southernese," so it became necessary to involve someone who could understand both parties and facilitate communication between the two. Without the mediator, our words were lost.

The high priest of God represents men and women before God. The task is carried out in two specific ways. The high priest was to offer gifts and sacrifices to God to atone for the sins of the people. Normally a dove or a lamb, without spot or blemish, was sacrificed on the altar by the priests to represent the repentance of the people so that the relationship between God and man could be established once more. Through the sacrifice of the animals the sins were carried away. God and man would be made at one again.

II. The Calling of the High Priest (vv. 2-4)

To become a high priest required the special calling of God. One could not seek the office, but rather the office would seek the candidate. God—in his own time and in his own wisdom—would call out those whom he wanted to serve. It would be a special person, with a very special calling of God.

The calling to become a high priest carries with it two distinct qualifications. First, the priest has to be empathetic with human frailty. Paul states, "He is able to deal gently with those who are ignorant and are going astray, since he himself is subject to weakness." A good high priest understands the needs, problems, and pains of those whom he was called to serve.

As a pastor, I am always struck by what is said to people in the midst of their grief. So often as we attempt to comfort those who have lost a loved one to death, we say things like, "I know exactly how you feel, I know just what you're going through." The truth is that many of us don't really know, nor do we really understand the depth of their pain. To fully appreciate all that their loss will mean requires the experience of having walked where they are now walking. The high priest understands intimately the needs of his people.

The second qualification involved the calling of God. Only God can know the hearts and minds of his people, and only God can call persons into service who will adequately fill the role of a just and fair mediator. It was not uncommon for people to seek the office of high priest in the Jewish world because of the fame and notoriety and to some degree the financial success that it would bring. Only those who had felt the true call of God to lead his people found ultimate and lasting success.

III. The Sufficiency of Christ (vv. 9-10)

Paul reveals that all of the duties and qualifications of the high priest are fulfilled in Christ Jesus. It is Christ who becomes *the* High Priest for the people of the world. He offers gifts and sacrifices for our sins. He is mediator between God and man. He who was without

blemish or sin died for us that our sins might be removed. The gap
between Holy God and sinful man has been spanned only through
the work of our High Priest.

As a Christian people we affirm that the Word of God became flesh
and dwelt among us. We believe Christ to be fully human and fully
divine. He understands humanity and he emphathizes with our needs.

He carries the calling of God. So Christ did not take upon himself
the glory of becoming a high priest. But God said to him, "You are
my Son, today I have begotten you . . . You are a priest forever . . . "
(vv. 5-6). From the beginning of time to the end of the age, it has
been the will and plan of God for Christ to serve as the connection
through which we come to God. God called him to serve us. He alone
is worthy. (*Jon R. Roebuck*)

THE ABUNDANT LIFESTYLE

MARK 10:35-45

Joseph Cardinal Bernadin of Chicago says that when he was made
an archbishop many years ago, his mother instructed him, "When
you walk down the aisle in the service, try not to look too pleased
with yourself." One could forgive a Christian leader for being moved
on such an occasion, but his mother's warning was both timely and
timeless. The church is all too prone to count success as the world
measures it: by salary, prestige, and power.

In evaluating a former student's career progress, a retired professor
at a Protestant seminary superciliously remarked that this minister had
"never served any really significant churches." The same criticism could
be made about Jesus' earthly ministry—and the same problem, longing
for "success," can be identified in the Twelve who followed him.

I. We Make the Wrong Assumptions

James and John were two of the three in the Savior's inner circle
of disciples. Along with Simon Peter, they witnessed our Lord's
Transfiguration and appear in the forefront of many gospel stories.
They loved Jesus, and wanted to remain close to him, but they
misunderstood what close discipleship entailed.

The setting of this episode in Jesus' ministry is on his way to the
cross. When he first predicted his suffering death (8:31), Peter

strongly objected to the concept. Peter was on the side of humans, not of God. He had a flawed understanding of the Messiah's mission, and what following Christ would mean. In Mark 10:35-45, we see that James and John made the same mistake.

The church is prone to the same error today: believing that visible power denotes importance to God, numbers equal faithfulness, and religious celebrity means success.

II. Jesus Turns Our Assumptions Upside Down

The Master's response to James and John is one of the rare occasions when Jesus did not do what was asked. He queried, "What do you want me to do for you," as he did before healing blind Bartimaeus. But in this instance, he told the disciples such a favor was not his to grant. Not only did the Savior deny their claim for places of privilege, but his answer also modeled for them the servant mindset they ought to emulate.

His response asserts that the "payoff" for discipleship is uncertain; there are no guaranteed successes as the world measures them. The "cup" and the "baptism" mentioned in verses 38-40 were later understood by the early followers as references to the sacraments: gifts of God's grace by which people have a share in the destiny of Jesus, as Albert Schweizer points out. Thus the cup and the baptism are not symbols of achievement or tokens of successful discipleship, but marks of our commitment to do as our Lord did.

III. Assume Following Means Serving

Jesus said, "Whoever would be first among you must be slave of all," in sharp contrast to James and John aspiring to places of honor. Isaiah 53 depicts Jesus as the suffering servant who was despised and rejected in his self-giving, not admired or loved.

The death of the Messiah as suffering servant offers freedom and forgiveness to all in the bondage of sin. While our following Jesus does not have the same redemptive power as his suffering, it does mean loving and serving others in Jesus' name. Far from being masochistic or self-destructive, our servanthood has a purpose: to reveal God's grace made incarnate in Jesus Christ. What is more, we can rejoice in the midst of any suffering such servanthood entails, confident that the road to the cross also leads to the resurrection. (*Carol M. Noren*)

OCTOBER 26, 1997

Twenty-third Sunday After Pentecost

Worship Theme: Christ is our great High Priest, interceding for us in heaven.

Readings: Job 42:1-6, 10-17; Hebrews 7:23-28; Mark 10:46-52

Call to Worship (Psalm 34:1-5, 8):

Leader: I will bless the LORD at all times; his praise shall continually be in my mouth.

People: **My soul makes its boast in the LORD; let the humble hear and be glad.**

Leader: O magnify the LORD with me, and let us exalt his name together.

People: **I sought the LORD, and he answered me, and delivered me from all my fears.**

Leader: Look to him, and be radiant; so your faces shall never be ashamed.

All: **O taste and see that the LORD is good; happy are those who take refuge in him.**

Pastoral Prayer:

Almighty God, the source of all life, we raise our voices in praise for your greatness. We thank you for the blessings you provide—for the blessings of family and friends, for food and shelter, for work and worship. Even as we thank you for these blessings, Lord, we pray for those who are alone this day—those who do not have family to love or friends with whom to laugh. We pray for those who lack the basic needs of life which we take for granted—those who do not have enough to eat, or who live on the street or in shelters, without a home to call their own. We pray for those who are unemployed—who lack

337

the sense of purpose that comes from meaningful work. Most of all, we pray for those who do not enjoy a relationship with you—those who do not have that joy and abundance of life which is possible only through surrender to your love and grace. Even as we intercede for these, Father, we thank you for our great High Priest, the Lord Jesus Christ, who even now intercedes on our behalf. We offer all these prayers in his name, Amen.

SERMON BRIEFS

SOUND, SIGHT, AND FAITH

JOB 42:1-6, 10-17

A new bride, just home from the honeymoon, was preparing a special meal with ham and lots of extras. The young husband was surprised when his wife cut off apparently two good ends of the ham before it went into the oven. "Why did you do that?" he asked. "That's the way my mother always fixed a ham," she replied.

On a visit to her folks he asked his mother-in-law about it and heard, "That's the way my mother always cooked a ham." The young groom made a special trip to grandmother's house to hear her explanation. "Son, that's the only way the ham will fit into my pan."

Do you respond to life the way others have, or do you make your own decisions? Is it truth for you because someone else said it, or do you have to see it for yourself? Job's testimony reflects the tension between sound, sight, and faith.

I. Responsibility Accepted

Job acknowledged, "I had heard of you by the hearing of the ear, but now my eye sees you" (42:5). In the pilgrimage of faith it can't be all hearing or all sight. Both are involved and we must make a responsible decision to both. Job accepted the responsibility for the word God spoke (vv. 3, 4), and for his own rash words. "I have uttered what I did not understand" (42:3). His personal encounter with God left him speechless at first (40:4-5).

"Faith comes by hearing, and hearing by the word of God" (Rom. 10:17, NKJV). When we respond by faith to God's word we begin to see God. The word spoken by Jesus will judge us at the last day (John 12:48). The rich man, concerned about his sinful family, was told, "If they do not listen to Moses and the prophets (the word of God), neither will they be convinced even if someone rises from the dead" (Luke 16:31). God has spoken through his word. Have you made a responsible decision and come to know him personally? Jesus said, "Blessed are those who have not seen and yet have come to believe" (John 20:29).

II. Repentance Acknowledged

Sound and sight came together in a fresh encounter between Job and God. He made the response the prophet made when he saw the Lord "high and lifted up" (Isa. 6, RSV): "Therefore I despise myself and repent in dust and ashes" (v. 6). Alexander Maclaren noted, "If we rightly understood His power, we can rest upon it as a Hand sustaining, not crushing us. . . . It is better to trust than to criticize, better to wait than to seek prematurely to understand."

True repentance was evidenced in Job's lack of demands. He asked for no vindication, nor for a healing touch. He was content with the presence of God.

III. Restoration Experienced

A turn from pride, rash demands, and self-sufficiency always brings one to a position of usefulness to God. Job was used as an intercessor for his friends (42:8, 10). He was restored to fellowship with his neighbors (42:11). New leadership in his family resulted (42:12-16). He died "full of days" (v. 17).

It doesn't always happen that way. Sometimes entrance into glory restores health. Sometimes the divorce goes through. Restoration to a vital relationship with God and full days in his will is always the best result. (*Bill D. Whittaker*)

ALWAYS ON THE JOB

HEBREWS 7:23-28

As the Chaplain of the Week at the local hospital, I am required to wear a "beeper" 24 hours a day so that I can always be reached in case of an emergency. I am, in effect, always on call and thus "always on the job."

There are a number of things that need to be always on the job. For example, for the safety of the nation, our National Defense system must always be on the alert, ready to respond anytime. We desire that our utility providers stay on the job. We need our power, our water, and of course our cable TV! Perhaps most important is the 911 emergency system. People are always on the job, waiting to help if there is an emergency. We need that kind of protection.

In the seventh chapter of Hebrews, as readers we are reminded of the great assurance and peace that Christ can offer. He does so because he is always on the job. Christ continues to work in our behalf, at all times, in every situation. In this passage, Christ is being compared to the high priests of his day. He is shown to be superior because, unlike them, he lives forever, he makes constant intercession, and he offers the perfect sacrifice.

I. Christ Lives Forever (v. 24)

In the old system of high priests and sacrifices, death meant there was a continual need for replacements. As soon as one priest died and new one would have to be appointed. Over and over the process of replacement went on.

One of the problems with computers and the software to run them is the problem of upgrades. No sooner is a program purchased and installed on the hard drive, than a new version, an upgrade is announced. There is a constant game of obtaining the newer, better, and faster program. Constant replacement can be tiresome.

Christ is superior to the finite high priests of his day. Christ is eternal and he holds the priesthood permanently. Christ will always serve as our high priest. Eternity is a difficult concept to comprehend. We have difficulty even visualizing such an expanse of time. But the truth of God's Word proclaims that as long as there is time, Christ will lead us, protect us, guide us and forgive us. He will open and maintain a channel to God. He lives forever and is our Priest forever.

II. Christ Makes Constant Intercession (v. 25)

To intercede means to "intervene" or to "mediate." Christ "always lives to intercede" on our behalf. Before Christ came, a mediator or priest was needed to act as a "go between" uniting man with God.

The priest became a middle man taking the petitions of each sinner to the throne of God's grace.

Most of us have been through the frustrating process of buying a car. It seems that at every dealership there is a middle man that we have to encounter. He takes our offer to someone else and then returns with the answer. It seems that we are never allowed to talk directly to the person who can make the deal. It is frustrating to play the game of indirect communication.

Christ comes to offer constant communication. He continues to petition God for our needs; he continues to provide the atonement for our sins. It is as if Christ says to God over and over again, "I know this man; he is one of mine." Christ intercedes on our behalf constantly; he mediates the relationship between God and man.

III. Christ Offers a Perfect Sacrifice (vv. 26-27)

On the Day of Atonement, the high priest would enter the Holy of Holies to make two important sacrifices. The first sacrifice offered was to atone for his own sins. The second was to atone for the sins of the people. It was a continuing action. It was repeated over and over, year after year. Christ died once for all! He has offered for us a complete and perfect sacrifice. When Christ died for our sins, it marked a complete and final sacrifice. His sacrifice met our needs. All that was, is, and will be needed to atone for our sins, Christ has already provided.

Sometimes dentists have the unpleasant task of filling cavities. On some occasions, a temporary filling is placed in the cavity until the permanent filling can be put into place. What agony as a patient, to go through the process over and over again. A complete and final fix would be the desired result.

Christ has done a complete work. His sacrifice has covered our sins for all of time. Christ is always on the job, making intercession and offering his love for us. (*Jon R. Roebuck*)

EYES OF FAITH

MARK 10:46-52

Every reporter has an agenda. Ask five people who witness an accident to give an account of what happened, and you'll get five different testimonies, even if they're all trying to be objective. Every retelling of a story has a purpose; it's true of current events, and it's true in biblical narratives. The way we remember and repeat the healing of Bartimaeus says something about us as well as him.

Our grandparents may have sung Homer Rodeheaver's interpretation of this passage, "Then Jesus Came:"

> When Jesus comes the tears are wiped away. . .
> For all is changed when Jesus comes to stay.

The remaining stanzas recall the healing of the Gerasene demoniac, the person who had leprosy, the person who could not hear or speak—the bottom line being that everything is different when Jesus comes to stay. A more contemporary rendition of the story, "Blind man sat by the road and he cried," emphasizes Jesus showing us the way to go home, that is, to be saved.

When Mark recounts this event of Jericho Road suggests *his* motive. He wasn't establishing that Jesus could heal the sick; that was already done at the beginning of the Gospel. The episode is set near the end of Jesus' earthly ministry. Earlier in the chapter we find the story of the rich young man, the account of James and John asking special favors, and Jesus' third prediction of his passion and death. Jesus was on his way to the crucifixion, and this is the final healing miracle Mark records.

How the story is framed tells us of Mark's purpose. The blind beggar perceived something those closest to Jesus couldn't see. Bartimaeus called him "Master"—the first time in Mark's Gospel the Lord is addressed that way. Bartimaeus proclaimed Jesus "Son of David" before the crowds of Palm Sunday used the title. Bartimaeus glorified God and inspired others to give glory. Faith and praise—even from someone considered an outsider—made a person whole, and gave him confidence.

Mark's depiction of the disciples make plain they didn't understand who the Messiah was or why they were going to Jerusalem. James and John's request resulted in a quarrel among the disciples. They showed an uncaring, even nasty attitude toward a blind man seeking the Great Physician. Mark's depiction showed even long-time followers getting in the way of God's power and purpose, when blinded by a merely human vision.

But the persecuted, Gentile church for which Mark wrote would also have heard it as a message of hope: that "outsiders" are included in the Kingdom; that God's purpose is accomplished even on the way to a cross; that those who are broken may still lead others to faith.

Today, Mark's perspective offers encouragement to Christians anxious about the future and tempted to close ranks against a sometimes hostile environment. Like Bartimaeus, we are to risk everything to proclaim the gospel, relying on God's promises rather than visible evidence. We are all blind or broken in some way, but by the grace of God we can be healed and used to the glory of Christ. (*Carol M. Noren*)

NOVEMBER

❧

Mending the Net, Sharpening the Hoe

Symbol: Bread

Bread is seen as the minimum need for human sustenance in God's providence.

Text:

"I am the bread of life. Your forefathers ate the manna in the desert, yet they died. But here is the bread that comes down from heaven, which a man may eat and not die. I am the living bread that came down from heaven. If anyone eats of this bread, he will live forever. This bread is my flesh, which I will give for the life of the world" (John 6:48-51 NIV).

Invocation:

"Almighty God, may your strong hand defend, guide, and empower my life and ministry today. In the name of Christ. Amen." (Reuben P. Job and Norman Shawchuck, *A Guide to Prayer*)

Scripture Focus:

- Matthew 4:3ff.
- Mark 6:41ff.
- John 6:48-51
- Exodus 16:4
- 1 Corinthians 11:24
- Philippians 4:19

Prayer Focus:

- Name persons you know who are living without heavenly sustenance.
- Express gratitude for heavenly sustenance provided for you and your family.
- Focus on ways to share heavenly bread with hungry people.
- Focus on preparing and receiving the heavenly bread.
- Pray that worship will provide heavenly manna abundantly to your people.

Prayer:

Eternal God, we thank you that we have found you and have experienced you in the intimacy of our being. We are grateful to have lived even for one hour in the fire of your trinity, the furnace of your unity. This makes us clearly say, "Now I understand." You alone are enough for me. Amen. *(Bill Self)*

NOVEMBER 2, 1997

❧

Twenty-fourth Sunday After Pentecost

Worship Theme: True love grows out of our commitment to Christ.

Readings: Ruth 1:1-18; Hebrews 9:11-14; Mark 12:28-34

Call to Worship (Psalm 146):

Leader: Praise the LORD! Praise the LORD, O my soul!

People: **I will praise the LORD as long as I live; I will sing praises to my God all my life long.**

Leader: Do not put your trust in princes, in mortals, in whom there is no help.

People: **When their breath departs, they return to the earth; on that very day their plans perish.**

Leader: Happy are those whose help is the God of Jacob, whose hope is in the LORD their God,

People: **who made heaven and earth, the sea, and all that is in them; who keeps faith forever;**

Leader: who executes justice for the oppressed; who gives food to the hungry.

People: **The LORD sets the prisoners free; the Lord opens the eyes of the blind.**

Leader: The LORD lifts up those who are bowed down; the LORD loves the righteous.

People: **The LORD watches over the strangers;**

Leader: he upholds the orphan and the widow, but the way of the wicked he brings to ruin.

346

All: **The LORD will reign forever, your God, O Zion, for all generations. Praise the LORD!**

Pastoral Prayer:

Our Father and our God, who has created us as a holy people, a royal priesthood, the body of Christ. We thank you for your steadfast mercy, for your compassion, for your grace. Forgive us for the way we so often fall short of your will for our lives—when we abuse when we could have encouraged; when we are silent when a word of witness is needed; when we ignore those who are hurting rather than extending a healing hand. And forgive us, Lord, when we fail to love, even though you have provided us a model of perfect love in Jesus Christ. Help us to surrender our lives to Christ so that love flows naturally from our hearts. We ask all this in the name of the One who loves us all the way to a cross, Amen.

SERMON BRIEFS

LOVE THAT LASTS

RUTH 1:1-18

The familiar words from Ruth (vv. 16-17) took on new significance when I heard them read at the wedding of two students. The bride was from Russia; the groom from Virginia. She had only been in America a year. Each of them is still learning the other's language; but they understand the language of love.

Through book and film Americans witnessed the "love story" about *The Bridges of Madison County*. In the story, a photographer and a married woman have an affair while her husband is away. For too many that defines love. Although spoken by a young woman to her mother-in-law, the words of Ruth provide a better model for love that lasts.

I. Love That Lasts Develops Through Loss

Naomi and Ruth shared grief in the loss of their husbands. They had experienced famine and other problems. Naomi affirmed that Ruth had treated her kindly through these times of loss (v. 8). The

347

prospect of separation brought tears (v. 9). No doubt these difficulties had strengthened the bond between Naomi and Ruth. Although Orpah also expressed her affection (v. 14), the bond was not enough to keep her from returning to her homeland.

Naomi felt Ruth would lose even more if they stayed together (vv. 12-13). But "Ruth clung to her" and insisted on accompanying her mother-in-law back to Judah. No possible future loss could be as real as Ruth losing the love of Naomi. She had lost her husband; she would not lose Naomi.

My wife and I grieved the loss of our first child. But from the grief came a stronger love for each other. Love that lasts develops through loss, if you are willing to seek the other's best welfare rather than selfishly continue to nurture the grief.

II. Love That Lasts Grows Through Commitment

Pollster George Barna describes our time as an age of decreased commitment. Authentic love involves commitment: "For better, for worse; for richer or poorer; in sickness or in health. This commitment of love has no boundaries. "Where you go, I will go." Love requires little to satisfy. "Where you lodge, I will lodge." Love will adjust. "Your people shall be my people." Love never ends. "Where you die, I will die,—there will I be buried."

III. Love That Lasts Comes from Faith

"The cord that drew her was twisted of two strands." Ruth loved Naomi but she also loved God. She declared, "your God, my God. The LORD do so to me, and more also, if anything but death parts you and me" (NKJV). The Lord became Ruth's Lord.

The fruit of the Spirit is love. Truly spiritual people have great capacity to love. Jesus said others would recognize his disciples by the love they have for one another.

"And now abide faith, hope, love, these three; but the greatest of these is love" (1 Cor. 13:13 NJKV). Authentic love lasts. It is the product of faith in Christ, our only hope for lasting relationships. (*Bill D. Whittaker*)

NOVEMBER 2, 1997

LIFE IS LIQUID

HEBREWS 9:11-14

In my view of life and its ebb and flow, there are four liquids that must be present in any home. My list includes: ketchup, Mountain Dew soft drink, Armor All protectant, and WD-40 lubricant. If I have those four liquids, I can survive just about any catastrophe!

There is, however, another liquid, without which we cannot survive: blood. Blood is the liquid of life. It surges through our bodies bringing oxygen and food to all the cells that comprise life.

Blood drives are always a fascination to me. If we are honest, most of us are a bit squeamish at the thought of giving blood. Needles and tubes bother even the bravest men and women. But have you noticed that when the need is great enough, when there is a crisis, then even the most anxious people step forward to offer their contribution.

Because of his love, and our need, Christ has offered to our world, the sacrifice of his blood. Through his death on the cross, Jesus has offered a superior sacrifice. In these verses from Hebrews 9, the writer illustrates the superiority of the sacrifice. It is superior in three ways.

I. It Was His Own Blood (vv. 13-14)

On the tenth day of the seventh month of each year, the high priest offered the sacrifice of animals to atone for the sins of the people. Symbolically, he took his own sins and those of his people with him into the Holy of Holies, and there he made sacrifice. Several different animals were used. The blood of bulls was used to atone for the sins of the priest (A little ironic, isn't it?), and the blood of goats was used to atone for the sins of the people. A special red heifer was used to wash away the sins of anyone having contact with the body of a dead person.

Rather than the blood of animals, Christ offered his own blood to atone for our sins. To offer his blood was to offer his life. His was a perfect sacrifice with no impurities. Even in our technologically advanced age, there is no synthetic substitute for blood. It is a precious human commodity. In the same way, there can be no substitute for the blood of Christ who offered his body on Calvary for the sins of humankind. His sacrifice was superior because it was the offering of his own blood.

349

II. There Was a Finality to His Sacrifice (v. 12*b*)

Verse 12*b* indicates that Christ entered the holy place—into the presence of Almighty God—"once for all." No more would a yearly sacrifice be made; the sacrifice of Jesus was a complete and final sacrifice. His blood offered that which no animal could give. The blood of animals removed the outward stains of sin; they cleansed the body but not the soul. They were unable to remove the guilt of sin.

Christ is able to forgive completely. The promise of 1 John 1:9 states, "If we confess our sins, he (Jesus) who is faithful and just and will remove our sins and cleanse us from all unrighteousness (guilt)." What freedom! In Christ, the believer never has to confess the same sins more than once. Christ's forgiveness is not like the old system of sacrifice where the sinner would feel the guilt of his iniquity over and over again. In Christ there is no guilt, but only freedom once that sin is confessed. Christ forgives and removes the guilt of our sins. There is a finality to his sacrifice.

III. It Was a Rational Sacrifice (v. 14)

On the cross, Christ offered himself. It was a voluntary and rational decision. Animals used for sacrifice never had a choice in the matter. They were selected and used by the High Priest. Yet Christ himself chose to offer his life, fully aware of the implications of his decision.

Could there be a greater illustration of the love of Christ than his pilgrimage to the cross? First came the agony of Gethsemane. Next would come the betrayal, the trial, the jeering crowds, and finally the crucifixion. At any point, Christ had the power to say No! and bring the process to a screeching halt. By his own choice, Christ died for us that we might have life. It was a rational sacrifice.

Christ offered his blood to atone for our sins, simply because of his love. (*Jon R. Roebuck*)

ANYTHING BUT LOVE

MARK 12:28-34

A recent Gallup poll on the faith Americans profess showed that a great majority of people in the United States believe in God. They also believe in heaven, and are confident they will go there after death. Those polled gave a wide variety of answers about what qualifies a person for heaven: being honest, acting kindly toward other people, obeying the Ten Commandments, giving one's life to Christ, and so forth.

Robert Bellah gives a face to this lack of consensus in *Habits of the Heart,* in an interview with a woman named Sheila. "Sheila-ism" is her religion; though she believes in God, it is a God whose values and standards are her own, who wants her to do what she thinks is best for herself. The suggestion of moral imperatives from outside oneself is more often than not regarded as repressive, bigoted, and an attack on individual liberty.

It's an ironic contrast to the spirit of the age in which Jesus lived and taught. In the nineteen references to "scribes" in Mark's Gospel, eighteen present these experts on the law in a negative light, obsessed with the letter of the law and trying to discredit Jesus. Far from discarding an external, communal standard for righteous living before God, the scribes devoted much time to measuring the extent to which they and others lived up to the standard. Some would say they were infatuated with the law itself.

There is a radical difference between the context in which Mark's Gospel was written and our own world, yet our Redeemer's words are equally challenging to both.

I. Hear, O Israel

Jesus answered the scribe's question, "which commandment is the first of all?" by quoting the *Shema* from Deuteronomy 6:4. These words were recited daily by Jews, who would have understood them as God speaking through Moses, the lawgiver. Therefore, they carried the weight of divine imperative, and also simultaneously reaffirmed Israel's corporate identity before God as "God's people."

Among followers of the Messiah, the *Shema* would have identified Christ as part of the prophetic tradition of Isaiah, Jeremiah, and others. Claiming this word as divine imperative to themselves had the additional effect of identifying themselves as people belonging to God in a special relationship.

II. Love the Lord Your God

The capacity for "hearing" the word of God or being called God's people is not the result of following rules successfully, nor the outcome of doing what feels right to an individual at a particular moment in time. Rather it is a gift from our gracious God, and the appropriate response is love that seeks expression through treasuring God's good purpose for us. As Saint Francis Xavier wrote, "E'en so I love thee, and will love, and in thy praise will sing; solely because thou art my God and my eternal King."

III. Love Your Neighbor

The scribe did not ask Jesus for the second commandment, though it, too, is found in the Torah (Lev. 19:18b). This command is echoed in Romans 13:9 and 1 John 4:7, 8. Eduard Schweizer wrote that it is impossible to keep the first commandment unless one lives according to the second. Jesus, as the fulfillment of the Law, obeyed the two great commandments perfectly, and gave his life for us out of love for the world and love for the Father.

Following Christ means, among other things, becoming like Christ in self-giving love. Like the scribe, we "are not far from the kingdom of God" if we know this—but we have not yet arrived unless we do it, too. Love is perhaps the most difficult commandment: impossible to do without God's enabling grace. *(Carol M. Noren)*

352

NOVEMBER 9, 1997

ૐ

Twenty-fifth Sunday After Pentecost

Worship Theme: Our trust must be in God rather than material things.

Readings: Ruth 3:1-5, 4:13-17; Hebrews 9:24-28; Mark 12:38-44

Call to Worship (Psalm 127:1-2):

Leader: Unless the Lord builds the house, those who build it labor in vain.

People: Unless the LORD guards the city, the guard keeps watch in vain.

Leader: It is in vain that you rise up early and go late to rest, eating the bread of anxious toil;

People: for he gives sleep to his beloved.

Pastoral Prayer:

Almighty and everlasting God, you are worthy of all praise. We worship your majesty, we adore your awesome love. All good things have flowed from your hands, O Lord; you have given us your truth, your love, your presence. Forgive us, Lord, when we focus on the foolish, temporal possessions that are in our hands for a moment and then gone; we are too often like children who see only what is immediate and do not see the greater truth. Help us, Father, to recognize that we are rich above all persons because of what you have done in our hearts and lives. Remind us, Lord, that there is no greater treasure than a forgiven life, a redeemed soul, a life indwelt by the Holy Spirit, and a future in your divine presence. Help us live each day worthy of the great future you have given us by your grace, for we ask it in Jesus' name. Amen.

SERMON BRIEFS

MATCH MADE IN HEAVEN

RUTH 3:1-5; 4:13-17

Fiddler on the Roof includes a scene where the heroine implores the town matchmaker to find the right marriage partner for her. "Matchmaker, matchmaker, find me a match." Would-be matchmakers should take lessons from Naomi. The brief love story of Ruth and Boaz reveals some excellent pointers on how to make a match; but more important, it contains vital decisions involved in having a marriage blessed by God.

I don't think marriages are made in heaven, but the Lord of heaven will bless a marriage that honors his will. "Seek first the kingdom of God and his righteousness, and all these things shall be added to you" (Matt. 6:33 NKJV), doesn't just apply to what we eat, drink, or wear.

I. Heavenly Matches Consider Earthly Realities

There is little doubt that Naomi's matchmaking was partly motivated by her own need for security (vv. 1-2). Cultural realities motivated her search for a near kinsman to perpetuate the family identity and retain ownership of her husband's land. Isn't God also concerned about earthly realities such as security, family, and compatibility?

A Gallup poll stated 47 percent of marriages now end with mutual incompatibility as the reason for the dissolution of the relationship. Most of the people who claim this were once madly in love.

We are warned "if anyone does not provide for his own, and especially for those of his household, he has denied the faith and is worse than an unbeliever" (1 Tim. 5:8 NKJV). Emotional, spiritual, and physical security stabilize marriage and enable the union to fulfill God's purpose.

II. Heavenly Matches Observe Life Actions

The untypical kindness of Boaz did not go unnoticed by Ruth (2:13). Apparently Boaz had also checked her out, "for all the people of my town know that you are a virtuous woman" (3:11 NKJV). In a moment when less principled people would have given in to lust, these two patiently waited. Ruth accepted his word and laid at his feet without fear (3:14a). Desire did not dethrone duty (3:13). The early hours of the morning brought renewed concern for their reputation (3:14b).

Every relationship involves risk. Observe life actions before you risk yourself to another.

III. Heavenly Matches Wait for the Lord's Blessing

Naomi told Ruth to "sit still, my daughter, until you know how the matter will turn out" (3:18 NKJV). That's good advice for all who seek a match. It is a good word for those who seriously court another, and sound wisdom newlyweds should heed. Heavenly matches take time.

"So Boaz took Ruth and she became his wife" (4:13 NKJV). Taking and becoming are continuing decisions of commitment. Insecurity visits again when the skin sags and wrinkles come. "Will he love me after the mastectomy?" "Will she be there when memory fails?" Browning penned the hope: "Come grow old along with me, the best is yet to be, the last for which the first was made."

All of creation was blessed through the union of Ruth and Boaz. From their son Obed came Jesse, then David, and ultimately the Savior of the world. Think about the future blessings jettisoned by couples who give up on their relationship at the first "big fight."

Your marriage may not have been "made in heaven" but it can become a heavenly match. *(Bill D. Whittaker)*

THE WELCOME MAT

HEBREWS 9:24-28

Do you have a welcome mat at your door? There is a difference between a welcome mat and a doormat. A doormat is a woven cloth on which you wipe your feet, leave the mud, or remove your shoes. Although it may look the same, a welcome mat says something quite different. It says, "We're glad you're here! You are among friends."

In our journey from earth to heaven, from the temporary to the eternal, we are received into glory with a welcome mat placed there

355

by a loving Savior. There is something better than a pot of gold at the end of life; because of the work of Christ there is a welcome mat receiving us into heaven with an enthusiastic reception. Christ welcomes us. We are welcomed into a relationship with God, we are welcomed into eternal life. We are welcomed into a forever fellowship with Christ.

How does the work of Christ welcome us into heaven?

I. Christ Appears for Us (v. 24)

Do you know what a sanctuary is? It is by definition a holy place, a shelter, a house of worship. It is a place where God and man have direct contact. According to Hebrews, Christ has not entered a man-made sanctuary. The writer clearly states that Christ did not enter the tabernacle, the temple—nothing built by human hands. Instead, Christ entered the one true sanctuary: heaven itself. Christ entered the place of God. It was there that Christ had directed communication with the Father.

When matters are serious enough, we desire that kind of communication. We want to talk directly. Maybe it's a big business deal, or a wedding proposal, or multinational negotiations; when the matters are of grave concern, we desire direct communication. No substitute for the real thing will do.

Christ has entered heaven, into the presence of God, to appear for us. Christ used direct communication to plead our case before God. Christ has taken our needs, our problems, our fears, and our pains to God. What joy there is in knowing that Christ has already paved the way for our journey. He has appeared for us!

II. Christ Sacrifices for Us (vv. 25-26)

In verse 25, the writer of Hebrews refers to the Old Testament sacrificial system. Year by year, the high priest entered the Holy of Holies on the day of Atonement and offered sacrifices for his sins and for the sins of the people. The sacrifice that was required was the blood of animals. In contrast to that system, Christ has made the one and only sacrifice. Instead of the sacrifice of animals, Christ offered the sacrifice of himself, which was sufficient for all our sins. Notice the key phrase of verse 26: "to remove sin by the sacrifice of himself."

To be a good host, to truly welcome someone into your home, you must make some sacrifice. There is the effort of cleaning the house, doing the cooking, preparing the table, working in the yard. Effort must be made for everything to made right. I remember as a child one of the most dreaded phrase in our home was, "The deacons are coming." Each year my parents would host a deacon/spouse cookout in our home. There was always much cleaning and preparation to be done. You couldn't mess up the dishes, walk on the floor, or enter into the forbidden living room. Everything had to be just right.

Christ has made everything just right by his sacrifice. By offering his life before God, we are no longer enslaved by our sins. We are no longer guilty under God's law. We are free. By his sacrifice, Christ has made it possible for us to be in God's holy place in fellowship with holy God.

III. Christ Saves Us (vv. 27-28)

The writer of Hebrews reminds us of the Judgment Day of God. There will be an ending to this life. We will be held accountable for what we have done or for what we have failed to do. Judgment will come. But verse 28 reminds us that Christ has removed our sins. He is coming again, not to remove sins a second time as though his first sacrifice was not complete. Instead, he comes to bring salvation.

The Day of Judgment, for those of us who are people of faith, will not be a day of fear but rather a day of grace. It will be a day in which we will be reminded that Christ loved us enough to die in our place. Instead of eternal punishment, Christ says, "Welcome, you are among friends."

My brother and I had fought all day. Mother had made the eternal proclamation, "Wait till your father gets home." We did so with great fear and trembling. He came in to make his I'm-about-to-spank-you speech. He pulled back the edges of his coat and said, "See this belt?" He had on sans-a-belt slacks, no belt in sight. We laughed until we cried. He did, too. How about that? We thought we were about to really get it, but instead we spent the day in laughter. We received something we did not deserve: grace. Christ saves us from what we deserve.

The road to God is made open by the work of Christ. The welcome mat is out at the end of our journey. Christ is there, offering us an enthusiastic reception. *(Jon R. Roebuck)*

357

WIDOW'S MIGHT

MARK 12:38-44

Nearly everyone likes to be identified with prestige and success, even in the church. Chapel attendance at one seminary more than tripled the day Robert Schuller was guest preacher; everyone wanted to see this Christian celebrity. Give any boy in the Sunday school a choice whether to be a king or a shepherd in the Christmas pageant, and you know which one he'll choose. The number at weekly Bible study will be higher when you study Joshua than when you get to Jeremiah.

Something in each of us gravitates toward those who have power; their stories allow us to enjoy their reflected glory and thus feel a little better about ourselves. Even if the powerful are oppressive and cruel, as in the cases of Pharaoh and Herod, we take satisfaction in comparing ourselves favorably to them.

This tendency in human nature makes it difficult to "get into" the story from Mark's Gospel. Jesus began by condemning those who enjoy their power and prestige. Their trappings of success—things to which any of his listeners might aspire—would be the means of their condemnation before God.

If that was not enough, Jesus drew their attention to a poor widow whose meager offering was all she had. He held her up as an example to his listeners. They were difficult words for them to hear. They knew a widow's economic standing was barely above that of a slave's. They received meager charity: being allowed to glean after the reapers had finished with a field. As Mark 12:40 indicates, widows were routinely swindled by the more powerful. Far from having a "big name," this widow's name wasn't even known.

I. Our Temptation Is to Stand with the Powerful

It is relatively easy to hear this story from the standpoint of those who stood beside Jesus. They looked at the widow, perhaps joined in praising her for her generosity. They could have exhorted one another to be more generous in their contributions to the temple, felt good about their increased level of giving, and might even have resolved to do something to lessen the widow's deprivation. They could have done all this without changing their self-understanding and protection of their own interests. But our Lord calls his listeners to do far more than write a larger check next time.

II. Our Challenge Is to Stand with the Widow

In contrast with those who watched the scene, or who contributed out of their abundance, the widow who gave all she had knew that her only hope was in God's mercy. Like the widow of Zarephath who gave the last of her sustenance to God's prophet, this woman committed all that she had to divine keeping. There is, among such people, the realization that "our help comes from the Lord, who made heaven and earth." Delusions of prestige and self-sufficiency may blind us until all other helpers fail, and comforts flee.

Standing with the widow means coming to the realization of our neediness. It also means acting on that realization: abandoning self-protecting strategies in favor of radical obedience in following Jesus' example. It is taking risks for and with Christ. And it means doing so with humility and thanksgiving, trusting the Lord's purpose and promise rather than human gain. The widow's might is the providence and love of Almighty God; worldly ideas of success pale in comparison. *(Carol M. Noren)*

NOVEMBER 16, 1997

❧

Twenty-sixth Sunday After Pentecost

Worship Theme: Christ's presence gives us confidence in the future.

Readings: 1 Samuel 1:4-20; Hebrews 10:11-14 (15-18), 19-25; Mark 13:1-8

Call to Worship (Psalm 16):

Leader: Protect me, O God, for in you I take refuge.

People: I say to the LORD, "You are my Lord; I have no good apart from you."

Leader: As for the holy ones in the land, they are the noble, in whom is all my delight. Those who choose another god multiply their sorrows; their drink offerings of blood I will not pour out or take their names upon my lips.

People: The LORD is my chosen portion and my cup; you hold my lot.

Leader: The boundary lines have fallen for me in pleasant places; I have a goodly heritage.

People: I bless the LORD who gives me counsel; in the night also my heart instructs me.

Leader: I keep the LORD always before me; because he is at my right hand, I shall not be moved.

People: Therefore my heart is glad, and my soul rejoices; my body also rests secure.

Leader: For you do not give me up to Sheol, or let your faithful one see the Pit.

People: You show me the path of life.

Leader: In your presence there is fullness of joy;

All: in your right hand are pleasures forevermore.

Pastoral Prayer:

Almighty God, who has resurrected our Lord Jesus Christ and through him has created us to be a unique community, his body, the church. We thank you for this day of worship, a time when you call on us to lay aside the week's agenda and focus our minds and energies on a greater purpose and a more certain future. Grant to us a sense of your presence, and give us the courage to act as children of God. We praise you for your love and mercy, which reach out to us even in the midst of sin and rebellion, and which call us to a life richer and purer than we could ever know apart from your grace. We praise you, Father, for the resurrection power that has come into our lives through the atoning sacrifice of Christ. Grant us confidence, O Lord, to live worthy of our divine calling; enable us to demonstrate in our words and actions that the risen One is even now alive and well and in our hearts. For we ask all these things in his powerful name. Amen.

SERMON BRIEFS

A MOTHER FOR ALL TIMES

1 SAMUEL 1:4-20

In Ponca City, Oklahoma, an artist depicted in a statue some of the women who helped settle the West. The pioneer woman has a bonnet and long dress. With in one hand she holds a Bible close to her heart. With the other hand she leads her child. Her face is turned upward and her eyes gaze into the distance. She is striding boldly across the prairie.

Consider this image for today's mother. Date book in hand, desktop computer on her shoulder, she heads to the car. Her child is running to catch up with her. They are eating a breakfast pastry, late for the car pool stops on the way to the child development center!

Both of these images contrast with Hannah, who is described in 1 Samuel 1. Hannah could probably identify more with the pioneer woman, but she still offers a contemporary model for today's mother.

I. A Mother with Sorrow

Many mothers today understand Hannah's struggle because your home isn't a bed of roses either. One news account listed the home as society's violent place. Jealousy tears apart family relationships. Couples who yearn for a child silently grieve with every news account of child abuse. Divorce pits family members against one another.

Mothers may even be misunderstood by the church. Hannah's preacher saw her praying at the altar and thought she was drunk (v. 13). A mother going through a divorce told me, "I guess I'll have to find another church. Not one member has said a word to me during this rough time. Maybe they don't know what to say, or they think I'm an embarrassment to the church."

Every mother, every home has problems, or will. For Hannah they continued "year by year" (v. 7). The tears easily flowed; her appetite diminished. Her husband worried. Instead of giving up she turned to God.

II. A Mother with Faith

A time of trouble is no time to give up on God and his people. Hannah kept fellowship in the house of God (v. 7). She prayed to the Lord, pouring out her soul before him (vv. 10-11, 15-16). Worship and prayer change the face of our problems. Perplexed by evil, the psalmist said, "When I thought how to understand this, it was too painful for me—Until I went into the sanctuary of God, then I understood" (Ps. 73:16-17 NKJV).

Faith finds new courage in the promises of God. Hannah received the word to "Go in peace; the God of Israel grant the petition you have made to him" (v. 17). The promise was enough. She "went her way and ate, and her face was no longer sad" (v. 18 NKJV). Sorrows and problems find resolution in the promises of God. Countless individuals have by faith "subdued kingdoms, worked righteousness, obtained promises" (Heb. 11:33 NKJV).

George Barna wrote: "What an incredible state of affairs. The family is deteriorating before our very eyes and little is being done to save it. Millions of Americans cannot even describe the meaning of "family values" (*Absolute Confusion,* Regal Books, 1993, p. 143).

Let's pray and work together toward the goal of letting both church and home preach God's will and God's truth. May both church and family be a place where we can find rest, comfort, and security in God's love. *(Bill D. Whittaker)*

FROZEN BY FEAR, FREED BY GRACE

HEBREWS 10:11-14, 19-25

Some animals have a tendency to freeze when overtaken by fear. Rather than run or scurry away, they stand motionless, until overtaken by that which is causing the threat. More than one deer, raccoon, or possum has been caught in the headlights of an automobile, only to freeze in terror and become struck by the automobile.

People can act likewise. Psychologists indicate that fear can grip us and keep us from action. I read of a man struck by a train at a railroad crossing. He lived to tell his story, saying he both heard and saw the train coming his direction, but he was unable to take a step. It was as if his feet had been cemented to the ground.

Other fears are equally paralyzing. The fear of rejection, humiliation, embarrassment, or failure can keep us from taking positive steps in relationships and in our daily living. Fear can even affect the way we relate to God. Because of our sin, our guilt, and our feelings of inadequacy, we may fear the presence of God. We fear his wrath, his judgment, his scrutiny.

The writer of Hebrews offers some good news to soothe our fears. No longer are we to allow fear to freeze us, but rather we are to let grace free us. Through Christ our Lord, we can have confidence as we relate to God.

As the perfect high-priest, Christ has offered a complete and final sacrifice. He now sits enthroned at the right hand of God (v. 12). Because of his work, Christians are being made holy and therefore are able to enter the presence of the Almighty God. As believers, we now have confidence to draw near to God, to hold fast to our hope, and to invest in others.

I. Christ Gives Us Confidence to Draw Near to God (v. 22)

We have confidence to draw near to God's presence. Separating the Holy of Holies from the common people was a huge veil.

Humans belonged on one side and God on the other. Only the high priest could go in, and only then on the day of Atonement. Christ has provided a "new and living way" to enter into the presence of God.

Through Christ, God reaches through the veil and draws us in. What we could not do on our own, Christ has done for us. We can draw near to God as a welcomed child because of the work of our Lord.

It is with great anticipation that we approach the throne of God. And yet there is to be no fear, only the calm assurance of Christ's confidence. We come in confidence because we have been cleansed. Our hearts are cleansed from all guilt and our bodies are cleansed from sin. And so in faith and in confidence we run to God and seek his face. We have been freed by grace to do so.

II. Christ Gives Confidence to Hold Fast to Our Hope (v. 23)

The ultimate hope of the Christian is contained in two simple statements. First, Christ arose from the grave. Second, Christ is coming again. These two words of affirmation and faith comprise our hope. The book of Hebrews reminds us to hold fast to our hope. We must never lose our grip on what we believe. The confidence for doing so is found in verse 23, "For he who has promised is faithful."

You've seen the bumper sticker that says, "God said it and I believe it." God is indeed faithful and therefore we can trust all of the promises that he has made. We need only look back to envision our hope for the future, for if we believe in the promises of God, we must also believe in the return of our Lord. We therefore build confidence in our lives and not fear, knowing that God has promised the faithful return of Christ. By holding fast, our faith is enriched and our hope is grounded.

III. Christ Gives Confidence to Invest in Others (v. 24)

As believers, we are to consider how we can constructively spur others on to Christian growth and maturity. We are to take up the ministry of encouragement. Through our faith, others should learn love and the doing of good works. We are not Christians merely for our own sakes, but for the sake of others. We must become contagious communities of faith, encouraging others to grow.

True disciples of Christ are called to make investments in the lives of people. To "spur" others toward maturity will require time, effort, prayer, and example. Though we may feel inadequate, perhaps even spiritually impoverished, God still can use us to build his kingdom if we will invest our lives into the lives of others.

When the automobile first appeared on the scene, thousands of Americans joyfully bought them. It did not take long for the joy to wear thin as many motorists found their cars bogging down along the roadways. The paths made by horses and buggies had too many ruts and puddles for cars to move about freely. To bring back the joy, Henry Ford started an ambitious campaign to introduce street paving to America. He assembled teams and provided them with equipment to begin paving "seed miles" across the nation. From town to town, these crews would pave a one-mile stretch of smooth road. When motorists first drove on the smooth surface, the exhilaration proved too great and soon miles and miles of roadway appeared as the joy of driving gripped the country.

Small investments can bring great rewards, especially those that are eternal in nature. In Christ, we can make a difference in others by spurring them to abundant life and good deeds.

God loves you and longs to enjoy fellowship with you. Rather than be frozen by fear at that thought, allow the grace of Christ to free you to experience the riches of his Kingdom. *(Jon R. Roebuck)*

COUNTDOWN WITHOUT NUMBERS

MARK 13:1-8

Americans who remember the beginnings of the space age will recall the excitement—and apprehension—about the nation's first orbital flight. Regular classes were forgotten as the children at my school gathered in front of a black-and-white television to watch the rocket launch. Would John Glenn really circle the earth and return safely? Could such a thing be done? We didn't know, but we kept our eyes on the screen and listened eagerly for each progress report. Our teachers assured us we were watching history in the making, and they were right.

Suspense, timing, and reminders from a Teacher are part of the scene from today's Gospel reading. Jesus had left the temple for the final time and had taken his disciples to the Mount of Olives, higher than the temple mount, where they could see the entire city. The odd remark by one disciple, "Look, Teacher, what large stones and what large buildings!" was met with an even stranger prophetic utterance from Jesus: "Do you see these great buildings? Not one stone will be left here upon another; all will be thrown down."

This interchange serves as introduction to the only long discourse in Mark's Gospel, often called "The Little Apocalypse." Verses 1-8 are part of an entire chapter dealing with signs of the end of the age. It is appropriate, therefore, to look at these verses in their context. What are the underlying themes in this prophecy shortly before the Passion, and how do they address the contemporary church?

I. The End of the Age Will Come

The phrase "second coming" does not appear in this chapter, though the revelation or appearance of the Christ is a theme. The destruction of the temple (which burned in A.D. 70), famines, earthquakes, wars and rumors of wars, are not signs of the end, but "birth pangs"—signs preceding the end and confirming Jesus' prophecy.

The church for centuries has declared its eschatological belief in reciting this line of the Apostles' Creed: "from thence he shall come to judge the quick and the dead." Ever since this conversation with Peter, James, John, and Andrew, followers of Jesus have believed the Savior will come again.

II. No One Knows When This Will Happen

The first question the disciples asked the Master was, "Tell us, when will this be, and what will be the sign that all these things are about to be accomplished?" It is a question followers (and nonfollowers) of the Messiah still ask. Throughout history and even today, self-appointed prophets have made a cottage industry of predicting when the end of the world will come. The Cold War, the Gulf War, and other events have all been accompanied by literature identifying current events with eschatological names and symbols. But Christ said to the disciples, "But about that day or hour no one knows, neither the angels in heaven, nor the Son, but only the Father" (v. 32). Christians should therefore be skeptical of anyone who claims to have inside information, for this contradicts the testimony of the Gospels.

III. Followers of Jesus Are to Be ready

Jesus' instructions were to take heed and watch, for we do not know when the time will come. For disciples of any age, this means striving to grow in the knowledge and love of God, witnessing and serving in Jesus' name, and trusting the Lord's faithfulness. It also means resisting "false Messiahs" and the temptation to second-guess God's timetable. Finally, it means looking forward expectantly to God's future. As the writer of Revelation concluded: "He who testifies to these things says, 'Surely I am coming quickly.' Amen. Come, Lord Jesus! The grace of the Lord Jesus Christ be with you all. Amen." *(Carol M. Noren)*

NOVEMBER 23, 1997

❧

Christuber King

Worship Theme: Jesus Christ is our Lord and King.

Readings: 2 Samuel 23:1-7; Revelation 1:4b-8; John 18:33-37

Call to Worship (Psalm 132:11-[13-18]):

Leader: The LORD swore to David a sure oath from which he will not turn back: "One of the sons of your body I will set on your throne.

***People:* If your sons keep my covenant and my decrees that I shall teach them, their sons also, forevermore, shall sit on your throne."**

Leader: For the LORD has chosen Zion; he has desired it for his habitation:

***People:* "This is my resting place forever; here I will reside, for I have desired it.**

Leader: I will abundantly bless its provisions; I will satisfy its poor with bread.

***People:* Its priests I will clothe with salvation, and its faithful will shout for joy.**

Leader: There I will cause a horn to sprout up for David; I have prepared a lamp for my anointed one.

***All:* His enemies I will clothe with disgrace, but on him, his crown will gleam."**

Pastoral Prayer:

With thankful hearts we bless you, eternal Father, for the awesome love and simple mercies with which you have showered us. In this season of thanksgiving, keep us ever mindful that you are the source of all that is good and pure in our lives. May our praises constantly flow into your presence, O Lord; may thanksgiving be perpetually on our lips, in gratitude for your love and grace. We thank you most of all for your Son and our Savior, Jesus Christ, who gave up the glories of heaven for a manger filled with straw; who poured out his precious blood at Calvary to atone for our sins; who rose up on the third day, conquering sin and death; and who even now intercedes for us. He is Lord of lords, and king of kings. He is worthy of all praise, and to him we gratefully lift our hearts in worship and adoration, as we offer these prayers in his name, the wonderful name of Jesus. Amen.

SERMON BRIEFS

CHRIST THE KING

2 SAMUEL 23:1-7

The peasants wait nervously outside the palace to learn the identity of their new emperor. The tribe sends its wisest elders to choose their new chief. Every four years Americans step into the voting booth with naive hopes that with this new leader happy days will be here again. The whole world longs for a good king and a brighter future.

I. Kings Begin with High Hopes

Coronations are often the high point of a king's reign. King David embodied the hopes of Israel. David's promise was evidence as he received anointment from Samuel, slew Goliath, and befriended Jonathan. The people sang ballads about the daring escapades of this one after God's own heart. David was King Arthur and Jerusalem was Camelot.

It was a kingdom where might was used for right, justice was for all, and shining knights, like angels in armor, battled to snuff out evil. For one brief shining moment this was "happily ever after." At his best, David was the most splendid king who ever sat on any throne, a king with high hopes and great dreams.

II. The Kings of This World Inevitably Fall

The dreams didn't last. By the end of his reign, David was king of a divided, disorganized, and disintegrating kingdom. His reign was a series of tragedies: David's sin with Bathsheba and murder of Uriah, the rape of his daughter Tamar by his son Amnon, the rebellion and murder of Absalom, continuous fighting between the tribes of Israel, and wars with the Philistines.

Finally David was judged too old to go into battle. The round table cracked. The shining moments are brief. The glimpses of glory fade. The kingdoms of this world are destined for collapse.

III. Jesus Is the King Whose Reign Will Last Forever

David comes to the end of a disappointing reign, and yet his farewell address is not sorrowful. The one dream that didn't die was of a king yet to come. One will come from David's line who will be a king like David at his best. The King of all kings did come, and one wonders if David would recognize him.

Peter Fribley wrote: "How can you be king who ruled with stories? Who walked to work and slept beneath the stars? . . . How can you be king who refused kingdoms, claimed no crown, walked to work, thumbed a ride to town?"

Jesus is a king unlike human rulers, who seek power and pleasure, who want celebrity and comfort. And unlike human kingdoms, the kingdom in which Christ reigns is a realm with no boundaries, no limitations, and no end.

IV. Our Lives Depend on Recognizing Jesus' Kingship

Those who stand against this king, the Lord of all, will not stand at all. David said those who don't recognize this king are like the thorny bramble thrown into the fire. If we live as subjects of the one true King, then we will be transformed. Jesus can free us from our small worlds and our self-centeredness.

The dream of Christ's kingdom will renew us. The One who is and was and is to come will bring grace and peace. He will make us a kingdom, priests serving God and one another. Every one of us longs for the One who will make our lives complete. Christ invites us into his kingdom, now and forevermore. *(Brett Younger)*

THE BOTTOM LINE: JESUS

REVELATION 1:4*b*-8

It is amazing the difference a few years make. It seems only yesterday when I wanted to write a letter to a friend and needed only paper and pencil. While a high school sophomore in Miss Liver-good's typing class, I used one of the first electric typewriters. Today I sit before a "one-eyed friend" who tells me how to type, warns me about spelling errors, and even corrects my poor grammar. While I'm writing my letter I can be listening to my favorite music on a CD—from within the computer! Writing a letter to a friend has never been so easy!

John did not have the convenience of a computer, but he did possess the heart of a writer. He probably chose seven churches to write to because they each had a special place or influence or authority within the Roman province of Asia, which included the western seacoast of Asia Minor on the shores of the Mediterranean. John wrote to the seven churches because the people knew and loved him, and in return he loved them the most. Through these seven churches the other congregations in the area heard the mes-sage—in fact every church in every generation has heard the truth. The truth of which he writes was that Jesus is Lord—the Eternal One. John writes about this Eternal One in several aspects.

I. Jesus As the Eternal Witness

A witness gives evidence to an act, event, or person. In verses 4 and 5 Jesus is an eternal witness of the truth concerning the Father. Jesus speaks from firsthand knowledge. Christ can identify person-ally with God's will, is able to speak with authority about God, and carries God's truth as no one else in the world could or can do.

His witness comes through the Resurrection. God, who loved him with all of his heart, raised Jesus from the dead. All who believe in him share in this resurrection. Because he lives I, too, can live!

II. Jesus As the Eternal Eraser

Do you regret the sins you have committed? Do memories of your pre-Christian life haunt you? Does Satan reinvent the wheel of past regrettable circumstances?

Marjorie Holmes related that a friend wrote to share how her granddaughter had made a wonderful observation. As Marjorie's friend and her granddaughter stood on a grassy hillside observing an airplane do its fancy skywriting, suddenly the words began to dis-solve. The girl asked her grandmother how the words disappeared.

As grandmother groped for an answer, the little girl's face brightened up. She exclaimed, "Maybe Jesus has an eraser!"

Holmes wrote that the day she received the letter had been an awful day. In fact for some time she had been extremely discouraged and depressed. She had been grieving over past mistakes, a cruel word, a moment to witness slipped by, a child unjustly punished, a friend let down. She stated, "No matter how much we mature as people, grow as Christians, try desperately to compensate, memories of our own failures rise up to haunt us, and sting. . . ."

The small child in her innocence and wisdom helped Holmes to realize that, like the writing on the sky that simply disappears, Jesus has wiped away all things that we can bitterly regret. Jesus does have an eternal eraser!

What does he need to use his eraser on in your life?

III. Jesus As Eternal Victor

The book of Revelation assures victory. Defeat is never mentioned—not once! We, the soldiers of the cross, catch a glimpse of the battleground. There will come a moment in history when heaven and hell will collide. Good versus evil; satanic hatred versus divine love. Amid the thunder and lightning, smoke and haze stands Jesus, the Son of God—the ultimate warrior. Spanning time from a manger to a cross, from a tomb to resurrection life—Jesus triumphs over Satan, Hell, sin, and all the forces of evil. As Christians we are assured of being on the victory side.

Forward March! (*Derl G. Keefer*)

WHAT IS TRUTH?

JOHN 18:33-37

In this text, Pilate is asking a question we all have asked: "What is truth?" This question must be addressed before you can trust the Bible, or commit your life to the Lord it proclaims.

I. How Can I Know Anything Is True?

There are several ways we gain information, or know something is true. Some things we learn through what our five senses experience. We learn some truths from what we see, touch, taste, smell, or hear. Some things we learn by figuring them out, such as through mathematics. Einstein didn't see or touch the theory of relativity; he discerned it rationally.

And some truth we can only know as God reveals it to us. Jesus does not look like a king to Pilate, and it certainly isn't logical. Since his kingdom is not of this world, Christ's kingship is one of those truths that must be learned through revelation from the Bible.

What is the difference in truths we can know by experience or logic and those we can only know from revelation? The first two can be proved to others, but biblical truth has to be accepted by faith. Or is that difference always true?

II. Can We Trust Everything We Know As "Truth"?

Our senses can fail us, or fool us. Everyone has seen an optical illusion that appears to be something it is not. Magicians rely on being able to fool your senses. Algebra—as exact and absolute as is mathematics—rests on a series of axioms and postulates. These statements, such as $a + b = b + a$, are called axioms instead of theorems, because they cannot be proved. Virtually all of mathematics is built upon some statements that cannot be proved (or disproved), and must simply be accepted "by faith."

Everything you know by experience, you know because you trust your senses—which can be fooled. Everything you know logically, you know because you trust your reasoning abilities—which also can be faulty. Everything anybody knows about anything ultimately rests upon faith assumptions. Philosophers call these assumptions "presuppositions."

Thus no one can say biblical truth, in general, is inferior to experienced truth or logical truth because biblical truth rests on faith. All knowledge requires a leap of faith to trust the methods by which we gained the knowledge. All knowledge is based upon presuppositions.

III. How Do We Know Which "Truth" to Trust?

A problem arises when truth sources disagree, such as when your eyes see something your logic tells you is impossible. You have to decide which source of knowledge is the authority. The Bible says Jesus walked on water, but experience and physics say that is impossible. The Bible says God loves you, but you don't feel loved. Which source of information do you believe?

Jesus told Pilate he came to bear witness to the truth. Elsewhere Jesus said he is, "the way, the truth, and the life." Jesus reveals God's truths to us. You can trust the Bible more than your experience or logic.

The problem is, too many people "test" the truth of the Bible at the wrong place. They begin with a promise saying God answers prayer, and test God by asking for a new luxury car. When they don't get a car, they conclude: the Bible is not trustworthy.

Start with Jesus, the witness to the truth. Do what he requires: confess your sinfulness, turn from your sin, ask to be forgiven, become a follower of his, and receive his gift of eternal life. Then you will know the truth, and it will set you free! *(William Groover)*

NOVEMBER 30, 1997

❧

First Sunday of Advent

Worship Theme: True satisfaction in life comes only through a life given to Jesus Christ as Lord.

Readings: Jeremiah 33:14-16; 1 Thessalonians 3:9-13; Luke 21:25-38

Call to Worship (Psalm 25:1-10):

Leader: To you, O LORD, I lift up my soul.

People: O my God, in you I trust;

Leader: do not let me be put to shame; do not let my enemies exult over me.

People: Do not let those who wait for you be put to shame;

Leader: let them be ashamed who are wantonly treacherous.

People: Make me to know your ways, O LORD; teach me your paths.

Leader: Lead me in your truth, and teach me, for you are the God of my salvation; for you I wait all day long.

People: Be mindful of your mercy, O LORD, and of your steadfast love, for they have been from of old.

People: Do not remember the sins of my youth or my transgressions;

Leader: according to your steadfast love remember me, for your goodness' sake, O LORD!

People: Good and upright is the LORD; therefore he instructs sinners in the way.

Leader: He leads the humble in what is right, and teaches the humble his way.

All: All the paths of the LORD are steadfast love and faithfulness, for those who keep his covenant and his decrees.

Pastoral Prayer:

Almighty God, who is from everlasting to everlasting, we worship you this day. In this too-busy season of the year, we step aside from the hurried and hectic pace of our lives to focus on what is truly important; we gather before you to seek your presence, to ask your forgiveness of our sins, and to intercede for others. We praise you for the fruitful earth, for the liberty we enjoy to worship and work, for family and friends who make our lives more complete. Yet we know, divine Father, that a full and complete life comes only through relationship with you through Christ our Lord. In this season of Advent—as we recall the Incarnation and as we look forward to Christ's second coming as King and Lord of history—help us to open our hearts that Christ might come anew and afresh into our lives. May Advent truly happen within our hearts this day, as we pray in Jesus' name. Amen.

SERMON BRIEFS

THE PROMISED ONE

JEREMIAH 33:14-16

According to a recent study, 1.6 percent of the world's population will commit suicide. On one hand, that percentage seems too high. On the other hand, it may be surprising that more people aren't in line for the highest windows.

When C. S. Lewis's wife died, in his grief he wrote: "What reason have we, except our own desperate wishes to believe that God is, by any standard we can conceive, 'good'? Doesn't all the evidence suggest exactly the opposite?"

I. Our Lives Can Seem Hopeless

In his darkest hour, the prophet Jeremiah cursed the day he was born. He spent his life telling the Hebrew people to shape up, with almost no results. The Babylonians had demolished Jerusalem and the temple and run off with all the best stuff and some of the best people. Jeremiah was left in captivity in Jerusalem. He is at this writing (v.1) confined to quarters. The Jews left behind at the exile lost their home, too, for they knew that life was not what it should be.

The whole world understands the feeling of hopelessness. Sinclair Lewis closed one of his novels with a successful businessman telling his beautiful wife, "Deep down we are all just the same. We are desperately unhappy about something—and we don't know what it is."

We spend our lives waiting. We bury our treasures. We are intimidated by the giftedness of others, incapacitated by our lack of discipline, and mesmerized by our fear of failure. Our lives aren't what they should be.

II. God Offers the Hope of His Grace

From captivity, Jeremiah speaks a word of hope. God promises that his people will be slaves no longer. The Messiah is coming from the line of David to fulfill the ancient promise of salvation. Jeremiah does not say a word about the people keeping up their end of the bargain. There is no bargain. There is only grace. This kingdom is dependent not on the goodness of the subjects, but the love of the King.

The game of hide-and-seek has occupied hours of many of our lives. In one version, the person who was "it" could shout, "Alley, alley, outs are in free." Anyone who was still hiding could return to home base without fear of being caught. The Creator of the universe stands at the home base of heaven calling "Alley, Alley, outs are in free." Everybody, come home. The game's over and you've won.

III. We Need to Accept God's Grace

Our refusal of grace does not change God's grace. We are forgiven even for putting off the celebration. We are not saved by anything

THE ABINGDON PREACHING ANNUAL 1997

we hold. We are saved by the One who holds us. We have only to accept grace and rejoice in God's unmerited favor.

During the days of sailing merchant ships, one ship was stuck off the coast of South America. Weeks went by without the slightest bit of wind. The ship was helpless and couldn't move. The sailors were dying of thirst when another ship drifted close enough to hear their shouts for help. They answered, "Let down your buckets." They found fresh water. Although they were at sea, they were surrounded by the current that came from the Amazon River. They only needed to recognize where they were. Thirsty people are surrounded by Living Water.

As children of God we are free to try and fail, free to make mistakes, and free to rejoice. At the end of it all, there is only grace. (*Brett Younger*)

A FULL LIFE

1 THESSALONIANS 3:9-13

I remember when I was young pastors and evangelists commenting that we never know when life will end. "Death is near," they would say. Even young people die.

During my junior and senior high school days, none of their predictions proved true among the young people I knew. But only two years out of high school, two college classmates and my favorite professor died. They weren't just names in a newspaper. They were flesh-and-blood people that I had laughed, cried, and prayed with at college. These were people I cared about deeply.

I was hundreds of miles away on summer break, August 4, 1967, when they died. They were traveling on assignment for the Christian college that I attended in Oklahoma. When I heard about the tragedy, I was overwhelmed with grief. One of the young men grew up in my hometown of Kansas City. I attended his funeral along with several other classmates. Their lives were too short. Even my "old" professor was only forty-two. Although their lives were short, they all lived full lives.

Paul summarizes what a full life is in 1 Thessalonians 3:9-13.

I. A Full Life Includes Joy

Look at many Christians today. There seems to be little joy in their lives. Why? Fear of failure, rushed hours, lack of trust, lack of prayer, a restless spirit, and anxiety are only a few reasons.

Vernon C. Lyons said that if doing God's holy will is all that matters to you, then no matter what the rest of life brings, you can find joy.

Do you have joy, real joy, wonderful joy in your heart? If not, let Jesus come into your heart.

II. A Full Life Includes Love

Often, love is misdirected, left out, hurt, and selfish. There are great cracks in the hearts and lives of the human heart. The world needs Godlike love poured down into those cracks.

Love demands ingenuity, consideration, and time. When we learn how to love, we learn how to give the center of ourselves to others and God. Real love gives, forgives, is open, waits, and promises full life. Love doesn't disappoint—it fulfills and satisfies needs.

The American Civil War began just as one New England couple planned to be married. The man was drafted into the army, so the wedding had to be postponed. The battles were severe, but the man escaped injury. He wrote regularly to his loving fiancé back home in New England. She would pore over his letters, reading and rereading them by the oil lamp of her home.

Abruptly, the letters ceased. Finally a much-anticipated letter arrived, but it was an unfamiliar handwriting. It stated, "There has been a terrible battle fought called the Battle of the Wilderness. It is very difficult for me to tell you this, but I have lost both of my arms. I can't write for myself. So a friend is writing this letter on my behalf. You are the dearest person to me, but because of my physical condition I feel I should release you from the obligation of our engagement."

The young woman never answered his letter. Instead, she took the next train and went directly to the hospital where he was being treated. A sympathetic army officer directed her to the young soldier's cot. The moment she saw her fiancé she tearfully threw her arms around his neck and kissed him. She cried, "I will never give you up! These hands of mine will be your hands."

A full life demonstrates this kind of love.

379

III. A Full Life Includes Holiness

I read about a plant in South America, called the pitcher plant. On the stalk of the plant just below the leaf is a little cuplike formation that, regardless the size of the "cup," is always full of water. It is a good illustration of practical biblical holiness. All that God asks is that the heart should be open completely to him and be filled with holiness. *(Derl G. Keefer)*

THE ULTIMATE SIGN

LUKE 21:25-38

This text is part of Jesus' response to a request for a sign of his return. Jesus' answer was better than what his listeners hoped to hear.

I. The Desire for a Sign

This was not the first time Jesus was asked for a sign. Often after proving who he was, people asked for more and more signs. He wanted people to believe in his message, to believe in the words of the Scriptures, and respond to God out of hearts full of love and appreciation for who God is. He did not simply want an army of miracle watchers.

Today people would love to know exactly when Jesus will return. Some would want to live like the devil up until the last minute, then repent and get ready for Christ in the hour prior to his return.

Before I accepted Christ as my Savior, I wished I could live my entire life in sin and then become a Christian in the hours before my death. Maximum pleasure, minimum discipleship. Jesus says in verse 34 to avoid that type of thinking. The parable of the foolish bridesmaids makes the same point.

Signs of the end times are not given so we can waste time until we know the day of Christ's return is at hand.

II. Specific, yet General Signs

The signs given were wars, earthquakes, and famines (v. 10). Rather than signs saying, "Jesus is coming this week," these events are constant reminders to the church of all ages, "Jesus could come anytime."

The events Jesus mentioned are all life-threatening events, and are all common around the world. They are intentionally general so that everyone, every week, everywhere, can be reminded: "Jesus could return this week." Every time you turn on the TV and Dan Rather tells you about the latest fighting somewhere, or an earthquake destroying buildings, or a famine in some little known section of the world, realize God is simply using the six o'clock news as a reminder: "Jesus could come anytime!"

Jesus used the example of a fig tree in verse 30. Is he saying he will return when the fig tree blossoms? Yes, and no. Every year when you see a tree blossoming, you know spring is coming in a few weeks. Likewise, every time you see a tree in bloom, you know Jesus is coming. Perhaps within a few weeks, like spring; perhaps not for another thousand years.

III. The Lesson of the Signs

Thus, the signs of Jesus are reminders he is coming, not warnings telling us when. Jesus warned us not to be deceived (v. 8) or terrified (v. 9), but to watch and pray (v. 36). This is the message of Advent.

Consider this: the people asked for a sign, proof Jesus is who he says he is, and when he is returning. And he gave them a sign: pray always!

They say, "Jesus, are you real? Are you coming? Give me a sign!"

Jesus responds, "Here is your sign: confess your sins, turn from them, take up your cross daily, and follow me. You do these things, and you will know! I will forgive your sins, I will carry your burden, I will change you from the inside out, and I will give you the assurance of your salvation!"

"Jesus, that's not what we were talking about! We want you to raise some more dead folks. Do something exciting!"

"I am offering a far greater sign than a miracle a stage magician or a skilled physician could duplicate. I'm offering the sign of a changed heart, the ultimate sign!"

Have you experienced that sign in your life? *(William Groover)*

DECEMBER

❧

Mending the Net, Sharpening the Hoe

Symbol: Light

The symbol of the presence of God in Scripture is light. The birth of Christ and the preparation for it are surrounded by light. People without light grope in darkness.

Text:

"This is the message we have heard from him and declare to you: God is light; in him there is no darkness at all" (1 John 1:5 NIV).

Invocation:

"Almighty God, who came to us long ago in the birth of Jesus Christ, be born in us anew today by the power of your Holy Spirit. We offer our lives as home to you and ask for grace and strength to live as your faithful, joyful children always. Through Jesus Christ our Lord. Amen." (Reuben P. Job and Norman Shawchuck, *A Guide to Prayer*)

Scripture Focus:
- Genesis 1:3
- Revelation 22:5
- 1 John 2:11
- Isaiah 60:1, 20
- 1 John 1:1-14

Prayer Focus:
- Visualize the light of Christ's star.
- Visualize the light of Christmas, including the Advent candle.
- Focus on people in your congregation who need to see the light, or need to see more light.
- Focus on people who need an expanded capacity to see the light.
- Visualize dark places that need the shine of light.
- Focus on ways of reflecting the light in the dark places.

Prayer:

"Come, Spirit of the Living God, fall fresh on us. Come, O Christ, your very coming is judgment on those in whose midst you arrive, and chasten and prepare us for the Father's presence. Grant that every man, woman, and child among us may begin to stay in a time of serious self-appraisal so that by Christmas we shall be appropriately humble and ready to receive and acknowledge the lordship in every part of our lives, in every shred of our being. Let the star that shone over Bethlehem when Christ was born shine once more in our troubled skies, and give hope to millions who dwell in darkness, doubt, and sin, for you are indeed a God of grace and kindness. We beseech you in the name of our Savior. Amen." (John Killinger, _The Abingdon Preaching Annual_ ed. Michael Duduit, 1996 edition) _(Bill Self)_

DECEMBER 7, 1997

☙

Second Sunday of Advent

Worship Theme: Advent is a time to prepare our hearts for Christ's arrival.

Readings: Malachi 3:1-4; Philippians 1:3-11; Luke 3:1-6

Call to Worship (Luke 1:68-79):

Leader: Blessed be the Lord God of Israel, for he has looked favorably on his people and redeemed them.

***People:* He has raised up a mighty savior for us in the house of his servant David,**

Leader: as he spoke through the mouth of his holy prophets from of old, that we would be saved from our enemies and from the hand of all who hate us.

***People:* Thus he has shown the mercy promised to our ancestors, and has remembered his holy covenant,**

Leader: the oath that he swore to our ancestor Abraham, to grant us that we, being rescued from the hands of our enemies, might serve him without fear,

***People:* in holiness and righteousness before him all our days.**

Leader: And you, child, will be called the prophet of the Most High; for you will go before the Lord to prepare his ways,

***People:* to give knowledge of salvation to his people by the forgiveness of their sins.**

Leader: By the tender mercy of our God, the dawn from on high will break upon us, to give light to those who sit in darkness and in the shadow of death,

***All:* to guide our feet into the way of peace.**

Pastoral Prayer:

Heavenly Father, creator and preserver of all, we gather before you in humility and gratitude. We praise you without ceasing, for you have forgiven our sin and made us your children, joint heirs with Christ. In this Advent season, we pray that you would prepare us anew and afresh for Christ's arrival. Too often we have allowed our attention to be turned away, our priorities to be disrupted; we have focused our energies on that which is secondary and temporary. Draw us again, O Lord, to Bethlehem; bring us anew, O Lord, to Calvary. Create within us a spirit of expectancy and openness to the Christ child; give us hearts of commitment and faithfulness toward the risen Christ. Prepare us to meet our Savior with new vitality, new courage, and new obedience. And even as you prepare our hearts to host Christ, prepare us to be dynamic witnesses to his good news, for we ask it in his name. Amen.

SERMON BRIEFS

I'M NOT RESPONSIBLE . . . AM I?

MALACHI 3:1-4

Phil, Oprah, Geraldo, and Sally Jesse spend their days with people who aren't at fault. If a wife cheats on her husband, whose fault is it? It could be the husband who was inattentive, her parents who caused her low self-esteem, the man who seduced her, or the society that glamorizes affairs. If a man steals a stereo, is he really to blame? It could be the fault of his friends who own stereos and make him feel inadequate, the advertisers who make stereos look so good, or the stereo's owner who left her car door unlocked. Our society is adept at avoiding responsibility.

I. We Don't Take Responsibility

Every day we see other people deny their responsibilities. It's harder to admit that we do the same thing. We have a list of excuses for our lack of commitment to Christ. We don't love our neighbors, but it's the neighbors' fault. They aren't very friendly. We don't pray as we should, but it's our family's fault. They're always finding something else we should be doing. We don't share the gospel, but it's our employers' fault. They don't want us to make anyone uncomfortable. The easiest way to avoid our real responsibilities is to say, "I have responsibilities."

II. We Are Responsible.

Martin Luther wrote: "A man is not responsible if a bird flies over his head, but he is responsible if that bird builds a nest in his hair." We are not accountable for all the sin in the world, but we are answerable for the apathy in our hearts.

Dennis Waitley argued that to match the Statue of Liberty in New York there should be a Statue of Responsibility in San Francisco. Without individual duty there can be no real freedom.

God's grace makes us accountable. Grace demands we live true to the trust we have been given. We are to be the salt of the earth and the light of the world. We are to live and speak the gospel. The ultimate folly is to accept the gift of grace without recognizing the responsibilities of Christian faith.

III. God Will Judge Us

Malachi understood that the day of the Lord's coming will be no Sunday dinner on the grounds. God's judgment will fall first upon the priests, for they are the most responsible. Church people usually think that judgment is for everyone else. We softpedal the many passages of Scripture that make it clear that judgment comes for all of us.

What percentage of what could be done for God do we actually do? Is it as much as 10 percent? Do we really believe that we bear no responsibility for the other 90 percent? Judgment is facing what we have done and what we have left undone. Judgment begins in the heart of God and reaches into our hearts. In the best families, children are concerned with disappointing their loving parents. This is the judgment feared by the children of the heavenly Father.

We need to repent and let God make us right. Malachi envisioned judgment day as cleansing. Christ will be a refiner's fire purifying his people. God will give us a scrubbing that one commentator described as getting caught in a car wash without a car. We should pledge ourselves to the God who leads us to a holy life. One day we will have to answer for what we have done. *(Brett Younger)*

A PRISONER'S PRAYER

PHILIPPIANS 1:3-11

Sitting in a drab, cramped house is a balding man writing a letter. His shoulders are stooped, his hand and foot are chained. Accompanying him in those chains is a rather large, muscular fellow with body armor displaying the seal of the Roman army. The year is around A.D. 63 or perhaps 64 in the city of Rome. The occasion that prompted this letter was a gift sent to the apostle Paul from his closest friends in the church that met in Philippi.

The tone of this prisoner's letter was not complaint, grievance, lament, or bitterness. It is a letter of joy, a treatise on hope. The beginning paragraph is a prisoner's prayer of thanksgiving. That's right—thanksgiving!

I. The Prisoner's Prayer Is for His Friends

Paul calls his friends "saints" in verse 1. He had a lofty view of the members of this parish. To him each one had great spiritual worth. He knew that they were "in Christ" and that Christ was "in them." God's grace, presence, strength, and power continually surrounded them.

This young congregation of men and women were relatively new Christians at Philippi. We might not call them saints due to their lack of maturity, but Paul saw them as saints in the making. He believed in their potential to deepen and broaden their relationship with God over the passage of years. His confidence ran deep in his converts.

Today the church is filled with many who are coming from the raw side of life. They are rough around the edges, hard to understand, illiterate of Bible truths and doctrines. But Christ sees in them great potential. Can we see any less? Our task is to be their friends, not their critics.

II. The Prisoner's Prayer Is for Spiritual Progress

There is a crisis moment when Christ comes in and all is forgiven. A new relationship is established between God and the individual.

In a sense this relationship is a *process*. Christ continues his wonder-working relationship. Paul prays for their spiritual development.

Today God desires the same for us. His dynamic and creative power is available to work in us, perfecting us so that some day we may hear him say, "Well done, good and faithful servant" (Matt. 25:21 NIV).

Robert Schuller relates that at the end of World War II the Allied armies searched everywhere for snipers. At a broken down farmhouse on a crumbling basement wall, a victim of Hitler's holocaust scratched a Star of David. In rough letters he wrote:

I believe in the sun—even when it does not shine;
I believe in love—even when it is not shown;
I believe in God—even when he does not speak.

Spiritual growth occurs even in the midst of adversity and the moments of silence.

III. The Prisoner's Prayer Is for Knowledge and Discernment

We seek a clear perception of who God is and what God is all about. We are in Advent. The Christ Child in the manger is the Jesus of history. Lyle Flinner said, "We need to see things as they really are and discern the highest and best for all involved." That discernment comes only through divine love, a love that is directed both to Jesus and to the people of the earth. It is divine truth seen through human eyes filled with a godly vision.

The spiritual battles of today are almost unparalleled in human history. Today's global Christian fights spiritual battles in a world that is blinded by New Age trickery, biblical ignorance (one-half of all American children by the year 2000—just over two years from now—will not have entered a church building), stark indifference, and in some areas of our world, outright torture and killing of believers.

We must be alert, knowledgeable, and discerning in our spiritual lives. Thanks, Paul, for your prayer for not only the church of Philippi, but for our church! *(Derl G. Keefer)*

UNDER CONSTRUCTION

LUKE 3:1-6

The idea that one must prepare for the coming of the Lord is nothing new, for the entire focus of the Advent season centers upon the celebration and anticipation of the birth of Christ. But in preparing for the "good news of great joy," Christians often overlook the one who actually paved the way, John the Baptist. Although John's ministry follows the Incarnation, it functions as an introduction to the redemptive purpose of Christ and the necessary human response.

Luke begins the third chapter of his Gospel with a list of earthly rulers from Rome to the synagogue in Jerusalem (vv. 1, 2). But aside from providing a chronological framework for the ministry of John the Baptist (A.D. 25–26), this roster contrasts the powers of earth against the Power of the universe. The inclusion of these leaders emphasizes their insignificance when compared to the impact Christ had on the history of the world. Every earthly ruler wants to be remembered for his contributions to civilization, but Jesus irrevocably modified society by changing humanity's relationship with God.

Like a herald proclaiming the arrival of a king, John prepared the hearts and minds of those who went out into the desert to hear his message. The quote from Isaiah 40:3-5 epitomizes John's prophetic role and the demands of God upon humankind. The call to make "paths straight" and "rough ways smooth" describes preparations for a royal visit. Before a king traveled to distant lands, roads and bridges were improved for the journey. Likewise, the beginning of Christ's ministry on earth required major improvements to lives in poor condition. So the townsfolk wandered into the desert to hear a strange man with a strong message.

There is something very intriguing about the desert. It is a place of introspection and self-reflection. With the distractions and pressures of city life absent, one becomes sensitive to the voice of God. Unfortunately, some people must journey to a barren land before they will hear God's call. Only when they are alone and totally dependent upon God will people stop to listen to his requirements. And with no place to hide, they must confront God's demand upon their lives.

THE ABINGDON PREACHING ANNUAL 1997

What does the Lord require? After wandering through the desert looking for the prophet of God, the people were told to "turn around," to repent and be baptized for the forgiveness of sins. John offers no soothing words of compromise or compassion. The command of God is clear. In order to receive the Lord and his salvation, one must pro-actively change his life by turning away from sin. The King is coming! And God's people must prepare themselves by straightening out their lives.

As an outward sign of their commitment, John baptized those who sought to turn their lives around. But this change of heart did not automatically elicit the forgiveness of sin. That activity would be accomplished by Christ's death on the cross. John could only prepare the people for the One who would reveal God's salvation to all humankind. So their lives remained under construction, paving the way for the Lord.

In this Advent season, all people must reflect upon the condition of their hearts and lives. As homes are being decorated and gifts wrapped, what internal improvements are we making in our relationship to God? Do not be fooled by the tenderness and innocence of a babe lying in a manger. As Christians celebrate the birth of Christ, remember the demands of our Lord. For God does not tolerate sin, and his people must repent to prepare for the coming of the King. (*Craig C. Christina*)

DECEMBER 14, 1997

⚜

Third Sunday of Advent

Worship Theme: The coming of Christ means both judgment and deliverance.

Readings: Isaiah 12:2-6; Philippians 4:4-7; Luke 3:7-18

Call to Worship (Isaiah 12:2-6):

Leader: Surely God is my salvation; I will trust, and will not be afraid,

People: for the LORD GOD is my strength and my might; he has become my salvation.

Leader: With joy you will draw water from the wells of salvation. And you will say in that day: Give thanks to the LORD, call on his name;

People: make known his deeds among the nations; proclaim that his name is exalted.

Leader: Sing praises to the LORD, for he has done gloriously; let this be known in all the earth.

All: Shout aloud and sing for joy, O royal Zion, for great in your midst is the Holy One of Israel.

Pastoral Prayer:

Almighty God, our creator and our redeemer, we praise your glory; we rejoice in your loving-kindness. Surely you are our salvation; apart from you there is no hope in this life or the next. Enable us in this Christmas season to be faithful witnesses of your love and grace. All around us are persons caught up in the pushing and shoving, the anxiety and anger that seem so inconsistent with a season of peace; empower us to offer a stronger and finer example, that we might reflect the love of Christ to a loveless world. In this

391

season filled with songs of love and joy, let us not forget that Christmas is a time of true happiness only as our lives are given to you in repentance and faith. May we come to know you more fully in these days, and may we demonstrate that knowledge day by day as we live for Christ, in whose name we pray. Amen.

SERMON BRIEFS

IN THE LAND OF THE LIVING

ISAIAH 12:2-6

The psalmist told us something important about the biblical faith when he said, "I believe that I shall see the goodness of the LORD in the land of the living" (Ps. 27:13).

Isaiah said, "The Lord has become my salvation." We have become accustomed to thinking of salvation primarily in terms of our hope for heaven beyond this life. As important as that is to us, it would be a mistake to limit our understanding of salvation to that hope. When Isaiah spoke of salvation, he was talking about something that can happen "in the land of the living."

I. Salvation Takes Place in the Land of the Living

Throughout the Old Testament, God is thought of as a God who saves. Israel's earliest experiences of salvation were things that God did in Israel's history. Notice the places in the Bible in which we find the words, "The Lord has become my salvation." In Exodus 15:2, they are part of a hymn of praise which Israel raised after God had rescued them from Pharaoh's army. In Psalm 118:14, they are parts of a ritual of thanksgiving to God for help in some very real crisis. In our passage from Isaiah, they are part of a psalm of thanks that follows a prophecy of the coming of a messiah to bring his people home from exile. These all have to do with saving works of God "in the land of the living."

In verse 3, there is a shift from past and present tense to the future tense. Isaiah says, "With joy you will draw water from the wells of salvation." Remembering enables us to anticipate the saving work that God will do in the future.

II. What Kind of Salvation Do We Need in the Land of the Living?

What are the great real needs of our world today? Do we need to be saved from war and oppression, from ecological disaster, from moral disintegration? What are the greatest real needs in your life? From what do you and those whom you love need most to be saved?

Is it inappropriate to turn to the God who "has become our salvation" for help with these needs? Isaiah would not have thought so.

III. The Savior Comes to Bring Us Salvation in the Land of the Living

During the season of Advent, Christians look forward to the coming of one whose name, Jesus, means "The Lord is salvation." Should we not expect that coming to have something to do with the real needs we experience in the land of the living? All three of the scripture passages in which we found the words, "The Lord has become my salvation," are passages that the early Christian community used to interpret the saving work of Christ.

That One who came and lived and worked among us in Jesus still comes and lives and works among us today. No, God does not often work through miraculous cures and spectacular interventions. But in many subtle ways, God is at work among us. When we see those saving works that were done through Jesus being done again, we can recognize God's saving work going on among us and respond.

In Philippians 4:6, Paul invites us to "let your requests be made known to God." This is not just an invitation to pray prayers that are like letters to Santa Claus. It is, rather, an invitation to take seriously the biblical belief that God is at work to bring about significant forms of salvation here "in the land of the living." (*Jim Killen*)

WHAT IF OR WHY NOT?

PHILIPPIANS 4:4-7

Worry changes nothing but the worrier, often to the negative extent that our creative juices are strangled and life is robbed of its vitality. A. J. Cronin states that only 8 percent of our worries are

393

legitimate, and the great majority of our concerns never occur! Emerson said it best:

> Some of your hurts you have cured.
> And the sharpest you still have survived,
> But what torment of grief you've endured
> From evils that never arrived.
> (From "Needless Worry" by Ralph Waldo Emerson)

From a positive viewpoint, worry is a distortion of our capacity to care. The irresponsible seldom worry. From a negative viewpoint, worry is a mild form of agnosticism. Since we feel God will not or cannot act, we feel we have to take matters in our own hands and play the destructive game of "What if?"

I. What If?—A Sit-Down Anxiety

This game of "What if?" is a wringing-of-the-hands, do-nothing, negative and inactive approach to life. We worry about the past, which ignores God's ability to forgive. We worry about the future, which ignores God's ability to teach us from our mistakes. We worry about people's judgment of us, which stems from our inability to love ourselves as God does. We worry about our health, which doubts God's ability to care for his own. We worry about finances, which ignores God's ability to give us the wisdom and discipline to manage, especially when we tithe. And we worry about dozens of other things.

Lloyd Ogilvie wrote a book entitled *Let God Love You!* This may be our greatest need. The word "anxious" (Phil. 4:6) means to "divide or share." When we let God love us, we no longer work against ourselves and begin to work with God. We also take the vital step in replacing a sit-down anxiety with a get-up audacity.

II. Why Not?—A Get-Up Audacity

A get-up audacity is an active, positive lifestyle that dares God to keep his promises and reaches out into every new day in the full assurance that he will. It looks at a situation not with a foreboding "What if?" but with a daring "Why not?"

I love the story of the first grader feeling the pains of leaving his beloved teacher upon being promoted to the second grade. In saying a tearful good-bye to his mentor, he said, "I wish you knew enough to teach me in the second grade."

One point of that story is that it is time to move on. Paul would agree. "Don't be anxious," he said, "do something—rejoice in God's goodness, show gentleness to everyone, and pray persistently with petition and thanksgiving" (vv. 4-6). Don't sit and fret. Get up and do.

Norman Cousins, in his book *The Anatomy of an Illness,* tells how he faced an "incurable," crippling disease and literally laughed himself back to health. Instead of giving in, he got up! We can as well when we put God first, seek his kingdom (Matt. 6:33-34), and remember that what God guides, God provides. As we do, we exchange the negative, "What if?" to a positive "Why not?" and begin to enjoy the abundant life. "And how!"

III. And How!—the Abundant Life

The Christian with a get-up-and-go audacity enjoys and expects the serendipitous surprises of God. He or she expects God to work. When a situation seems hopeless, the Christian is praying, working, believing, expecting. The believer knows that "surprise" is God's other name and that God will strengthen us in the problem, teach us from the problem, or God may remove the problem altogether.

Arnold Lemerand, on November 1, 1980, while taking a daily stroll, witnessed a tragedy at a construction site. A massive cast-iron pipe dislodged and rolled onto five-year-old Phillip Toth, suffocating him. With no one else around, Lemerand instinctively did what he could. He lifted the 1800-pound pipe off Toth's head, saving his life. Later on, neither he nor his sons could budge the pipe. Not bad for a fifty-six-year-old who had recently suffered a heart attack and was told by his doctor not to lift anything heavy. I am not saying that God will use you to perform a miracle, but I'm not saying he won't either.

The abundant-life-living Christian expects God's surprises, is sustained by his power, and is kept by his love. "And the peace of God, which surpasses all understanding, will guard your hearts and your minds in Christ Jesus" (Phil. 4:7). The word *guard* paints the image of a faithful sentinel on duty. In this Christmas season, often haunted by the worry of unfulfilled expectations and loneliness, let God hold you guarded and secure in love. Why not? *(Gary L. Carver)*

AND YOU CALL THIS GOOD NEWS?

LUKE 3:7-18

We think of Advent as a happy time. This is the season when our attention is drawn to the most significant and wondrous event in the history of humanity—the inbreaking of the Savior into a world that has lost its way. We look upon Jesus as the hope and the healer of our globe which is sick unto death. And so we see Christmas as the beginning of a new age, an age of health and harmony that will come in fullness when our Lord returns. The message of the coming of Christ is indeed good news.

Or is it? It is really a matter of perspective. If we look at the news of the coming of the Savior from a certain angle it is deplorable news. John the Baptist makes that distressingly clear. John was an odd character, firmly embedded in the prophetic tradition. His dress and habits were strange, symbolizing his rejection of corrupt society. Both his lifestyle and his message shouted to the world that big changes were on the horizon. No longer could people rest easy with the status quo. Rather, John warned them that the coming of the Promised One would sweep over them like a raging fire in a bone-dry forest.

John's announcement of the Messiah's coming fell softly on no one's ears. He certainly didn't try to lull his audience into believing that they could welcome the Savior with an unreflective enthusiasm, like a child who looks forward to Santa Claus. John the Baptist's words were troubling. The harshness of his tone made it evident that he had no patience with those who would require coaxing or cajoling before they would be receptive to his message. John spoke with brutal frankness.

The great church reformer Martin Luther once stated, "The most consistent outcome of the Word of God is that on its account the world is put into an uproar." Personally, I would not have wanted to bear the brunt of John's preaching. In the very first verses of our text, we find John apparently lashing out at his audience, calling them names. "You brood of vipers! Who warned you to flee from the wrath to come?"

Evidently John stuck such an undignified label on them because he anticipated their reaction to his message. You see, they were confident they had a guaranteed place in the plan of God. It wasn't as though they were going to be forced to try out for a part in the divine drama. God couldn't get along very well without them. After all, they reasoned, they were irreplaceable because they were the children of promise. Despite any illusions that they cherished, or that we might cherish, God is not dependent upon any particular group of people—not Israelites or Americans, not blacks or whites, not Catholics or Baptists. As John proclaimed, "I tell you God is able from these stones to raise up children to Abraham."

The strangest thing is that our scripture text concludes by saying that John "proclaimed the good news to the people." How is it that John's message, with all of its name-calling, threats, and warnings, can still be labeled "good news"?

Above all, it is because the bad news of God's judgment implies the good news of God's mercy. In the proclamation of darkness, the light of hope always shines. Imagine going to the doctor for a routine examination. As far as you know, you are perfectly healthy. You're feeling well and have had no symptoms of illness, or at least you didn't recognize the symptoms or take them seriously. After the test results are back, the doctor sits down with you. The results of your examination indicate that you have diabetes. If you do not drastically change your eating habits, you will surely face dire consequences. Bad news. But at the same time, the good news implied in the bad news is that your condition is not hopeless. Something can be done. It may be tough to make the adjustments, but still there is hope for a full and fruitful life.

With God, every apparently bad word about judgment implies a good word about salvation. Divine warnings are given so that divine mercy might be accepted. Judgment is a way that God shows his care for us. If God were uncaring, God would simply abandon us without notice. But our Lord loves us enough to redemptively hurt us. The word of God is painful the way surgery is painful. The agony it causes is but a stage on the way to health.

The Christ that John the Baptist announced is certainly a threat to anyone who has become complacent and overly comfortable with his or her life, values and opinions. The Christ that John called people to prepare for was One who came to interrupt the normal course of life in order to introduce the way of God. *(Craig M. Watts)*

DECEMBER 21, 1997

❧

Fourth Sunday of Advent

Worship Theme: Christmas transforms the world as well as our lives.

Readings: Micah 5:2-5*a*; Hebrews 10:5-10; Luke 1:39-45 (46-55)

Call to Worship (Luke 1:47-55):

Leader: My soul magnifies the Lord, and my spirit rejoices in God my Savior, for he has looked with favor on the lowliness of his servant.

People: **Surely, from now on all generations will call me blessed;**

Leader: for the Mighty One has done great things for me, and holy is his name.

People: **His mercy is for those who fear him from generation to generation.**

Leader: He has shown strength with his arm; he has scattered the proud in the thoughts of their hearts.

People: **He has brought down the powerful from their thrones, and lifted up the lowly;**

Leader: he has filled the hungry with good things, and sent the rich away empty. He has helped his servant Israel, in remembrance of his mercy,

All: **according to the promise he made to our ancestors, to Abraham and to his descendants forever.**

Pastoral Prayer:

Almighty God and everlasting Father, we have seen your light and have come to worship you. We have seen your light in the lives of

Christian brothers and sisters, who have willingly sacrificed themselves in response to your call. We have seen your light in the lives of those who have been transformed by your grace, whose lives have moved from hopelessness to hope, from anger to love, from sin to salvation. And we have seen your light most perfectly displayed in your Son and our Savior, Jesus Christ—who stepped out of heaven's glories to share in our earthly experience; who taught a new way of life, characterized by love and forgiveness; who gave his own life willingly that we might be freed from sin's bondage and restored to our true humanity. In these days of Christmas, help us to lay aside the season's tumult and frustration; help us to see Jesus only, and in the seeing may we be transformed by his holy light. For we pray in his most precious name. Amen.

SERMON BRIEFS

THE DYNAMICS OF EXPECTANCY

MICAH 5:2-5*a*

When the wise men told Herod the Great that a new king had been born within his realm, he was deeply disturbed because he knew of Israel's tradition of expectancy—and he considered it dangerous. When he asked his advisors where the new king was to be born, they turned to our passage from the book of Micah for an answer. The book of Micah is part of the prophetic heritage of the people of Israel. It can teach us a lot about the dynamics of expectancy.

I. Expectancy Grows Out of a Combination of Memory and Belief

When people remember that good things have happened in the past and believe that the One who made those good things happen is still at work in the world, then they can face each new day of life with expectancy.

The passage from Micah suggests that Israel should look to Bethlehem for a new messiah, because the great King David had come from that town. The central theme of the prophetic message is that the God who had acted to save his people in the past will also work to save them in the present and in the future.

Are there memories and beliefs in your life that can generate expectancy in you?

II. Expectancy Is Not Always Welcomed

People who are beaten, who have given up, find expectancy annoying. It challenges their complacency. It keeps them from being comfortable in their cynicism.

Those who want to exploit or oppress others also find expectancy threatening. Herod had good reason for finding the idea of the birth of a messiah threatening. The first three chapters of Micah, like so much of the prophetic literature in the Bible, is full of condemnations of such oppressive practices as he had employed in his reign.

Have you ever felt resentful or annoyed when someone else insisted upon taking a positive, expectant attitude toward some situation in which you were both involved? If you have, maybe you had better ask yourself why.

III. Expectancy Gives People the Ability to Persevere and to Keep On Trying

The belief that something has happened that will eventually make things better can give us a hope to hang onto. The prophets gave the people of Israel such a hope, and it sustained them through years of defeat, exile, and suffering.

In her book *Legacies,* Betty Bao Lord tells the story of a Chinese businessman who was imprisoned in his own office for years during the persecutions of China's great cultural revolution. He was able to persevere because each day he could look out between the boards that had been nailed over his window and see a little vermilion kite. He knew that his young son was flying it there to let him know he was not forgotten. He held onto life as he had once taught his young son to hold onto the string of a kite, because he knew someone outside waited faithfully. Someone cared.

Can you remember ways in which expectancy has enabled you to persevere? How great is the hope, how great is the perseverance, that can come with believing that the eternal God remembers you and is working for your good!

When you recognize the saving work of God actually happening in your life and in your world, expectancy will prepare you to enter into the new possibility. *(Jim Killen)*

HOW CAN I BE HOLY WHEN I CAN'T BE GOOD?

HEBREWS 10:5-10

When the text begins with a "therefore," we ask, "What's the 'therefore' there for?" In this case, the "therefore" serves as a bridge over which we travel from the writer's argument in verses 1-4, to his resulting conclusion in verses 5-10. He states that the old sacrificial system existed only to remind us of our sins and was totally insufficient to deal with the depth of our sinfulness. "Therefore . . . Christ came into the world" (v. 5).

Because of the inadequacy of burnt and sin offerings (v. 6), Jesus bowed his will to the will of the Father and became the eternal, once-and-for-all sacrifice for our sins. "And by that will, we have been made holy through the sacrifice of the body of Jesus Christ once for all" (v. 10 NIV).

Made holy? To that we are tempted to say, "I believe that he died for me, but me—holy? How can I be holy when I can't even be good?" To which God responds: "You are right, you can't." But he can make us so, and already has. The word *holy* means to "be separate" or "to be set aside." God makes us holy. It is totally his work. Already, he has "separated" us as believers.

I. God Separates Us from the World

As God's children, we are called to live a life that is distinctively different. We are to live moral, upright, spirit-filled lives that reflect the character and nature of Jesus. This does not mean that we ever attain a moral perfection or that we live in an ivory tower existence far removed from reality. We shall always have our frailties and be in constant need of confession, repentance, and faith. But it does mean that we are to be separated from the world's standards of judgment and measurement and be attuned to God's.

God's ways are not the ways of the world. He says that the first shall be last and the last shall be first. If we seek to find our life, we will lose it, but if we lose our life for his sake, we will find it. To be the greatest, we must become the slave of all. To be "separate" means that we seek to play our life to an "audience of One" and to be salt and light that reflect God's glory.

II. God Separates Us for His Service

Just as Jesus came to do God's will, we are separated to do his will and be Jesus in the world. Our talents, time, and potential are placed at his disposal. Just as Jesus found his ultimate fulfillment and satisfaction in doing the Father's will, so do we (v. 9). God doesn't ask us to do the impossible or even the uncommon. He expects us to do the common with an uncommon fervor. As Major Ian Thomas is fond of saying, "God is not so much concerned about our ability as he is concerned about our availability."

III. God Separates Us unto Himself

Holiness is not a code of conduct or a set of practices. It is a personal relationship to the living Jesus Christ who died for our sins. We conduct our lives in and through that personal relationship to him. We are a part of God and God is a part of us making us whole and holy. Peter Gomes said, "To be holy is to be out of sync with the world and not out of balance with God."

The old fable may say it best. An ancient kingdom faced a dilemma when the grain crop became poisoned. Anyone who ate the grain became insane. Faced with extinction or insanity, the wise king made a wise decision. He said, "We will eat the grain and we will suffer the results. But we will set aside a few to follow a different diet. That way there will always be some who know that we are insane."

In this often mad rush of busyness and preoccupation with material things we call Christmas, could there not be some who are different? Could there not be some who show the world love and generosity in the name of One who came to give his all? *(Gary L. Carver)*

SINGING MARY'S SONG

LUKE 1:39-55

People like Christmas for a variety of reasons. The family gatherings, the heart-warming music, the decorations. For children, receiving presents plays a significant role in their fondness for Christmas. But at heart for those of us in the church, our pleasure in Christmas is rooted in our love for the Christmas story, the story of the birth of Jesus.

But not everyone loves that story. And sometimes the people who dislike it the most understand its meaning the best. The Christmas story—and the Christmas event behind it—is not a placid and harmless happening. To the contrary, Christmas is not safe. The reason it is not safe has nothing to do with the traffic hazards around the malls, harmful toys for children, or the possibility of Christmas tree fires. Christmas is not safe because the Christ Child is not safe. He came not only as a promise but as a threat. Most of us have gotten so comfortable with Christmas because we have not seen Christ's coming as a threat as well as a promise. But Mary saw it, and it made her sing.

I. Mary Longed for a Better World

Just as we experience Christmas as safe, we tend to think of Mary as timid. She is usually portrayed as a pleasant and compliant figure rather than a defiant one. Meek and mild, humble and quiet—that's the Mary Christmas pageants and Hollywood movies give us. Not often are we provided a glimpse of a Mary who has a vision of a revolutionary world sparkling in her eyes or a passion for justice throbbing in her heart. But that is the Mary of the Bible. The woman God chose as the one to bear Jesus, the Savior, recognized the ugliness of inequality. She was incensed by the brutality of oppression. Mary longed for a better world.

II. Mary Recognized God Was Bringing a New World

It was sometime after her encounter with the angel that Mary went to visit her older cousin, Elizabeth, who was also pregnant. By that time Mary had begun to consider how the birth of this baby, the promised Savior, would affect other people besides her. The prospects were thrilling. When Elizabeth declared to Mary that she was blessed among all women for being chosen to give birth to the Lord, Mary couldn't contain herself. She began singing a visionary song of a changed world. With the power of a God-inspired protest singer, she belted out the words,

my soul magnifies the Lord, and my spirit rejoices in God my Savior,
for he has looked with favor on the lowliness of his servant.

In tones more likely to shake her hearers than to soothe them, she
sang of God and the promised Savior.

> He has brought down the powerful from their thrones,
>   and lifted up the lowly;
> he has filled the hungry with good things,
>   and sent the rich away empty.

Not everyone who has called Jesus their Lord and Savior can sing
Mary's song. Many prefer a tamer tune. But there have been people
who through the centuries have sung her song in their hearts, if not
always on their lips. Though they live in the misshapen and unjust
world of the present, by the power of God they envision a just world
to come and they sing God's future. That kind of song is subversive.
It calls into question the present world order. It speaks of new
possibilities. It lifts up the spirit of people who have been brought
low.

In 1973, in Santiago, Chile, the democratically elected government of Salvador Allende was toppled by the forces of General
Pinochet. Pinochet put in place a rule known for its horrible and
oppressive methods. During the overthrow, 25,000 people were
crammed into a sports stadium and detained at gunpoint. Periodically, individuals were taken out to be tortured and abused. All
hope for justice seemed to be battered to pieces.

Among those huddled in the stadium was a popular Chilean folk
singer, Victor Jara. He had managed to bring his guitar with him.
There in the midst of the brutality and abuse, he began to play and
sing. He lifted his voice against the violence and destruction that was
being imposed upon his people. The crowd hushed in order to listen
to his songs, songs of courage and hope. His songs helped them to
see beyond the pain and defeat of the moment to possibilities yet
unrealized.

The soldiers knew his music was undermining their fear-inspiring
work. They confronted Jara and declared, "If you don't stop that
song, we'll cut off your hands." Victor lifted his eyes to theirs and
kept playing his music. They carried out their threat and chopped
off his hands. The soldiers laughed at him and taunted, "Now try to
play your guitar." He couldn't play. But again he began to sing. He

continued to sing out his heart, sing of his vision of a better world. The furious soldiers stopped him only when they took their guns and shot him.

But even that did not stop the song. The people who heard it remembered. Throughout the time Pinochet and his forces ruled Chile, the oppressed people sang the song of Victor Jara.

Mary sang because she knew that the child she was to bear would change the world. When and how it would change, she did not know. But heart by heart, life by life, community by community, the change comes. *(Craig M. Watts)*

DECEMBER 28, 1997

❧

First Sunday After Christmas

Worship Theme: We have been made a part of the family of God.

Readings: 1 Samuel 2:18-20, 26; Colossians 3:12-17; Luke 2:41-51

Call to Worship (Psalm 148):

Leader: Praise the LORD! Praise the LORD from the heavens; praise him in the heights!

People: Praise him, all his angels; praise him, all his host!

Leader: Praise him, sun and moon; praise him, all you shining stars!

People: Praise him, you highest heavens, and you waters above the heavens!

Leader: Let them praise the name of the LORD, for he commanded and they were created.

People: He established them forever and ever; he fixed their bounds, which cannot be passed.

Leader: Praise the Lord from the earth, you sea monsters and all deeps,

People: fire and hail, snow and frost, stormy wind fulfilling his command!

Leader: Mountains and all hills, fruit trees and all cedars!

People: Wild animals and all cattle, creeping things and flying birds!

Leader: Kings of the earth and all peoples, princes and all rulers of the earth!

People: **Young men and women alike, old and young together!**

Leader: Let them praise the name of the LORD, for his name alone is exalted;

People: **his glory is above earth and heaven.**

Leader: He has raised up a horn for his people, praise for all his faithful, for the people of Israel who are close to him.

All: **Praise the LORD!**

Pastoral Prayer:

Almighty God, who is beyond human comprehension and beyond human experience, you are worthy of all honor and glory; you are from everlasting to everlasting. We are not worthy to enter your presence, yet in your grace you have not only brought us into relationship with you, you have even allowed us to call you Father. Truly we cannot fathom such love, yet we gladly and gratefully accept your invitation into this divine family, this blessed community. Even as you make us one with you, our Father, so bind our hearts together as your church, your family of faith. Too often in the past year we have fallen short of being family; we have allowed pride or greed or some other evil to disrupt and harm your church. Forgive us, Father, and prepare us in this new year to find new unity and peace and purpose as your church. Give us a deeper and more meaningful love for one another, even as you love us and as Christ gave himself for us. Help us to honor you with all of our lives during this new year, as we pray in Christ's name. Amen.

SERMON BRIEFS

A REASON TO KEEP GROWING

1 SAMUEL 2:18-20, 26

A person who has a purpose for which to live has a reason to keep growing. And when a person keeps growing, life becomes an adventure.

I. Are You a Growing Person?

We admire people who are alive and growing. Are you that kind of person?

That question has a unique importance for young people. Their lives are often intentionally planned around becoming all that they can become. They go to school to push back the horizons of their knowledge. They go out for sports and discipline their bodies to achieve. They set goals and work at accomplishing them. At its best, youth is a time for exploring brave new worlds.

But there are always some young people who just don't see the point in it all—or who really don't believe anything will come of it. They may drop out and drift into some stagnant or self-destructive existence.

What is true for young people is true for all of us. Aren't the most interesting people you know people who are still growing and learning? Aren't they the people who are studying to advance in their careers or developing latent talents or traveling to broaden their perspective? Winfred Garrison, a great Christian teacher in the first half of this century, undertook to learn Chinese in his eighties just to keep his mind alive.

Of course, it is easy for adults to drop out and quit growing. Some think that is what they are supposed to do. But the results are sad.

II. A Person with a Purpose Has a Reason to Keep Growing.

Our scripture lesson tells of the boyhood of the prophet Samuel. Samuel's parents had dedicated him to God and brought him to live with the old priest, Eli. Eli must have brought the boy up knowing that he had a special purpose in life. In fact, God was preparing Samuel to be one of the pivotal leaders of Israel. The text says that, "Samuel continued to grow both in stature and in favor with the LORD and with the people" (v. 26).

Something similar was said about Jesus. No one ever had a greater purpose than he. In preparation for it, he "increased in wisdom and in stature, and in favor with God and men" (Luke 2:52, NKJV).

We need purpose to keep us growing. Those young people who are making the most of their educational opportunity are often those who have a clear sense of purpose. And the adults who keep a growing edge on their lives are usually those who are committed to something.

III. Where Can We Find a Purpose to Bring Our Lives to Life?

The purpose is there. We just have to discover it and put ourselves into it. There is a current in human life and history that is the purposeful movement of God working to bring his creation to fulfillment. That movement calls out to us all to follow.

The biblical story can help us recognize what God is doing among us. Where can you see that same movement going on around you and within you? What within you would move you toward the fulfillment of God's purpose for you? Say yes to it. What in the world around you moves the world toward the fulfillment of God's purpose for us all? Lose yourself in serving it.

Allow that purpose to take over your life. It will push you to become a growing person. It will turn your life into an adventure. *(Jim Killen)*

TABLE TALK AND HOME FOLKS

COLOSSIANS 3:12-17

It is as if in our text today, the apostle Paul's positioning himself at his rightful place at the head of the table and remarks to the gathered fellowship at Colosse, "Now here is the way we do things in the family of God." We must continue to "put to death" the old life with its unregenerate ways (vv. 5-9) and "put on" as clothes the life of the new person in Christ (v. 10). In relationship to each other there is no racial or class distinctions in the fellowship (v. 11).

This is family talk. As members of the family—chosen, beloved, and set aside for service—there are certain values that should characterize our relations with each other.

I. We Should Put on Virtues of Family Unity (vv. 12-14)

Paul relates seven virtues with which family members should clothe themselves. Family members should genuinely and compassionately care for each other. We should show kindness to those who would seek to do us harm. Our own powers should be brought under the Father's control, resulting in gentleness with each other. Our tempers should have a long fuse. We should be patient with each other's peculiarities. We should grace each other with forgiveness, just as the Father has graced us.

Above all, we are united as we embody the selfless love so evident in Jesus Christ. What we hold in common, Christ, is greater than anything we could ever hold in difference.

II. We Are to Reflect the Nature of the Family Name (vv. 15-17)

Whatever we say or do should be done in the name of Christ (v. 17). In Paul's day, a name was more than just a handle affixed to an individual; it *was* that individual—his nature, character, and personality. When we pray in the name of Jesus, we pray in his character and nature. We seek to pray the prayer that Jesus would pray.

So the nature of family life should reflect the character of Jesus— for we are Christians, "little Christs." Our relationship within the family should reflect the peace, graciousness, wisdom, and joy of our joint heir, Jesus Christ (vv. 15-16).

Sigurd Bryan said, "If we can be a Christian in our own homes, we can be a Christian anywhere." And it also may be true, "if we aren't a Christian at home, are we a Christian at all?"

Keith Miller tells about his early struggles to develop a prayer life. Waking early to pray he stumbled around disturbing everyone in the house. His young daughter came to him as he knelt in prayer.

"What are you doing, Daddy?"

"Don't bother me, Honey, I'm trying to pray."

She persisted, "What are you doing, Daddy?"

"Go on, Honey, Daddy's busy."

"Let's play, Daddy."

Exasperated, Miller screamed, "Will you leave me alone. I'm trying to pray!" She ran crying to her mother, now also awake and preparing breakfast.

"What's wrong with Daddy?" the daughter asked.

"Leave Daddy alone, Honey," her mother replied. "Daddy's got to pray so he can be a Christian to the people downtown." Ouch!

I heard a story years ago from an elderly preacher. One of many children, he grew up poor during the depression. As the large family gathered around the table for the evening meal, the father would come in fresh from milking the family cow. The family watched this nightly ritual as he first strained the milk and then filled each child's glass full and then the mother's. He would turn his back to the family, pour what little was left into his glass, and then used water to make his glass full of liquid. The preacher said that it was years before he realized the selfless love and devotion of his father, whom he thought liked water in his milk.

How are you doing in reflecting the family name? *(Gary L. Carver)*

WHAT'S A KID TO DO?

LUKE 2:41-51

I'll bet there is hardly a person in America between the ages of five and forty-five who hasn't seen the movie *Home Alone*. Some of you have probably seen it a half dozen times. My kids have memorized a fair amount of the dialogue and can anticipate every scene. But for the benefit of you culturally disadvantaged few who have not seen the movie, I'll give you a thumbnail sketch.

Around Christmastime, a large family is preparing to leave for a vacation in Europe. They plan to get up early in the morning to catch their flight. Unfortunately, during the night the electricity in the neighborhood gets knocked out. Consequently, the alarm clock goes off late. The house breaks into total chaos as the family frantically dresses, packs, loads up, and dashes off to the airport to make their flight.

Once the plane is in the air, the mother has this haunting feeling that she forgot to do something. Were all the doors locked? Yes. Was the garage closed? Yes. Was newspaper delivery cancelled? Yes. With an explosion of realization, she cries out "Kevin!" In the rush and jumble of leaving, Kevin—the youngest child in the family—was left behind. The rest of the movie deals with his antics as he copes with being alone and as he foils the efforts of two bungling burglars from robbing his house. Kevin, who began the movie as a little boy who can't tie his own shoes or pack his suitcase, quickly learns to be independent.

I can't help thinking of *Home Alone* when I read our text for this morning. Of course, the star of the story is not Kevin but Jesus. In the bustle and confusion of getting ready for a trip, he gets left

411

behind. Jesus' mother, Mary, was even slower than Kevin's mother to realize he was missing. Instead of a few hours, it took a whole day for Jesus' parents to notice that his seat was empty.

The family had been in Jerusalem for the Passover, the most important religious holiday of the year for Israel. After the festivities, they packed to head back home to Nazareth, their hometown. Jesus' family was traveling with a group of others. Apparently his parents thought he was with some other people. I can't imagine the shock they must have felt when they realized they left him alone in the big city.

It took Mary and Joseph three days to find Jesus. Three days of anxiety, tears, and guilt, I imagine. I can hear it all now. "We should have been paying more attention. We should have been absolutely certain he was with us. How could we have left him there? What rotten parents we are." But after three days of frantic searching, they neared the great Temple. They turned a corner and there he was. He wasn't crying and worried. He didn't blame his parents for neglecting him. Instead, Jesus was sitting with the teachers, the religious experts, asking questions and listening to their answers. It seemed that the people who heard Jesus were pretty impressed with what he had to say.

His parents were more appalled than impressed. When they saw that Jesus was not frightened or in any kind of danger, they got upset in a different way. Parents are like that. Sometimes, if they think their child is lost or in trouble, then they find out he's all right, they don't know what to do first—hug him or spank him for not listening to them in the first place. It seems that's the way it was with Mary and Joseph.

When they found Jesus, his mother said, "Child, why have you treated us like this? Look, your father and I have been searching for you in great anxiety" (v. 48). In other words: "Jesus, we've worried ourselves to death because we thought you were lost. You should be ashamed of yourself for making us feel so terrible."

What did Jesus say? "Mom, Dad, I'm sorry. I'll never do something like that again." Is that what he said? No! What he said was, "Why did you seek for me? Did you not know that I must be about my Father's business?" (v. 49 NKJV). Jesus' earthly father, Joseph, was a carpenter. Jesus wasn't sitting there with a saw and hammer. He wasn't talking about his earthly father's business but that of his heavenly Father, God. Jesus had left his parents and caused them a lot of worry by going to the temple to get involved in divine business.

There are several lessons that this story about Jesus suggests. First, *there is something more important than parents and families.* Now, I recognize this is the last thing many of you parents want me to say, but it is the God-given truth. Families are important. Children are important. Parents are important. But the living, loving knowledge of God is more important.

Second, *kids need to be patient with their parents.* Maybe like Jesus, a child feels that she is ready to be a lot more independent than her parents think she is. But sometimes parents hold her back because they know the world is more dangerous than she thinks it is, and she really might not be as prepared for it as she believes.

Third, *children should listen to their parents.* Even though Jesus did fine in Jerusalem all on his own, when his parents told him how upset they were, he paid attention. The scripture tells us that when he went back home with his folks, "he was obedient to them."

Despite the occasional fight and disappointments, no one else is likely to love us as long or as much as our family. A wonderful African church leader, Desmond Tutu, reminds us: "You can't choose your family. They are God's gift to you, as you are to them." *(Craig M. Watts)*

BENEDICTIONS

ॐ

Advent

We journey toward Bethlehem, O God, where you will reveal the glory of heaven and the hope of earth. May the light of your glory brighten our path to the future, and may the brilliance of your hope beckon us to new beginnings.

May the One born in Bethlehem—who joined divinity and humanity, love of God and labor for people—unite heaven and earth, in us as in him.

Christmas

L: We came with haste. We found Mary and Joseph keeping watch in the night, and the baby crying in a manger.
P: Glory to God in the highest, and peace to all on earth!
L: Now, as we return to our fields, we will not forget;
P: We will keep all these things with gladness, pondering them in our hearts.

L: There is a people sent from God whose name is Hope.
P: And the people named Hope shall bear witness to the light; despair shall not overcome us.
L: There is a people sent from God whose name is Love.
P: And the people named Love shall bear witness to the light; hatred shall not overwhelm us.
L: There is a people sent from God whose name is Life.
P: And the people named Life shall bear witness to the light; death shall not overpower us.

Season After Epiphany

May God go with you as you depart into the desert, there to meet the temptations of the soul. May the Spirit lead you to an oasis where waters run deep and clouds rise high, and where the voice of heaven whispers in the cool of the trees.

O God, make us vessels worthy of the wine of the new covenant. Let us carry it across an earth drenched with blood, anointing the wounds of God's peoples and raising the cup to their feverish lips. For long has the covenant been promised to the world, and long shall its wine be poured out for many.

Lent

Dear Lord, who calls not the well but the sick to repentance, anoint us to be agents of your healing ministry. Send us forth as heralds of the fasting to which your prophet Isaiah calls us—the fast that loosens the bonds of wickedness, frees the oppressed, feeds the hungry, houses the homeless and clothes the naked—so that, when people ask, "Where are you, Lord?" you can answer, "Here I am."

O God, you send us forth not into the world in which Jesus was born but into the world in which we were born. You will not save us *from* our world, because you have saved us *for* our world. And you have promised to go with us into that world, enabling us to do even greater works than those of Jesus. Go with us, dear Lord, and we shall become the keepers of your promise.

Easter

O God, who in Jesus Christ turned the defeat of Good Friday into the victory of Easter, bringing dawn out of darkness and life out of death, make us faithful witnesses to the life-giving power of your crossbearing love. Keep us ever mindful of the Risen One's promise that we would do even greater works than he. And send us forth, with hope renewed and zeal aflame, to labor in the vineyard of the Lord.

O Lord, as you have made disciples of us, now you send us into the world to make disciples of others. Go with us and be our guide, that the witness of our lives may confirm the testimony of our lips.

Season After Pentecost

Return now to the world, and go gladly, despite your fears. Though afflicted, you will not be crushed; though perplexed, you will not be driven to despair; though lonely, you will not be forsaken. The Lord of life dwells in you and among you, now and forever.

Do not lose heart, for *there* is the abode of God. If your heart be troubled, God will share your agony; if your heart be triumphant, God will share your gladness. Do not lose heart, for there is the shelter for your neighbors. May you share *their* agony and gladness, as you trek, arm-in-arm, to the mountaintop.

Special Occasions

Almighty God, as you have drawn us together in honor of your prophets, send us forth to settle the Promised Land that they saw from the mountaintop but were not allowed to enter. Give us, as you gave them, tough minds and tender hearts, that we too might become apostles of nonviolence in a land of violence, champions of justice in a society of injustice, and heralds of peace in a world of conflict.

O God, as here we have expressed gratitude for our nation's ideals, let us go forth to praise them in speech, codify them in law, and translate them into deed. As they turn our eyes from the successful to the struggling, give us the grace to remember that these ideals did not come to us without price, and will not survive without sacrifice.

TEXT GUIDE

THE REVISED COMMON LECTIONARY (1997), CYCLE B*

Sunday	First Lesson	Second Lesson	Gospel Lesson	Psalm
1/5/97	Jer. 31:7-14	Eph. 1:3-14	John 1:1-18	Ps. 147:12-20
1/12/97	Gen. 1:1-5	Acts 19:1-7	Mark 1:4-11	Ps. 72:1-7, 10-14
1/19/97	1 Sam. 3:1-10	1 Cor. 6:12-20	John 1:43-51	Ps. 139:1-6, 13-18
1/26/97	Jon. 3:1-5, 10	1 Cor. 7:29-31	Mark 1:14-20	Ps. 62:5-12
2/2/97	Deut. 18:15-20	1 Cor. 8:1-13	Mark 1:21-28	Ps. 111
2/9/97	Isa. 40:21-31	1 Cor. 9:16-23	Mark 1:29-39	Ps. 147:1-11, 20c
2/16/97	Gen. 9:8-17	1 Pet. 3:18-22	Mark 1:9-15	Ps. 25:1-10
2/23/97	Gen. 17:1-7, 15-16	Rom. 4:13-25	Mark 8:31-38	Ps. 22:23-31
3/2/97	Exod. 20:1-17	1 Cor. 1:18-23	John 2:13-22	Ps. 19
3/9/97	Num. 21:4-9	Eph. 2:1-10	John 3:14-21	Ps. 107:1-3, 17-22
3/16/97	Jer. 31:31-34	Heb. 5:5-10	John 12:20-33	Ps. 51:1-12
3/23/97	Isa. 50:4-9a	Phil. 2:5-11	Mark 14:1–15:47	Ps. 31:9-16
3/30/97	Isa. 25:6-9	1 Cor. 15:1-11	Mark 16:1-8	Ps. 118:1-2, 14-24
4/6/97	Acts 4:32-35	1 John 1:1–2:2	John 20:19-31	Ps. 133
4/13/97	Acts 3:12-19	1 John 3:1-7	Luke 24:36b-48	Ps. 4

*This guide represents one possible selection of lessons and psalms from the lectionary. For a complete listing see *The Revised Common Lectionary.*

...lest Lord Jesus ("Crusaders' Hy...

Reading – Kathy (niece)
(Song of Songs

Howland

Song – "Old Rugged Cross"

Bill Siegfried

"Hymn of Promise"

Sunday	First Lesson	Second Lesson	Gospel Lesson	Psalm
4/20/97	Acts 4:5-12	1 John 3:16-24	John 10:11-18	Ps. 23
4/27/97	Acts 8:26-40	1 John 4:7-21	John 15:1-8	Ps. 22:25-31
5/4/97	Acts 10:44-48	1 John 5:1-6	John 15:9-17	Ps. 98
5/11/97	Acts 1:1-11	Eph. 1:15-23	Luke 24:44-53	Ps. 47
5/18/97	Ezek. 37:1-14	Acts 2:1-38	John 15:26-27; 16:4b-15	Ps. 104:24-34, 35b
5/25/97	Isa. 6:1-8	Rom. 8:12-17	John 3:1-17	Ps. 29
6/1/97	1 Sam 3:1-10	2 Cor. 4:5-12	Mark 2:3-3:6	Ps. 139:1-6, 13-18
6/8/97	1 Sam. 8:4-11, 16-20	2 Cor. 4:13-5:1	Mark 3:20-35	Ps. 138
6/15/97	1 Sam. 15:34-16:13	2 Cor. 5:6-17	Mark 4:26-34	Ps. 20
6/22/97	1 Sam. 17:1, 4-11, 32-49	2 Cor. 6:1-13	Mark 4:35-41	Ps. 9:9-20
6/29/97	2 Sam. 1:1, 17-27	2 Cor. 8:7-15	Mark 5:24-34	Ps. 130
7/6/97	2 Sam. 5:1-5, 12b-19	2 Cor. 12:1-10	Mark 6:1-13	Ps. 48
7/13/97	2 Sam. 6:1-5, 12b-19	Eph. 1:3-14	Mark 6:14-29	Ps. 24
7/20/97	2 Sam. 7:1-14a	Eph. 2:11-22	Mark 6:30-34, 53-56	Ps. 89:20-37
7/27/97	2 Sam. 11:1-15	Eph. 3:14-21	John 6:1-21	Ps. 14
8/3/97	2 Sam. 11:26-12:13a	Eph. 4:1-16	John 6:24-35	Ps. 51:1-12
8/10/97	2 Sam. 18:5-9, 31-33	Eph. 4:25-5:2	John 6:35, 41-51	Ps. 130
8/17/97	1 Kings 2:10-12; 3:3-14	Eph. 5:15-20	John 6:51-58	Ps. 111
8/24/97	1 Kings 8:22-30, 41-43	Eph. 6:10-20	John 6:56-69	Ps. 84
8/31/97	Song of Sol. 2:8-13	James 1:17-27	Mark 7:1-8, 14-15, 21-23	Ps. 45:1-2, 6-9
9/7/97	Prov. 22:1-2, 8-9, 22-23	James 2:1-10, 14-17	Mark 7:24-37	Ps. 125

Date				
9/14/97	Prov. 1:20-33	James 3:1-12	Mark 8:27-38	Ps. 19
9/21/97	Prov. 31:10-31	James 3:13–4:3, 7-8a	Mark 9:30-37	Ps. 1
9/28/97	Esther 7:1-6; 9:20-22	James 5:13-20	Mark 9:38-50	Ps. 124
10/5/97	Job 1:1; 2:1-10	Heb. 1:1-4; 2:5-12	Mark 10:2-16	Ps. 26
10/12/97	Job 23:1-9, 16-17	Heb. 4:12-16	Mark 10:17-31	Ps. 22:1-15
10/19/97	Job 38:1-7, (34-41)	Heb. 5:1-10	Mark 10:35-45	Ps. 104:1-9, 24, 35c
10/26/97	Job 42:1-6, 10-17	Heb. 7:23-28	Mark 10:46-52	Ps. 34:1-8, (19-22)
11/2/97	Ruth 1:1-18	Heb. 9:11-14	Mark 12:28-34	Ps. 146
11/9/97	Ruth 3:1-5; 4:13-17	Heb. 9:24-28	Mark 12:38-44	Ps. 127
11/16/97	1 Sam. 1:4-20	Heb. 10:11-14, 19-25	Mark 13:1-8	Ps. 16
11/23/97	2 Sam. 23:1-7	Rev. 1:4b-8	John 18:33-37	Ps. 132:1-12, (13-18)
11/30/97	Jer. 33:14-16	1 Thess. 3:9-13	Luke 21:25-38	Ps. 25:1-10
12/7/97	Mal. 3:1-4	Phil. 1:3-11	Luke 3:1-6	Ps. 85:1-2, 8-13
12/14/97	Isa. 12:2-6	Phil. 4:4-7	Luke 3:7-18	Isa. 12:2-6
12/21/97	Mic. 5:2-5a	Heb. 10:5-10	Luke 1:39-55	Ps. 80:1-7
12/28/97	1 Sam. 2:18-20, 26	Col. 3:12-17	Luke 2:41-51	Ps. 148

CONTRIBUTORS

Don M. Aycock
Editor, Special Projects
SBC Brotherhood Commission
1548 Poplar Avenue
Memphis, TN 38104

Barry Beames
Pastor
First Baptist Church
523 N. Polk Street
Jefferson, TX 75657

Gerald Borchert
Professor of New Testament
Southern Baptist Seminary
2825 Lexington Road
Louisville, KY 40280

Rick Brand
Pastor
First Presbyterian Church
222 Young Street
Henderson, NC 27536

Michael Brown
Pastor
Central United Methodist
Church
27 Church Street
Asheville, NC 28801

Harold Bryson
Professor of Preaching
Mississippi College
PO Box 4013
Clinton, MS 39058

Joseph Byrd
Pastor
Stewart Road Church of
God
14539 Lincoln Road
Monroe, MI 48161

Gary L. Carver
Pastor
First Baptist Church
401 Gateway Avenue
Chattanooga, TN 37402

Craig Christina
Ph.D. Candidate in
Preaching
2825 Lexington Road
Louisville, KY 40280

Earl C. Davis
Trinity Baptist Church
780 Walnut Knoll Lane,
Suite 3
Cordova, TN 38018

Michael Duduit
Editor, *Preaching* Magazine
P.O. Box 7728
Louisville, KY 40257-0728

Paul R. Escamilla
Pastor
Munger Place United
   Methodist Church
5200 Bryan
Dallas, TX 75206

Travis Franklin
Chaplain
Methodist Children's Home
1111 Herring Avenue
Waco, TX 76708

Bill Groover
Pastor
Bethany Baptist Church
2319 Taylorsville Road
Louisville, KY 40205

C. Thomas Hilton
Pastor
Amelia Plantation Chapel
20 Painted Bunting
Amelia Island, FL 32034

R. Leslie Holmes
Senior Pastor
First Presbyterian Church
320 Sixth Avenue
Pittsburgh, PA 15222

Derl G. Keefer
Pastor
Three Rivers Church of the
   Nazarene
15770 Coon Hollow Road
Three Rivers, MI 49093

James L. Killen, Jr.
Pastor
Williams Memorial United
   Methodist Church
4000 Moores Lane
Texarkana, TX 75503

Gary G. Kindley
Pastor
St. John's United Methodist
   Church
311 E. University Avenue
Georgetown, TX 78626

Robert R. Kopp
Pastor
Logans Ferry Presbyterian
   Church
730 Church Street
New Kensington, PA 15068

Alton H. McEachern
Pastor
Cornerstone United
   Methodist Church
50 Rockland Way
Sharpsburg, GA 30277

J. Lawrence McCleskey
Pastor
Myers Park United
   Methodist Church
2335 Richardson Drive
Charlotte, NC 28211

David N. Mosser
Pastor
First United Methodist
   Church
410 E. University
Georgetown, TX 78626-6899

Carol M. Noren
Professor of Preaching
North Park Theological
  Seminary
3225 West Foster
Chicago, IL 60625

Jerry E. Oswalt
Academic Dean and
  Professor of Preaching
Florida Baptist Theological
  College
1306 College Drive
Graceville, FL 32440

Kathleen Peterson
Pastor
Palos United Methodist
  Church
PO Box 398
Palos Heights, IL 60463

Jon Roebuck
Pastor
First Baptist Church
PO Box 347
Gatlinburg, TN 37738

L. Joseph Rosas
Pastor
Union Avenue Baptist
  Church
2181 Union Avenue
Memphis, TN 38104

William L. Self
Pastor
Johns Creek Baptist Church
7500 McGinnis Ferry Road
Alpharetta, GA 30202

Thomas R. Steagald
Pastor
First United Methodist
  Church
511 Robert Street
Marion, NC 28752

Billy D. Strayhorn
Pastor
Methodist Church
5309 Ridge Springs Court
Arlington, TX 76017

Carolyn Volentine
PO Box 658
Logansport, LA 71049

Douglas C. Walker, III
Vice President for
  Institutional Advancement
Southern Baptist Seminary
2825 Lexington Road
Louisville, KY 40280

Craig M. Watts
Pastor
First Christian Church
7700 US 42
Louisville, KY 40241

Bill D. Whittaker
President
Clear Creek Bible College
300 Clear Creek Road
Pineville, KY 40977

Brett Younger
Pastor
College Heights Baptist
  Church
2221 College Heights Road
Manhattan, KS 66502

INDEX

❧

OLD TESTAMENT